Beauty, Mystery and Power

Come, explore the ancient magical and spiritual practices of the Norse, Slavs, Russians and Germans. Take charge of your life. Seize your destiny. Experience the remarkable strength of this compelling way of life that has much to offer the world of today.

Rituals, traditions, lore and mythology all combine to demonstrate the simple, yet profound truth that each of us is uniquely important. You are responsible for your own destiny. The family and friends who constitute your extended family are also important: by working together and helping one another, you create a powerful force for healing, happiness and prosperity.

Live life with passion and honor, the way your ancestors once did. *The Rites of Odin* has been assembled from the best sources available in Scandinavia, Germany and Eastern Europe. The background lore and rituals are fully integrated into a complete religious and magical system. Here are mystical teachings and magical rites for the solitary practitioner, groups of seekers and even special materials for those families who choose to explore their heritage together.

The way to Valhalla still awaits those who are bold enough to walk this unique spiritual path that has endured for over a thousand years.

About the Author

Ed Fitch is one of the founders and major scholars of modern Paganism. Initiated into Gardnerian Wicca during the mid-1960s, he has continually added to the existing background lore on Wicca and mainstream Paganism, and is widely considered to be one of the best and most influential writers of rituals in the U.S. today. His ceremonies are poetic reconstructions of ancient rites in a modern and magical form, using original material researched from historical, anthropological, and literary sources worldwide.

The son of parents from a Russian immigrant community, Ed traveled widely as a boy, living in construction camps in the Southwest desert, mining camps in the West, on a ranch far back in the northern California wilderness, on a farm in Virginia, and on an old southern estate near Washington D.C. As an Air Force officer he traveled the world before settling down into a civilian job as an aerospace engineer in Southern California.

To Write to the Author

If you wish to contact the author or would like more information about this book, please write to the author in care of Llewellyn Worldwide, and we will forward your request. Both the author and publisher appreciate hearing from you and learning of your enjoyment of this book and how it has helped you. Llewellyn Worldwide cannot guarantee that every letter written to the author can be answered, but all will be forwarded. Please write to:

Ed Fitch
℅ Llewellyn Worldwide
2143 Wooddale Drive, Dept. 978-0-87542-224-4
Woodbury, MN 55125-2989, U.S.A.
Please enclose a self-addressed, stamped
envelope for reply, or $1.00 to cover costs.
If outside the U.S.A., enclose international postal reply coupon.

The Rites of Odin

Ed Fitch

Llewellyn Publications
Woodbury, Minnesota

FIRST EDITION
Eleventh Printing, 2007

Cover Art: Martin Cannon
Interior Illustrations: Robin Wood and Christopher Wells

Library of Congress Cataloging-in-Publication Data
Fitch, Ed.
    The rites of Odin / by Ed Fitch.
      p.   cm. — (Llewellyn's Teutonic magick series)
    Bibliography: p.
    Includes index.
    ISBN 13: 978-0-87542-224-4
    ISBN 10: 0-87542-224-1
    1. Northmen—Religion. 2. Magic. 3. Rites and ceremonies.
I. Title. II. Series.
BL863.F47   1989
293—dc 19   89-2490
                                                        CIP

Llewellyn Publications
A Division of Llewellyn Worldwide, Ltd.
2143 Wooddale Drive, Dept. 978-0-87542-224-4
Woodbury, MN 55125-2989
www.llewellyn.com
Llewellyn is a registered trademark of Llewellyn Worldwide, Ltd.
Printed in the United States of America

Other Books by Ed Fitch

The Castle of Deception

Magical Rites from the Crystal Well

A Grimoire of Shadows

Dedication

To the folk of the immigrant community where I grew up, who taught me that together we could work hard, keep each other honest, improve our places in life, and stand against the world.

To the good people of Caer Calliech, who taught me that a tight-knit group of friends can be far closer than one's own blood kin, and can indeed accomplish miracles.

To my children, who taught me to understand the heights and the depths of love.

Acknowledgments

To Evan McCallum and Lothar Oehmichen for advice and guidance, and long, stimulating discussions of history and philosophy.

To the Brewers' Guild of the Asatru Free Assembly for permission to adapt their own excellent instructions on mead-brewing, as modified by my own experiences and misadventures.

And for permission to use the following articles and passages:

"On Versatility," from *The Notebooks of Lazarus Long*, by special permission of Robert Heinlein.

Lines from "Little Gidding," *Four Quartets*, by T. S. Eliot, Faber and Faber, Ltd., and Harcourt, Brace and World, Inc.

"Crafting a Drinking Horn," by Mara Schaeffer, *Crystal Well*, Vol. 13, No. 3.

"Frau Holle—Folk Tale and Ritual," by Ed Fitch, *Gnostica News*, Summer 1976.

Contents

Foreword xiii
Preface xv

The Calling of the Grey Wanderer xix
Introduction to Odinism—An Old Religion in a New Age xxi
The Way of the Rainbow Bridge 1
The Gods of Valhalla and Before 3
How We Stand Before Our Gods 21
The Rede of Honor 23
Sayings Concerning the Gods 27
Sayings for Oneself and One's People 29
Concerning Secrecy 37
Concerning the Body 38

RITES AND CEREMONIES 39

Leaders of the Rituals 41
Sample Altar Arrangement 44
Seasonal Festivals of the Folk 45
Blessings, Charms and Prayers 47
General Rite in Honor of Odin 51
Torch Processional and Ceremony 59
The Blot Rite 61
The Sumul Celebration 67

Seasonal Festivals for the Gathered Folk 71
    The Vala's Vision (Maiden's Day) 71
    Spring Evenight 76

Walpurgia Feast (May Eve) 80
Summer Sunstead 84
Hloaf Festival (Lammas) 89
Fall Evenight 93
Night of the Specters 97
Heroes' Day 103
Winter Sunstead and Yule 108

Household Seasonal Celebrations 117
The Vala's Vision (Maiden's Day) 117
Spring Evenight 120
Walpurgia (Beltane) 122
Ostara 123
Summer Sunstead 125
Hloaf Festival (Lammas) 127
The Week of the Spirits (Halloween) .129
Festival of Odin 132
Yule 135
Family Day (Mothernight) 137
Festival of Light (Christmas) 139

Solitary Rites 141
The Vala's Vision (Maiden's Day) 141
Solitary Spring Evenight 145
Solitary Walpurgia (May Eve) 150
Solitary Summer Sunstead 154
Solitary Hloaf Rite Festival (Lammas) 159
Solitary Fall Evenight (Autumn) 163
Solitary Night of the Specters 168
Solitary Salutations to the Heroes 174
Solitary Winter Sunstead and Yule 178
Solitary Affirmation Ritual 186

Protection in Travel 190
Bonding of Brotherhood 193

Betrothal Ceremony 196
Wedding 200
Birth Pledging of an Infant 207
Coming-of-Age Rite.......................................209
Rite of Pledging for a Child 214
Divorce 224
Funeral Rite...227
Rite for Healing of the Body..............................233
Rite for Healing of the Spirit 237
The Runner's Seid 241
Seid: Casting the Ball of Light 243
Rite of the Flaming Spear 245
Lust Seid 250

LORE 253

Runes...255
Runes Symbolizing the Gods and the Festivals 269
Rune-Talisman Rite 272
Rune Divination 275
Ritual Implements and Costumes 277
Crafting a Drinking Horn 279
Brewing Your Own Mead.................................289

Readings 295
   The Philosophy and Theology of the Nordic World Tree 297
   Yule Journey 303
   Frau Holle: Folk Tale and Ritual 317

Principal Sagas 325
Zodiacal Houses...329

Recommended Reading 331
Additional Bibliography 335

Disclaimer

Norse mythology and folklore is a large and complex field of study. As with other systems of legend, these myths were modified and altered with the centuries, and different versions also came to exist in various geographical locations. While my studies have been fairly extensive, I cannot claim to be totally comprehensive in my researches. When legends varied with time, I generally tried to use the older, more primal, and/or more psychically appropriate folk traditions as bases for lore and ritual.

The folk tradition is that body of lore not recorded in the Eddas and other written mythological texts, but which was genuinely believed in and practiced by ordinary people for unrecorded centuries. In some instances, folk tradition is at variance with Eddic mythology; however, the folk ways upheld by the common folk are no less valid than the poetry of the skalds.

I welcome any comments and suggestions, and will try to correct any errors in scholarship in future editions of this book.

Also, I have made some ritual departures from the original. Primarily, the ancient Norse religion tended to be patriarchal, with the three major gods of Odin, Thor, and Frey being most honored. The feminine aspect provides a much-needed balance to religious systems, especially so in this era, and hence the inclusion of Freya in lieu of her brother.

Freya, as included here, is the goddess in her earlier, more all-encompassing female form. Scholars will note that as the generations proceeded the earlier, matronly "household" aspects of Freya were transferred over to Frigga. I have chosen in these rites to view Freya more in the three full meanings of Maiden, Mother, and Crone; perhaps as Jord or Erda would have been seen in yet earlier times. In a few places, of course, the Frigga-aspect of household, child rearing, and mothering is by far the goddess form most appropriately honored, and I have done so. It works, and works well, I think.

Of course, for those who feel the rites should be modified to give more specific attention to various god/goddess powers, then by all means they should do what feels right. After all, we are all different, and our gods differ as much as we do!

Foreword

Once again the Gods and Goddesses fare forth out of the northern light and ride in the wild hunt across the sky. They seek fellowship once again with those who sprang from their beings in the dim mists of ages past. The tide has turned: the age of awakening to the thunder clap of Thor, the whisperings of Odin, and the touch of Freya has come. Again we are roused from deep within by the mystery of *Runa* as it spreads its song within our souls.

The Rites of Odin is an important new contribution in the latest phase of the long-standing Teutonic rebirth. This northern Renaissance has been underway since the late 1500s throughout the Teutonic world—in Scandinavia, England and Germany. Only now its heart beats more true than ever. This is an ideal addition to the Llewellyn Teutonic Magick Series, as it gives us a complete religious system based on the timeless images of the northern Gods and Goddesses.

The author is a well-known and respected writer and authority in the Neo-Pagan world. His perspective on the northern rebirth is invaluable. In *The Rites of Odin* he presents a system which combines the ritual technology of contemporary Neo-Paganism with the rich and powerful imagery of the northern tradition.

In many ways *The Rites of Odin* represents the beginnings of a synthesis of the Norse or Teutonic way and that of their sister-folk, the Celts. The lore and magick of these two great northern peoples, the Teutons (which includes the English, Germans and Scandinavians) and the Celts (Irish, Scottish, and Welsh) are the depth foundations of the true spirituality of those descended from their ancient stock.

In this synthesis, combined with the contemporary magical technology of Neo-Paganism, *The Rites of Odin* is a tremendous contribution toward the unfolding of a real "Norse Wicca." Here the author begins to retrace the way back to the reconstruction of the true Vanic faith of the ancient Teutons; a faith in which the Lord (Frey) and the

Lady (Freya) reign supreme.

The treasures you will uncover in working with *The Rites of Odin* are many and manifold. They are the inborn spiritual treasures of your ancestors you have inherited from them. These treasures are their greatest gifts to you. Take them, work them and awaken to their wonder!

Edred Thorsson
Consulting Editor for the Teutonic Magick Series
September 15, 1989, Austin, Texas

Preface

Years ago, somewhere in the Jutland peninsula of Denmark, I experienced a time of magic and awe.

I had arrived in Copenhagen a few days earlier, and had spent a delightful (but entirely too short) time in the aptly nicknamed "Paris of the North," then took a pleasing rail trip to Kolding to meet with old family friends. I had spent time in that quaint town, often wandering through the shadowed, echoing halls and the outlying ruins of Koldinghus Castle, usually completely alone in the huge, medieval fortress-turned-museum (itself built on the site of some far-prehistoric fort), while rain pattered against the windows of old, thick glass.

In a couple days the weather lifted, and the Sun came through in all its summer glory. We decided to take advantage of the fine weather for a leisurely drive through a countryside of immaculate farmsteads and well-groomed forests to work our way up the ancient "Soldiers' Road," the northernmost remaining segment of a major trade and military route that once stretched from the Black Sea up through eastern and central Europe, gradually wending its way to end at Cape Skaagen at the far northern tip of Jutland.

In times long past the Soldiers' Road had been one of Europe's major thoroughfares, and was used for thousands of years by merchants, armies, minstrels, migrating tribes, gypsies, farmers, thieves and many others for every possible type of human endeavor. It came into being perhaps shortly after the last Ice Age, and was in regular use up until a couple of centuries ago. Occasional segments of it are still in use here and there, though the rest has been swallowed up by pastures, dirt country lanes, farmers' fields and forests. Far to the south it has become a part of autobahns, railroad right-of-ways, and all manner of roadways through a dozen countries.

The day was spent looking at various sites where fortresses, defensive walls and trade towns had once stood. A placid field marked the soft outlines of what had been fortifications where a massive and bloody battle had once been fought, long ago. The causes of that war, the names of those who lived and died, and even the names of the princes and leaders themselves have long vanished. Both eternal Nature and hundreds of generations of prosaic farmers have long erased all but a few rounded ridges and shallow depressions in this placid locale.

Spearheads, bronze arrowheads and bits of armor still show up in the spring ploughing, but are usually left to be swallowed up by the Earth once more.

As sunset approached I was wandering alone through the empty heath some few kilometers away, when I saw a row of burial mounds, great earthen hillocks, which were the final resting-places of nobles and chiefs dead a thousand years or perhaps much longer.

I climbed up the steep side of the nearest mound and reached the top to see a row of similar brush-covered tomb-hills stretching in a line to the west, with the midsummer Sun setting exactly at the end of the line of mounds. I stood there, taking in the silent scene.

I couldn't help thinking, "There's a truth here, if you can figure it out. These ancient, forgotten ones sleeping beneath my feet may have known it. *Think!*"

At that time and at that place there seemed to be a final balancing of man and Nature, though I never was able to put it into words. If I had, perhaps it might have been something like T.S. Eliot's thoughts,

> We shall not cease from exploration
> And the end of all our exploring:
> Will be to arrive where we started,
> And to know the place for the first time.
> —*Little Gidding*

Years have passed since then. I've traveled to quite a few other countries, been in a war, taken part in the hidden espionages between nations, worked on projects that will ultimately send humankind toward the stars, married and had my own children.

I've found myself looking back to that place and time, and to others like it, considering.

In the intervening years, my experiences with Paganism and in Nature have been very rewarding to me, and I've managed to pass some of that value on to my sons. Yet the Paganism I have lived for these years does not, to me, seem to be complete. The theology and magic is rich and full, but some of the people, groups and tenets seem stuck in the 1960s.

I personally came full circle in my attitudes and outlook, watching the free and easy idealism and experimental lifestyles of two decades ago grind inexorably down into nihilism, diseases, narcotics and a variety of politics that only seems to favor losers and totalitarian ideologies. It's been disappointing.

Further, this is a less civilized era than the earlier part of this century. It's painful to see that children and women seem to be routinely victimized and abused. Crime, drugs, perversions and fashionable hypocrisies have made every urban area into a decaying jungle zone, while the media seems intent on idealizing the negative. One who must earn a living within a city is gnawingly aware that rearing children and maintaining a household in such an environment is perilous at best.

If I could, I would take my children back to the ranch or to the farm where I myself grew up. It was safe and wholesome (and essentially Pagan) there.

But it can't be done; the ranch is gone and the farm belongs to another branch of the family. The next best plan is to bring to my family and friends, and to others like us, through my writings and researches, some of the strength and character factors that shaped my own growing years. Frequent vacations into the wilderness, to old and beautiful places, is of course a recommended part of it.

And so also is a solid, no-nonsense religion that nonetheless possesses magic, mystery and high ideals.

The ancient Norse had much to recommend them. They built on a little-known social and religious structure that preceded them, and which had been there from earlier eras of folk migrations. Their system of religion and of society influenced lands from Finnmark to the northern Mediterranean, from central Russia (my own ancestral land) to Britain and Iceland, and even touched the shores of Vinland, which would not be known as "America" for yet half a millennium. The times and the lands were often hard, but the culture of the Northlands prospered.

With the help of some very inspired friends I've tried to codify the essence of ancient Odinism into a format and a ritual system which is applicable to today's world. Much research was involved over a period of years, and all the key materials herein are from a wide variety of original sources, from the Eddas to Jacob Grimm, from Russian folklore to German and Bohemian folk traditions, and from archaeological and literary volumes obtained across northern and central Europe.

As I began the actual writing of this book I began visiting some of the currently-existing Odinist groups. I have liked the people that I've met: They were (and are) solid working-class folk much like the farmers, ranchers, carpenters and construction workers among whom I grew up. Existing Odinist groups tend sometimes to incline a little toward a survivalist and warrior ethos though, while my own personal slant, and the one in this book, is more toward creating and maintaining close-knit mini-societies of friends and extended families.

I think it can be said that I've tried to re-create Odinism somewhat as it might have been, though not necessarily as its enclaves exist today. I have instead re-created the Way of Valhalla as it should be— nurturing and strongly protective of the things that have always mattered, like children, family and friends, and oriented to using means that are physical, spiritual and magical to build success in this uncertain world of ours.

There is magic and mystery here, but it is the echoing of like-spirited peoples from the past, the beauty and strangeness and awe of Nature, and the treasured love of those who are closest. It echoes the pragmatism of a farmstead in Virginia, in Jutland, in Free Ukrainia, or in Bohemia.

And it has a bit of what I felt alone out on those Danish moors, long ago.

Ed Fitch
Orange County, California
August 1988, C.E.

The Calling of the Grey Wanderer

O far traveling, Sky-Cloaked Wanderer
From the far, ancient lands,
We call to you across mountain and forest,
And the far, limitless grasslands;
We call to you across distant time,
And a hundred hundred slow turnings
Of the vast spindle of the sky.
We call to you in lands of mystery
Where ravens wheel in darkling skies,
And the far calling of wolves,
Echoing eldritch through crisp night wind,
Brings close the strange far worlds
Where humankind never has trod.
We call to you beyond the distant icy tundra
And the vast plains of snow
Beneath the unearthly rippling and flowing
Of the dark northern skies' boreal lights,
To the golden gates of far Valhall
Where the shimmering bridge of rainbow
Links the dark Middle Earth of men
With the shining realms of the Gods.
Come to us now and be with us here,
Great Odin!

Introduction to Odinism:
An Old Religion in a New Age

"Odinism? In the present day? Aren't we beyond all that?" Such is likely to be the response of many to the re-introduction of a faith that has not been practiced for a thousand years. It seems more than a little strange that the Gods and Goddesses of Valhalla should now be finding increasing numbers of adherents in the modern era, when humankind has built a technological civilization far beyond anything ever dreamed of in ages past, and when we have begun pushing out even into the infinite vastness of space toward frontiers that will never end.

Yet this era has its troubles, and they are serious ones, hearkening ominously back to the chaotic events of the Dark Ages. Governments grind down on the means of honest citizens in order to sustain vast organizations that seem to do little, if any, good. Increasingly large numbers of people have come to depend completely on the public dole, while drugs and perversions seem particularly to victimize the young. Abroad, artificial and alien creeds seize and hold power brutally, their twisted principles reducing millions to starvation and choking out the last embers of freedom. Those who should provide learned discourse on the guidance of our civilization seem sadly lacking in an understanding of the most fundamental facts of what life really means, and are all too far from knowing those who must actually work (and work hard) for their living. They seem to have lost touch with reality long ago. Everywhere the truth seems twisted, with honest words, deeds and good ideals vilified, forgotten or trivialized. Sadly, the religions of the present era only seem to make matters worse, and have long been a part of the problem.

Now there is a great need to concentrate on the most basic aspects of life, the ones which have been proven over millennia of human experience. A person must grow to maturity, seek adventure and experience as much of the world as possible, push back the boundaries of knowledge, seek out good friends, find a lover who is a kindred soul, and provide the best possible means for oneself and one's family. Above all else, children must be nutured, raised and protected against a harsh and oftimes decadent world; they must grow to adulthood with love and with education that will leave them strong and free from the world's questionable values. One's family and folk must together build an island of warmth and hope, defending it resolutely, if need be. One should seek out more of the folk and build toward a saner, better future.

The ancient religion of northern Europe left us with ideals of strength, individuality and honor, stressing the value of family, friends, and folk. Although even the Eddas were altered in their re-editing by Christian writers, these principles have remained constant.*

The Old Ways never quite died out. They were kept alive here and there by a few devotees and passed down through their families. From time to time sympathetic scholars gathered together, among what they could find to preserve for succeeding generations, some hint of the solidity, the magic, the beauty and the mystery that our ancestors knew. Then with the latter part of the 20th century came a renaissance in all varieties of ancient European Paganism, and a wide realization that the Old Religion, wherever one might seek it, fulfilled the empty, echoing voids in hearts and souls that had lost the true paths in centuries past.

Stern times bring forth stern creeds. None knew this better than the American Indians, the peoples of the Siberian steppes, or the Norse and Teutons. This era is one of peril and danger, as old ways decay and as the world seems to everywhere sag dangerously toward chaos. The path of Valhalla, and the lesser-known ones that existed alongside it, provide the inward strength that is so needed today: Odin's hard-gained wisdom; Thor's strong arm, protection and sturdy humor; Freya's beauty and magic, warmth and protectiveness; even Loki's sly jokes and outrageous pranks. Less known but with equal importance and possibly deeper roots is the Dark Lady Hulda, sometime companion of Odin and always wise beyond all understanding, equally at home in the realms of men, the lands of the dead and the shining realms of the Gods.

The Old Ways still have great strength and magic to them; they are alive and well and growing here and now. The shining paths give magic, mystery, beauty, common sense, a love of family, close friends, and one's own home and land. They've been around for a long time though, like Odin himself, they have usually not been recognized by the once-born.

Now is the time. They are needed, and the Old Gods come!

---

*Ed. note: This editing was more typical of the fate of Celtic (Irish/Welsh) mythology.—E.T.

The Way of the Rainbow Bridge

It is deep within our souls. The wind whispers in the high evergreens as we stand on the shore of a crystal lake and watch the clouds drift among the high peaks that tower above us. Across the smooth, cold lake we can see the thin waterfalls that drop ribbon-like down the sheer cliffs, falling free into the blue waters with a soft sound. There are five, perhaps eight separate streams, all as white as spun crystal.

Off to the west, on a high foothill, are the high earthen mounds that mark the final resting places of the Great Ones, those who have done the most for our folk in the past. It is said that on moonlit nights when the wolves howl long and eerie, and the boreal lights ripple and flow, that their words can be heard and even their forms can be seen by those who are sturdy enough of heart to remain among the steep, grassy mounds. It is good, though; they protected our people and attained great things in their lifetimes, and now, long after death, they still protect and advise us. Who but our people could be so fortunate?

To the east, where yet another hill rises is a lighter place, a spot where our children love to play, and where the first rays of the rising Sun will caress the meadow through the warm seasons. The oak grove atop the knoll is as old as the mountains themselves. Huge, tall stones stand there in the high clearing, with words of devotion chipped deep across their faces. Some have markings of fire from the sky that flash during summer storms. The old stories tell that the Great One visited there once, resting his great hammer and laughing with the folk. He had flashing eyes and a bristling red beard. His sky-cloaked comrade quietly drank of the ale we had given him and looked about with his one good eye that seemed to see into the hearts of everyone. The wiry and mischievious third one was always grinning, always weaving words, always chipping in with his outrageous jokes.

At other times, even recently, has come the Woman. Her strong, wild wolves are always near her, yet other creatures seem to feel safe in her presence. Sometimes in spring she is said to be a golden-tressed maiden in blue or white, sometimes in summer a beauteous, full-blooded woman with a flowing mane the color of the sunset and a cloak of the same rich hue. When the seasons are cold and harsh she is in black furs, her ebon hair streaked through with silver, and the rustlings that follow her cannot be entirely of this world. Our elders seem to talk often with her, and even the children speak of meeting her in the forest and along the lake from time to time, and say that she is wise and kindly.

And then there are our folk, our people. We are all close, and we know each other very well indeed, for we labor together in the fields, we hunt and fish together, we join for celebrations and laughing and worship. Sometimes we disagree, and these rough areas must be worked out by the quarrelers themselves or with the help of others. Yet we are all like a great family, and indeed we are mostly all related, close or far, by blood. Some like living with the bustle at the center of the village, and others, solitary off in the woods. We all fit together with near perfection, it seems, and none from the outside could match so closely as we do, one with the other.

The children are our jewels and our treasures, and we love them with a height and a depth that only the Gods could possibly understand. They are conceived in love, and each birth makes the months of concern and the hours of pain seem worthwhile. As they grow we encourage them, discipline them when necessary, worry, agonize and fear when they take sick, laugh and cavort with them when all is well. If we lost one it would seem to be the end of the world. We take them on adventures into the high mountains and to other far lands as they grow, to teach them of the world. They are so small, young and tender, and they try so to understand the world, to be grown-up, to seek the Light and to reach for the skies. What can we do for them but the very best we can possibly manage?

So here we stand, where the air is as pure and clean as the shining waters before us. We know our Gods and we know our people. We have pride in our past and an eternal confidence of the future. The skies are open, and the world is good!

The Gods of Valhalla
and Before

Odin

The prime deity in our ancient path is one who is really at the center of the Gods, rather than a solitary being claiming omnipotence, and who is not at all adverse to having other deities called upon for aid or blessing. In the Eddas and the various related lore he never demanded to be chief of the Gods, but due to his vast wisdom was respected and consulted by Gods and men alike.

Odin may be seen in two ways, both aspects of the same way, and valid. The more common way is in his persona of All-Father, a view more commonly ascribed by those with a Christian background. It is this aspect on which we call in matters pertaining to family, folk and land, where wisdom and guidance are valued above all. In this aspect Odin is sometimes pictured as a heroic, strongly built patriarch, a view which is valid much of the time.

The second aspect is similar to Mercury, or Hermes: sharpness of mind, quiet, adept at magics and the altering of the flow of circumstance, always wandering, wise in the ways of the world, yet always interested in learning more, and giver of victory in conflicts. Since earliest times he has been pictured as a tall, lank individual wearing a wide-brimmed hat and a cloak of grey or blue, and carrying a staff which, while useful for walking, also possessed immense powers. This is the manner in which he was most often viewed in ancient times.

Odin is also one-eyed. The legends say that he treasured knowledge so greatly that he gave his right eye in ransom for it. He is possessed of vast strength and will power. The same legends say that he had himself fixed to a tree to gain the deepest of wisdom, and hung alone on the tree for nine days and nine nights. "Word by word I sought out words. Fact by fact I sought out facts," he said.

Often it is said that he roamed the world alone and solitary, accompanied only by a pair of wolves or a pair of ravens. Sometimes he rode a strange, eight-legged steed "Slepnir," who represents time itself. His son, who would often ride behind him, is the yearly reborn spirit of life.

3

The legends indicate that Odin has always preferred to be involved with people, families in particular. He takes an interest in dynasties that show promise, and follows them through the centuries. Odin cares for people, even if at times it must be a stark and hard caring that comes up against fate itself, and presses against the very boundaries of possible and impossible, of life and of death.

Psychologically, Odin is the patron who wakes each of us from our earlier, magical world view to a more mature and intellectual outlook on life. He represents abstract thought and the ability to make the abstract come into complete reality. Odin also gives godlike inspiration and solid worldly success to those who strive for and deserve them.

In many ways, Odin seems to be the ultimate priest for Gods as well as for men. His way of gaining the knowledge which he treasures so much is strikingly similar to the way in which a Siberian shaman, or priest, will seek the secrets of life and death. His self-crucifixion on the Tree to gain wisdom is a ritual which looks strikingly similar to the Native American Sun dance. Based on this, some have felt that Odin may originally have been an ordinary man who sought godhead and ultimately attained it. Whatever the truth, this story provides the ultimate inspiration and challenge to humankind, saying, "Where I am now, so also may you be, if you are willing and strong."

Thor

Odin's close friend and companion on their many wanderings was the Thunderer, the red-bearded and powerfully built Thor. In Pagan times Thor was always popular, and in some lands even supplanted his friend, the One-Eyed.

Thor sends lightning, thunder and life-giving rain. He has always been a strong protector of his folk, and gives gifts freely to his human friends. He has a liking for farms, fields, forests, mountains and streams. Thor has a hearty and oftimes bawdy sense of humor. He likes drinking, banqueting, storytelling and good company in general.

His one weapon is his mighty hammer, Mjolnir, a magical weapon which strikes with the lightning and roars with the thunder as it is used, and which always returns to his hand. In ancient times and even

THOR

occasionally to this day those who call him their patron will wear a miniature tau-shaped hammer about their necks. It is of particular interest that warriors and those who must face stressful situations will find wearing a Thor's-hammer to be appropriate.

Whereas Odin rewards intelligence, Thor rewards hard work. From a psychological viewpoint their long-standing partnership makes excellent sense, especially when leavened with Loki's curiosity and sense of humor.

Thor is similar to Freyr in that he represents "the good life." It can truly be said, "Thor is the working-man's God!"

Loki

The jokester of Valhalla became its chief villain toward the end of the legend cycle, and set forth the events that brought the realm of the Gods to its end. Yet it is thought that in doing so he was acting as an agent for that which was fated to happen. Loki is a very real personage and a very real God, and whatever is said by those who comment on the Eddas, he is still very real today. The legends should be viewed as giving not only his good features of humor, wit, questioning, pranks and parodies, but the darker side of these aspects as well—an object lesson of what can happen when these go wrong. The darkness that slowly rose in Loki's personality can happen very actually in the soul and spirit of any human being, and can eventually have similarly destructive consequences. He is like the child portion in each and all of us: either fun-loving or destructive.

Also, he can be a personification of a sometime dark aspect of the Great Goddess known in the most ancient legends of all peoples and all lands, named in northern Europe as Erda, Erce, or Hulda, and along the rim of the Mediterranean as Eurynome. There are times when destruction is needed and inevitable, to clear away the decadence of the past. Robert Graves most aptly wrote her words:

> When the water stinks
> I break the dam.
> In love I break it.

LOKI

Loki would not want to mention "love," but he would break the dam anyway.

Loki is Thor's half-brother, being born from the Elder Gods who held sway before Valhalla. The legends state that Odin, Thor and Loki went on many adventures together, and together accomplished great deeds.

He has domain over fire, and is a master magician and conjurer as well as a shape-changer. Bearing always in mind Loki's dark side as well as his good one, he is most valuable as a witty, entertaining acquaintance, and someone to call upon when his positive aspects are needed. Additionally, his cleverness and sharp wit are most useful in dealing with the deceptiveness and decadence of a world which has lost the Old Ways.

Loki represents both our divine intelligence and also the free will whereby we can choose for good or ill, and if we make a mistake, to correct it. He typifies the human mind: on one hand clever, foolish, immature. On the other hand, he personifies the elevating, aspiring traits in human intelligence.

Freya

Freya was the sister of Freyr. Especially in early times, she was very all-encompassing in her attributes, and seemed to have inherited many of them from various personifications of the Great Goddess who far preceded the Gods of Valhalla. Freya is famed for her great beauty, and indeed is often known as "The Fair One." In the earlier days, she also rewarded good housewives, though in later times Frigga has become more the patron of the home.

Freya is quite independent, being chief of the Valkyries, the demi-goddesses who select the noble and heroic dead and carry them to the Realm of the Gods. (Some of the legends say that a quarter, or even a half, of the dead go to Freya, which must be a fine reward indeed for these worthy ones!). She is patroness of women who attain wisdom, status, and power, since the Valkyries had been ordinary women, then priestesses, and after being Valkyr became Norns, the Great Goddesses who weave the fates and histories of people and of nations.

Freya is the Daughter of Time, as well as the patron and protec-

FREYA

tress of the human race. On her breast she wears "the jewel whose power cannot be resisted," Brisingamen (*brising*: fire, specifically the fire of the enlightened mind, *men*: jewel). In ancient times the winter constellation which we today know as Orion was at that time called "Freya's Gown" by the Norse and Teutons, and the sword belt in Orion was called "Freya's Girdle."

She is as strong, beautiful and wise as any of the "Eldest Ones."

Balder

The God most beloved by all living things as well as by the other Gods, the Eddas say, was Balder. Blond, fair, and handsome, he is good and loving in every way, always willing to sacrifice himself for others. He may be viewed as being similar to Christ, or as the Green Man of the world's legends whose death is the sacrifice that brings new life to the Earth, and whose rebirth in spring symbolizes the inevitable rebirth of all things. There are traces of Balder being part of a very ancient life-religion of which we now have no records, but which preceded the Gods of Valhalla. In it, Balder and his brother Hodur would have been the symbolic, yearly rivals for the favors of the Goddess.

He is the patron of light and of day. Balder is always cheerful and caring, willing to listen and to help.

Tyr

The invincible warrior of the Nordic pantheon, and far older than all the others of Asgard was Tyr. He is said to have sacrificed his right hand to help bind Fenrir, the wolf who, when set free, is destined to devour the Sun. Tyr symbolizes will and desire. It is thought by scholars that he may have been the original father-god of the archaic Indo-Europeans, long before the dawn of our histories.

Heimdall

A bright and gracious God, Heimdall guards the heavenly rainbow bridge that leads to the realm of the Gods. He is the watchman and warder of the Gods, and good to call upon at any time that watchfulness and guarding are required.

The old legends told that he was born of the Elder Gods, that he wants less sleep than a bird, sees a hundred miles off by night or day, and hears the grass on the ground and the wool on a sheep's back both grow. It is said that his horn will alert all living things when the great conflict of Ragnarok comes, bringing with it the end of the world.

Bragi

The patron of poetry and eloquence, Bragi was the skald, bard, and minstrel of the Gods. He likes wells and springs, is easy to like and is enjoyable company at any time. He is the personification of poetic inspiration, the wisdom of the skalds, and divine illumination in the soul.

Freyr

Patron of fields, crops, and green growing things, he is the peaceful and fruitful protector of farmers, and a personification of the basic male principle in the universe. Freya and Freyr were originally Vanir: pre-Valhalla deities who together shared the seasons. Quite probably the spring and the summer were hers, and the fall and winter were his.

Aegir

God of the sea and patron of sailors, and similar to Neptune. He can be fearsome and awe-inspiring to the extreme, as is the ocean itself. He has power over sea serpents and water monsters of all kinds, yet Aegir is invariably a very genial and pleasant host to those who visit him.

Hodur

The blind brother of Balder who, according to the legend, threw the mistletoe at his bright brother, not knowing that this small plant was the one thing in existence that could hurt or kill Balder. Some have said that he personifies ignorance and darkness, though it may be said that he is the personification of age and aging, and the dissolution which clears the way for the rebirth of new life. There are some indications that before the time of Valhalla there was a life religion, now forgotten, in which Balder was the king of the waxing year, Hodur the winter king (or the king of the declining year), and Nanna the eternal Goddess for whom they contended.

Hermodur

The messenger of the Gods, personifying quickness. He is a son of Odin.

Ostara

The patroness of spring, fertility and new life, after whom our holiday of Easter is named. Lovely, cheerful, bright and sensual, she enjoys dancing and good company. Traditionally, fertility cakes are offered to her and eaten in honor of her during Easter-tide. "Hot cross buns" originated as offerings to Ostara.

SIF

Sif

The Goddess who was consort to Thor, and who was famed for her long, beautiful golden hair with which she preferred to work her magic and her enchantments. She is the patroness of harvests and the comfortable wealth that comes from them.

Hulda

Also known as Holle or Berchta. She is one of the earlier Gods, or Giants, and represents an earlier goddess tradition that far preceded Valhalla. For those who are drawn to the folk magics of ancient Europe, particularly those during the era and in the lands of the Norse religion, an understanding of Hulda is very useful indeed. Although Hulda has no direct part in the Eddic cycle of legends (she is mentioned indirectly and her magic-user followers, asadherents of an older tradition, are mentioned as often being in conflict with the followers of Asgard), her worship once spread over all of north, central and eastern Europe, and contributed greatly to the common peoples' traditions in following the Norse religion.

There is a vast amount of her folklore still surviving and there are probably millions in those regions who still follow Hulda, though under a different name. Over the past thousand years a thin veneer of Christianity has been applied and the Goddess has been re-named as "Mary," with her deeds and sayings transferred mostly intact as part of the local versions of Judeo-Christianity.

She is the Goddess of the burial mounds and the fairy-mountains. (As a result of their extensive researches, the Brothers Grimm felt that she was Venus in the ancient legend of Tannhäuser.) Hulda is the Eye Goddess associated with grave mounds, and whose spiral eye carvings mark ancient grave sites across all of Europe. (She may well have been the potent "fairy godmother" in the original German version of "Cinderella" in which Cinderella is stronger, magically adept and somewhat darker than in our present, popular version.)

Sometimes comely and dignified, though more often appearing as an old crone or a wise woman, she is kind, benignant and merciful.

Hulda (or Holle) likes lakes and fountains, creates rain and snow, and rules her own garden-like realm in the nether world. Apple trees are particularly sacred to her. She is the patron of flax and weaving, and is often mentioned in eastern European legends as going through houses and blessing the infants.

There is another side to Hulda: she is the Goddess of the Witches, and also the Goddess of winter and the underworld. At the depth of winter she leads a procession of wolves, elves, witches and spirits of the dead through the moonlight and snow, carrying away the souls of those whose time has come to die. Oftimes she can appear as a beautiful woman from the front, though look like a tree from behind.

Hulda is both the kindly bringer-in of life and the dark, austere one who takes it away at life's end. She is the forerunner of Hel, and later gave many powers to the Asgardian Queen of the underworld.

She often carries a spindle for spinning the threads of fate and destiny. Some legends state that her spindle is magically linked with the axis that runs from the middle of the Earth, out through the North Pole and to the North Star. This she later gave to Freya.

Hulda is the original patroness of housewives and of families, though in later times this was passed first to Freya and then to Frigga. She loves singing and the playing of musical instruments, and was thus also the orignal patroness of music. In some parts of northern Europe she is said to be the wife or mother of Odin, although this admittedly conflicts with the better-known and more recent legends. In ancient times some peoples in northern Europe called the Milky Way "Hulda's Road," though more recently this "road of souls" was said to belong to Freya, who has also inherited many of Hulda's other strong attributes.

Some scholars have felt that she precedes the Old Gods, and that her name is also Huldana, Erda, or Earth. If so, then Hulda is perhaps the most ancient of all the High Ones, and deserves honor as the Ultimate Source.

Ran

Queen of the Sea and consort of Aegir, the Sea God. (In the legends of northern Europe she has always been considerably more important than Aegir.) Ran is queen of the undines, or mermaids, and hence is known for her music, her ability to prophesy the future, her spells of enchantment and her great beauty. The souls of those who have drowned are said to go into her realms. She is the patroness of girls and of young women who have not yet married. Ran's daughters are the proverbial "nine waves of the sea," and the entrance to her abode is through the Maelstrom, the vast whirlpool said by legends to exist somewhere in the higher latitudes of the North Sea.

Hel

Loki's daughter is queen of the realms of the dead, and is as fearsome as the darker aspects of the ancient Greek Hecate. Hel (also called Hella or Hellia) is sister of the chaos wolf Fenrir and a vast earth dragon; she is pictured as half-black and half-white. Hella sits in judgment of souls which have not been able to attain either the high state of Valhalla or the elemental beauty of Ran's sea realm.

There are different traditions, and the legends of Hel changed with time. She was preceded by the archaic Lady Hulda, and apparently received all powers from this Elder Goddess. Hel's realms, according to the early legends, are deep within the Earth, at the root of all existence (which in the Eddas was figuratively called the base of the World-Tree, Yggdrasill) and can be quite pleasing or severely unpleasant, depending on what a soul truly deserves.

(Interestingly, Jungian psychology places Hella deep within the subconscious of every living human, in the "racial memory" itself!)

Hella is not death nor any evil being; she neither kills nor torments. She takes the souls of the departed and holds them with an inexorable grip. She is the hard reality which lies at the end of all things.

Iduna

The Goddess of youth, she also represents our Earth. Iduna supplied the Gods with the source of immortality, magical apples. There is metaphysical importance here, for the apple has always been equated with the wisdom of how the universe really works. Apples are the sweet fruit of the soil which, when sliced crossways, show a five-pointed star, symbolizing humankind made perfect, the ages of man, eternal rebirth and much more. One should refer to the writings of Robert Graves' *The White Goddess* for an in-depth discussion of this ancient, universal symbol.

Nanna

Balder's wife was a Goddess who was good, loving and devoted. It is said that after Balder's death she died of heartbreak. Her spirit comforts those who have lost a member of their family, since Balder himself existed happily and with good friends in Hel's realm after death. He was, in time, joined by his beloved wife. In some very ancient legends she is the ageless and beautiful Goddess for whom Balder and Hodur eternally contend; she finally descended into the underworld to confront Hodur, and successfully bring the slain Balder back up into the world of the living once again.

Gerd

The wife of Freyr, her beauty was so great that it left sparkles in the air after she passed. She was given the choice of immortality or annihilation under the pressure (or inspiration) of Freyr, and consciously made the decision to become an immortal goddess.

Bil

The Goddess of weaving, as mentioned in "The Saga of Gisli the Outlaw." Weaving, like spinning, seems to have been a means for effecting magic as well as a very common household routine.

The Norns

The three Goddesses of fate who spun the destinies and histories of men, women, nations and Gods—even the history and ultimate destiny of the universe itself!

Frigga

The patron of mothers, parenting and households, Frigga was the wife of Odin and the chief of the Asynjor. Her son was the Bright One of Valhalla, Balder. Originally Frigga and Freya were probably one deity, but in most of the legends she is separate, being the older and highly competent matron whose common sense and family love holds the home together. Frigga is perhaps one of the most basic and important goddesses: without her influence the very basis of all society, the family and the home, could not exist. She rewards good housewives, watches the home and is the guardian of women in childbirth.

Ullr

A stepson of Thor and Sif, and a minor hero of Nordic myth.

Vali

The son of Loki by Siguna or by Rinda, and one of the Aesir.

Skadi

The Giantess who was the mother of Freyr, and is the patroness of all who love wild, snow-covered wilderness mountains. She became the wife of Njord.

Forseti

One of the Aesir, and the son of Balder and Nanna. He is the patron of justice and uprightness.

Njord

A Giant who was the father of Freyr and Freya, and may originally have been consort to the earth-mother Goddess Jord.

Vidar

"The Silent One," who was the son of Odin by a Giantess, and who was almost as strong as Thor. One of the Aesir, the legends tell that he ultimately destroys the chaos-wolf Fenrir at the world's end of Ragnarok.

Aesir

The entourage of Gods and Goddesses who were the attendants of Odin.

Asynjor

The entourage of Gods and Goddesses who were the attendants of Freya and Frigga.

Vanir

In Nordic myth these appear to have been the seafaring gods of a race which preceded the Aesir in Scandinavia. After a defeat by the Aesir, the Vanir fused with them.

Giants

The Elder Gods of Nordic myth who were displaced by the Aesir, the Asynjor and the Vanir. They could be of normal human stature and were known for their magic, and often for their beauty.

How We Stand Before Our Gods

One could say that we view our Gods as Christians view their saints: entities to be called upon for favors in time of need. This is an oversimplification. The Odinist stands tall and proud before his or her Gods, arms out and eyes on the skies. We talk to the Great Ones who are our friends, and they talk back to us, if only in our minds.

The High God, whether viewed as Odin, Thor, Heimdall, Balder or even Loki, is friend and comrade, father or brother, depending on the worshipper's needs. The Lady, whether viewed as Freya, Frigga, Hulda, Sif, Ran, or even Hel, is friend and confidante, mother or sister, depending on the worshipper's needs. The follower of the Rainbow Bridge strives to become one with his or her Gods, to see through divine eyes, to gain the deep and far understanding which only a Goddess or God might only know. His or her Gods are friends, and in the rites of Valhalla the devotee meets with the Gods as an equal.

When they are used, images or symbols of our Goddesses and Gods provide concentration points for meditation and the seeking of purpose and serenity. These icons need not have any intrinsic magical or spiritual power to be effective, although with continued use they will be imbued with a greater Power.

Odin, Thor, Loki, Freya, Hulda, Frigga, Hel and all the others are primaeval and archetypal. Their essential being is unchanged in whatever personal form or forms one chooses to salute and acknowledge them.

That which we term "Divine," or "Goddess and God," represent the totality of consciousness and preconsciousness of all sentient and elemental things within the universe. The Divine is infinitely complex. It exists across time and dimensions so that the panoramas of the past and the many alternate futures are visible to it. It perceives and is part of past histories that might have been, and existences which are not in this time and space. The Divine is the repository of all knowledge and wisdom. It is capable of vast powers and magics which have no limit. The Divine is each of us personally, along with countless others who have lived, will live, or may never live.

In order to have a oneness, a rapport and a personal closeness with the Divine, the Odinist chooses to recognize at least a small portion as Gods whom he or she can name and visualize, as friends that can be known and understood. This is a true and valid approach, and with the soul-binding of family, best friends and of our own unique folk comes the keying of that deepest part of the mind which opens the portals to the wisdom of the Gods, and brings their presence through to help us in this world.

The Rede of Honor

1. In all that you do, consider its benefit or harm upon yourself, your children and your people.

2. All that which you do will return to you, sooner or later, for good or for ill. Thus strive always to do good to others, or at least strive always to be just.

3. Be honest with yourself, and with others. "This above all; to thine own self be true."

4. Humankind, and especially your own family and folk, has the spark of divinity within it. Protect and nuture that spark.

5. Give your word sparingly, and adhere to it like iron.

6. In the world, your first trust and responsibility should be to your own people. Yet, be kind and proper to others whenever possible.

7. What you have, HOLD!

8. Pass on to others only those words which you have personally verified.

9. Be honest with others, and let them know that you expect honesty in return, always.

10. The fury of the moment plays folly with the truth; to keep one's head is a virtue.

11. Know which battles should be fought, and which battles should be avoided. Also, know when to break off a conflict. There are times when the minions of chaos are simply too strong or when fate is absolutely unavoidable.

12. When you gain power, use it carefully and use it well.

13. Courage and honor endure forever. Their echoes remain when the mountains have crumbled to dust.

14. Pledge friendship and your services to those who are worthy. Strengthen others of your people and they will strengthen you.

15. Love and care for your family always, and have the fierceness of a wolf in their protection.

16. Honor yourself, have pride in yourself, do your best and forgive yourself when you must.

17. Try always to be above reproach in the eyes of the world.

18. Those of our people should always endeavor to settle any differences among themselves quietly and peaceably.

19. The laws of the land should be obeyed whenever possible and reason, for in the main they have been chosen with wisdom.

20. Have pride in yourself, your family and your folk. They are your promise for the future.

21. Do not neglect your mate and children.

22. Every one of our people should work according to the best that s/he can do, no matter how small or how great. We are all in this world together, thus we must always help each other along.

23. One advances individually and collectively only by living in harmony with the natural order of the world.

24. The seeking of wisdom is a high virtue. Love of truth, honor, courage and loyalty are the hallmarks of the noble soul.

25. Be prepared for whatever the future brings.

26. Life with all its joys, struggles and ambiguities is to be embraced and lived to the fullest!

Sayings Concerning the Gods

There is much discussion as to whether the Gods are real, or whether they are a creation of men. There are records of a very great "King Odin" in the Black Sea area several thousand years ago, whose history of great attainments may have grown in the retelling by the descendants of his people, until his legend made him to be a God. Yet also, the Gods of Valhalla (Odin included) have always provided spiritual sustenance as well as inspiration to their followers for as long as any religious artifacts or written records of them have existed. Each person chooses his or her own reality. Our Gods evolve as do we, and take new qualities as we need them. A child must know that the Deities are very real and very immediate, though as one matures, his or her concepts may change. At the very least, all Gods do indeed exist firmly within the mind. Beyond that, form your own opinions, and test them continually.

That which is called "supernatural" does indeed exist and is often experienced. But the term "supernatural" is erroneous: It is very "natural" indeed, being usually a reflection of some facet of existence which may be rarely seen and not, as yet, explained by our sciences.

The Eddas and the sagas tell of bravery and of great deeds, yet always bear in mind that they spoke for a very distant, very harsh, era. Also, they were changed and altered by unbelievers over the centuries. Thus one should take their guidance primarily in matters of spirit, as far as today is concerned.

The Eddas tell of those who are particularly good, wise, strong, or heroic as being worthy of rebirth in another life, while those who are weak, common and ordinary are forgotten by the Gods and disappear into the ocean of life as a mere drop of water into the shining sea. One should strive always to be worthy of rebirth, and to urge one's children and kin to be the same.

The ancient lore suggests that great Odin himself was once a man like any other, but by his own search for knowledge, wisdom, courage

27

and much work he became a master shaman, ultimately attained kingship and then godhood. Remember: he is not the only one who can do such a thing! "Where I am, there ye may be also." Attain to excellence by all means, and to greatness if you can.

The stories of Loki tell much of the problems that can occur with different personalities. They are worth studying, and considering, to avoid his mistakes.

Our Gods grow as we grow. Or perhaps it is our perception of them that changes as we mature.

In the times of our ancestors, Odin gave victory in battle. Nowadays he also gives success in life.

Thor has always been "the working man's god."

An unfortunate legacy of Christianity is that it has, for 2000 years (and Islam for slightly less time), sought to break down close ties between families, friends, clans, tribes or peoples. The goal seems good and noble at first glance: "Devote yourself and all you have to the true God and to all men. Bring the whole world together before Him." But it hasn't worked. Most wars and repressions for the last two millennia have been due, directly or indirectly, to this thrust for universalism. Study history, and see for yourself.

One who worships the Old Gods will proudly stand to pray, and look to the skies.

A God who made iron would not permit his followers to be slaves. A God who is famed for his knowledge and wisdom would not accept followers who allowed themselves to be slaves. Therefore, all of our folk must treasure wisdom, thought and freedom.

Sayings for
Oneself and One's People

Our People

"Our people" is a term taken as being "those who are close to us." Certainly this would be our own personal families: husbands, wives, children, parents, uncles and aunts, but also it includes close friends with whom we have much in common, proven by a long time of knowing each other well. If our close friends are similarly linked with others whom we may not know well, but with whom we mutually feel we have much in common as within a clan or tribe during past eras, then these too are considered to be the "folk," or our "people." Also, one's own folk or people may definitely include wartime comrades, for more is shared in battle than can be expressed in words. Perhaps we all may be physically located in the same community, though it is much more common nowadays for members of the "folk" to live widely apart from one another, even though we might get together whenever possible.

We draw our strength from the natural world, from the land, the mountains and the seas. One must have lived with Nature to have a full understanding of what life truly involves. Those who know nothing but the city are missing a crucial part of their own souls.

Insofar as it is possible, we should form our people into a mosaic of families, family groupings and communities. Together we can help each other and be better prepared for whatever the future holds.

Society

The word "society" has two quite different meanings. The usual is that of the ofen ambiguous and chaotic world about us. The other meaning is that tight and firm relationship between ourselves, our families, our friends and our own people.

Family and Friends

Always respect your children's tastes. Do not hurry them to be as adults, nor ridicule their tastes in stories and other literature. With proper upbringing, they will mature at their own individual times and ways.

Young people should endeavor to learn some trade or skill even at an early age so that at first they can have money of their own, then support themselves, and ultimately be able to support their future mates and themselves without much trouble. When this is done, it is easier for their parents to help them, and eventually their families, as needed during the years to follow. Of course, it is best to have two or more very different skills or professions at which one is capable; it increases your security and flexibility in the world.

Parents must care for their children, even when the young ones become mature. When youths become of age, it is well that, if at all possible, the parents provide for the first home of the new husband, wife and infants. For their part, the young adults must realize that their parents represent a rich lode of experience, and continually pay attention to their advice. (Costly mistakes are easy to make when one is young.)

It is good for parents to provide some monetary support for their children as they get started in adult life, for inheritances seldom come when they are most needed, and few look forward to the deaths that make these bequests possible. Also, inheritances invariably are heavily taxed. Conversely, grown children are obligated to see that their parents are secure in old age, keeping them as honored elders of the family for the remainder of their natural lives.

The attainment marks of your own children, as well as those of your folk, should always be much higher than the sludge levels that seem often to be the accepted standards of others.

If it is possible, larger household groupings of family members are desirable. Younger people need occasional care for their children, and older folk need companionship. Each family member must have necessary privacy, though "many hands make light work." But it is important that everyone must contribute as much as they can to such an extended family.

The Elders, with their treasure trove of experience, have the responsibility to formulate the morals of the folk. These cannot be artificial or contrived. They must be realistic, and help the people to continue and prosper. Our folk must validate these morals by their daily lives so that they very naturally become an intrinsic part of our faith.

A father's first duties are to his children and his wife. A wife's first duties are to her children and husband. Both should be involved with other close, like-minded friends, helping and supporting, for in working together much can be accomplished.

The Eddas and the sagas are of particular value in educating our younger children into the values of honor, truth, bravery, knowledge and wisdom. A parent should acquire copies of this ancient literature to pick out anecdotes that would be both entertaining and instructive to the young ones. Following the old traditions, these tales should be told by word of mouth, rather than be read.

Guilt, even for the worst of crimes, should die with the guilty. It should not be passed on to the next generation. The world will give them enough else to contend with!

Debts of all kinds should most properly die with the debtor, and not be passed on to his widow or heirs. (Note the reason above.)

> A man's first duty over all else is to support his children, even if he can't support his wife. (She may, after all, be a crazy woman.). But then, for exactly the same reason, a woman's first duty is to her children.
> —Evan McCallum

We must not keep our children away from reality. The world is real, and a child's or a youth's capability for understanding may surprise you.

It is advisable not to call unwarranted attention to oneself by being particularly different, bizarre, threatening or bothersome to others. You can have a more relaxed time being yourself when the outside world isn't wondering and worrying about you.

Oneself

It is with our feet firmly placed in the good Earth that we can best reach toward the stars.

A young man or a young woman should endeavor to learn as much of the world as possible, to experience as much as possible (but with caution because the world has treachery, as well as adventure and beauty), to meet and understand as many differing races and nationalities, and stations in life as possible. Seek out adventure and search for truth. Also, they should gain as much formal learning as possible and acquire a trade, profession or business. As they advance themselves they forward their people, helping and supporting.

Any man who goes to war should be married with at least one son or daughter, or at least have his wife to be pregnant with child. Thus, if the worst happens and he does not return, his heritage and the results of his love will not be lost to his people.

No matter what your station in life, or how good (or bad) you have been dealt with by circumstance, society, and others, you can always improve your own lot and those of your people. Nothing is impossible if you use your brains and work hard at it.

That which you have chosen for your work and your life's tasks should by all means be something that you enjoy.

> Thou shalt honor thine ancestors, for they created our society and the world in which we live.
>
> —Evan McCallum

Man's basic instincts are to succeed. One should use these instincts to the maximum extent.

Don't try; do, and succeed!

Forgive yourself at least once yearly for any and all transgressions. From time to time, late at night, put your own negative feelings and guilt before the ancient Dark Goddess Hulda that she may consume and destroy them. Make a solitary confessional rite of this, in your own words.

> If you believe in Hell, you're probably already there.
>
> —Lothar

If one has an interest in things arcane and occult, then such things should be studied, and one should become Godi (Priest), or Godia/Gydia* (Priestess) in addition to whatever else is done for livelihood or pleasure.

Our imperative is to strive constantly to expand our powers of body, mind, and spirit.

The Odinist always gives full, outstanding service to the

---

*Godia is the form preferred by the author, although the historical Old Norse word for priestess is gydia.—E.T.

chieftain to whom he or she chooses to serve.

Good manners are always to be admired, not only in dealing with your own people, but with all others as well.

Always seek to expand your own station in life, your personal wealth and your well-being, and also those of your family and your people.

Seek out those whom you can trust, and make it a practice to consider their advice.

Seek always for the truth. It may be hidden, and fools or evil ones may try to alter it, but it is always there.

Use caution in dealing with those you do not know. Discern what they really mean, rather than accepting their words as spoken.

Other peoples and other groups have their own outstanding, brilliant individuals. Seek these out and, if they are willing to be amiable, cultivate their acquaintance. Friends, contacts and people of influence can always be of value.

Try to judge every man and every woman by their own virtues and faults, and avoid making generalizations when you can. If someone seems constantly to be hostile, then be prepared to avoid or counter them when possible.

Someone whom your dog likes and whom you would trust with your children will probably make a worthwhile friend.

Remember always your responsibility to your family and your close friends, and when you have them, to your actual children. Let these considerations always guide your decisions in important matters.

It is good for the soul as well as for the body for one to decide, occasionally, to go hungry for a day or two.

Your body is the temple of the Gods. Do not desecrate it with drugs, immoderate alcohol or other harmful dross. Care for your body. The Gods give you only one per lifetime.

If you have no children you are a genetic dead end.
If you have no family you are a social dead end.
If you have no folk you are a cultural dead end.
Think of the future, plan carefully, live fully,
And do the very best you can.

The World

The world is not always a pleasant place; yet we owe it to ourselves, our friends and our families to give them places of safety and security. Above all, our children are our own personal immortality; they are young, and tender. They have an untrammeled sense of beauty, idealism and wonder that must not be crushed by the world's harshness. We owe it to the Gods and to ourselves to care for our young, our own families and our good friends.

Pay attention to all that you see and hear, and discern what is omitted, wrongly stated or hypocritical (that sort of thing seems to be fashionable nowadays). Discuss your thoughts often with your children, family and friends. The nature of truth should be explained to the young ones until they fully understand.

In the world at large, one should usually keep his or her deepest goals, thoughts, and opinions to oneself. This yields an immediate advantage when dealing with others.

Sayings of the Ancients

Work, be aggressive, and succeed, for:

> The sleeping wolf rarely gets a bone
> Or a sleeping man victory.
>
> —Hávamál

> The fir tree withers on a dry knoll without shelter of bark
>   and needles;
> So too does a man whom no one loves.
>
> —Hávamál

> Even though a man's health may be poor,
> He may not be unhappy in all things:
> One may be blessed with good sons,
> Another with friends,
> A third with full barns,
> A fourth with good deeds.
> Better to live and be happy.
>
> —Hávamál

Cattle die; kinsmen die; you likewise must die;
But the voice of honor never dies
For him who has a good reputation.

—Hávamál

Never mock a wandering man or a guest,
None is so good that he lacks all fault,
None so wretched that he lacks all virtue.

—Hávamál

If evil thou knowest,
Then *proclaim* it to all as evil,
And make no friendship with foes.

—Hávamál

This above all: to thine own self be true.
And it must follow, as day follows the night,
That thou canst not then be false to any man.

—Shakespeare (from *Hamlet*)

Whenever possible, be truthful, but use discretion as to how the truth may be taken by others:

A man about to speak the truth
should keep one foot in the stirrup

—Old Mongolian saying

In Summary

Care for your children above all; they are your most direct legacy to the future. Care for your family next, your spouse, brothers, sisters and especially your parents. Tend to your uncles, aunts and cousins. Be certain to help your good friends also, for they may be closer than your own blood kin. If you have any energy left over after all this, then perhaps you can consider saving the world!

Be versatile!

A human being should be able to change a diaper, plan an invasion, butcher a hog, conn a ship, design a building, write a sonnet, balance accounts, build a wall, set a bone, comfort the dying, take orders, give orders, cooperate, act alone, solve equations, analyze a new problem, pitch manure, program a computer, cook a tasty meal, fight efficiently, die gallantly. Specialization is for insects.

—Robert Heinlein

On Perseverance and Strength

The world will not always be kind to you. In spite of caution, in spite of a closeness to our Gods, you may well at times be burdened by illness or misfortune. Money may be short and the demands on you may be long, or the law and the world of men may treat you harshly. The best course for the Odinist is to bear it through stoically while working incessantly to lighten or to remove the adversity. Remember, you have a responsibility to your family and to your people. "Take off the pressure" from time to time if you must, in order to retain your mind, but always aim steadfastly to overcome your difficulties. Do not become sodden with opiates or alcohol, for abandonment to these admits failure and will ultimately kill you. If you must accept help from others, plan on paying them back, in full, when it is possible.

It is worthy to stubbornly adopt the creed that, "The world may be full of harshness and illness, but by Great Odin and all the Gods I shall build myself to something better." Hang on grimly and tenaciously if need be, and if you have those who depend upon you, care for them in spite of all circumstance and misfortune, but survive.

As your situation betters, as strength and health and prosperity return, take every means to better your position and your physical self. Regain your joy in life, and improve your position in all ways so that it cannot happen to you again.

> That which does not kill us
> Makes us stronger.
>
> —Nietzsche

Concerning Secrecy

Odinism is not a creed for everyone. Any Grove which is formed should carefully screen all who express interest and admit for visits those who have been specifically recommended by a member and who would fit well with the rest of the people. For close-knit groups of family members and good friends there should be a probationary period of a year and a day at least, followed by a discussion of all members. A unanimous vote should be required.

Outdoor rites should similarly be for grove members and recommended and screened visitors. The place of camping, ceremonies, feasting and other activities should be closed to any outsiders. Although it may cost more, isolated and private campgrounds should be obtained for outdoors rites, unless one has sufficient privacy on his or her own property. (It is recommended that the leaders or spokesmen arranging for a place in a state park or other such retreat cultivate a good relationship with the forest service officials and with the park rangers. They are almost invariably good people who share the Odinists' love for the world of nature. Of course it is obvious that the rules of the park be observed fully, and that any Odinist group leave its area cleaner than they found it.)

Concerning the Body

Know your goals, design an effective way of attaining them and keep at it.

One should strive always to keep his or her body in very good physical condition, with much exercise, a balanced diet of nourishing food, sufficient sleep and a calm state of mind. Drugs and immoderate use of alcohol are to be avoided, as they weaken the body and can make one a slave who would neglect or betray his family and people in pursuit of more worthless dreck with which to harm himself.

A regular workout routine is a must. Remember: when you are in good shape, you feel good, look good and are a lot healthier!

Rites
and Ceremonies

Leaders of the Rituals

Those who lead the rites to Odin are the *Godi* (pronounced "gothi," with the "th" as in "then"), or Priest, and the *Godia* (pronounced "gith-ya," with the "th" as in "then") or Priestess. If possible, they should have training in conducting ceremonies, in helping other people with their problems, and a good knowledge of the lore and practice of Odinism. A Godia who is particularly talented in magical healing and of working seid (pronounced "seeth," with the "th" as in "then"), who has ability to forsee the future, has proven excellent knowledge of people and the world, of the arts, and of the sciences, would be termed a *Vala.*

Whenever possible, it is customary for the Godi or Godia to have various members of the group take portions of each ceremony.

The Sign of the Hammer

This is a self-blessing, a protection and a salute to the Gods. It is frequently used in the rites. You may wish to speak the names aloud when making the hammer while off by yourself, and voice them in your mind when you are with others. The right fist is used.

Touch forehead, saying
Odin
(intellect, wisdom, creativity, victory, The Father)

Touch breastbone or heart, saying
Balder
(kindness, mercy, forgiveness, love [agape], redemption, the Son)

Touch left breast, saying
Freya
(beauty, sensuality, love [eros], nurturing, magic, good fortune, the Mother)

Touch right breast, saying
Thor
(strength, adventure, challenge, work,
hearty joy, the Protector)

Sample Altar Arrangement

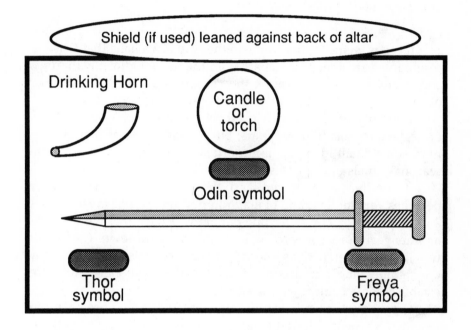

Shield (if used) leaned against back of altar

Drinking Horn

Candle or torch

Odin symbol

Thor symbol

Freya symbol

A staff (if used) may be leaned against the altar. The altar could be the surface of a flat rock or the top of a table or box, or simply lean implements against the side of a firepit or the base of a tree (an oak, if possible). Try to include some seasonal decorations.

Seasonal Festivals of the Folk

It often seems to those new to the way of Valhalla that seasonal ceremonies are something apart from the usual Odinist gatherings, and perhaps in some groups the seasonals are performed as an obligation—as a remnant of our fertility-cult ancestry.

Certainly much has been lost through the centuries and millenia of neglect, persecution and wars; but enough remains that we may have some small idea of the importance and the power which the seasonal rituals once possessed.

If one lives close to the land, the yearly cycle of the seasons becomes very familiar and of major importance; crops must be good and cattle fat, or you and your people will have to "live lean" for another year. For those who live in the cities and the towns (as most do now), an attention to the seasonal rites and festivals can help to draw our families and our friends closer together, and can help to re-establish some contact with the Earth.

Since the most archaic times the cycle of the year has been represented by the glyph of the eight-spoked Sun wheel. There are, of course, the four major seasonal festivals (Spring, March 21 or 22; Midsummer, June 21 or 22; Autumn Harvest, September 21; and Yule, December 25; and the cross-quarter days that come between them (the Vala's Vision or Lady Day, February 2; Walpurgia or May Day, May 1; Lammas or "Hloaf-Mass," August 1; and Halloween or "Specter Night," October 31).

Taken as a whole, the eight yearly rituals originally told the myth of a semi-divine king or hero, his dark twin brother, and the immortal Lady for whom they are rivals—a symbolic representation of the way that all crops yearly grow, ripen, die and are reborn anew from the immortal Earth. The yearly festivals can tell of birth, life, fruition, harvest or conflict, death and of the pilgrimage into the lower realms to bring back life once again.

The yearly cycle of our people's festivals, as symbolized by the

Sun wheel and as told in the original stories of the seasonal cere-monies (though the original forms of some festivals have been lost over the centuries) is nothing less than a telling of the birth, life, des-tiny, death and inevitable reincarnation of all things, and an explana-tion of them. The rites say clearly that all things are linked through all of the world and through all of the universe.

There are many levels of understanding of the seasonal rites: they speak to the highest reaches of the intellect and to the deepest realms of the subconscious. Many feel that such ceremonies can open sources of power that allows one to draw on certain fundamental energies of our biosphere.

Metaphysical theories, and the implications of ancient traditions, state that there are seasonal tides about the Earth and all things living—even extending into other dimensions and to the realms of what we would call the Gods. This cthonic/vital energy is little under-stood, but it seems to flow from and about particular areas on the globe, some of which are marked with enigmatic prehistoric mon-uments and some at the crossing points of the strange traces called *ley lines*.

By a ritual which completely involves those partaking, it is said that it is possible for a Grove and all its members to tap into this power. A sort of "magical pumping" takes place which has many facets of understanding, and many subtle and obvious effects.

Of course, most will enjoy the seasonal festivals for the obvious opportunities to enjoy the good company of friends and family in a small celebration, and perhaps to sample a touch of the "sense of magic" which comes of a service in honor of the Gods. The deeper meanings are there, when one chooses to think and to consider.

Blessings, Charms and Prayers

On a fine, sunny day, or early in the morning the following salutation would be made by various of the ancient English:

> Erce, Erce, Erce.
> Hail Earth, Mother of All!

or

> Erce, Erce, Erce.
> Eorthan modor!

("Erce" is thought to be an extremely ancient name of the Earth Goddess.)

When pouring a libation upon the ground in honor of the Gods in general and Hertha (yet another name of the Earth Goddess) in particular, the ancient Lithuanians would say:

> Blooming Earth,
> Bless the work
> Of our hands!

It is proper, when one is partaking of food and drink outdoors, particularly in the mountains, forests, along a lake or seashore, to make a libation to Hertha as Earth Mother. Either before or after eating, whichever seems more appropriate or is more practical, go to a growing tree or bush and drop a few crumbs of food at its base, and pour out nearby a few drops of drink. Then say this following salutation, adapted from an old Anglo-Saxon charm):

Hail Earth, Mother of All!
May your fields increase and flourish,
Your forests grow and spread,
And your waters run pure and free.
Accept my offering, O Earth Mother.
Bring forth that which is good, and sustaining
For every living thing.

Before going into a stressful or potentially dangerous situation:

Odin, far-wanderer, grant me wisdom,
Courage, and victory.
Friend Thor, grant me your strength.
And both be with me.

(You may wish to touch the hammer if you are wearing one. Otherwise you may wish to make the Sign of the Hammer: touching the clenched fist of your right hand to your forehead, breastbone, left shoulder and right shoulder.) Then go ahead and do the very best you can.

In blessing a friend's departure, raise your right hand before him or her in an attitude of blessing and say:

May Odin give you knowledge of your path,
May Thor grant you strength and courage on your way,
And may Loki give you laughter as you go.

If he is so inclined, upon seeing a beautiful woman, a young man may touch his lips to his hand and hold it out in salutation toward her, saying:

The Lady Freya shines through you.
May her blessings go with you, lovely one.

She needn't see your salutation, but it might be flattering to her if she did. It depends upon the occasion.

If she is so inclined, upon seeing a handsome man, a young woman may touch her lips to her hand and hold it out in salutation towards him, saying:

> *The Lord Odin is within you,*
> *May his blessings be with you, O handsome one!*

Depending on the God aspect she prefers, she may instead say, "The mighty Thor," "The golden and handsome Balder," or similarly refer to her favorite God. Only your imagination need be your limit.

In blessing a child:

> *May great Thor protect you*
> *With his strong arm and mighty hammer,*
> *May the good Mother Holle*
> *Hold and comfort you,*
> *And may all blessings be upon you,*
> *Small and holy one!*

Salutation before a meal, with all linking hands as they sit around the table:

> *Lord Odin and Lady Freya,*
> *We give our greetings to you!*
> *Bless this bounty set here before us*
> *And enjoy this good food with us*
> *As we do enjoy it.*
> *Hail and love to you!*
>
> All: *Hail and love to you!*

Lighthearted blessings or a well-wishings for a friend:

> *May you be feasting and drinking*
> *In Valhalla for a full night*
> *Before the Christian God*
> *Knows that you're dead.*
>
> *May you live to be a hundred and ten.*
> *And may mine be the last voice*
> *That you hear!*

It is proper, even when drinking a casual beer or a bit of wine, to briefly raise one's cup and give a salutation such as, "Hail Odin," or "Odin Bless."

General Rite in Honor of Odin

*(This rite may be held when there is need,
or at any time the celebrants desire.)*

The place where the ritual is held should have an altar set up near the north of the ritual area. Beyond it hang a banner of the Odin Rune done in black cloth with silver or gold rune markings. At the center of the altar have an image symbolizing the Lady Freya with a raven or wolf image (or other representation of Odin) to her left. An incense brazier is placed to the right of the images, and lit shortly before the rites. A sword or dagger is placed before the images.

Odin Rune

Have mead or ale available, and a drinking horn or tankard; this all should be placed beneath or beside the altar. Each person carries a tankard or horn attached by a thong or strap. (The Godi or Godia may wish to have extras available.) Set one additional tankard or chalice on the left side of the altar in honor of the Great Ones. Have copies of this rite available for all in the rite, with the Godi or Godia giving copies of the ceremony to as many of the celebrants as possible, marked for easy reading in the dim light.

The ritual area may be lit only by flame. Also, have eight candles or torches on or immediately beside the altar, to be lit during the ceremony. Four will be set at the far quarters (directions) of the ritual area while four others will remain on or immediately adjacent to the altar. Additionally, burn a small taper on the altar from before the start of the ceremony in order to light the other candles or torches, which the Godia (Priestess) and Godi (Priest), and any others so appointed may use during any readings. Place it immediately before the representations of Odin and Freya.

If a hand-held banner or standard of the Odin Rune is available, it should be carried by the Godi. Other standards with runes of the Goddesses and Gods of Valhalla may be carried by the devotees if such are on hand. Play appropriate music if it is available. Wagner's "Entry of the Gods into Valhalla," followed by "Siegfried's Rhine Journey" are ideal, though other music or even storm and nature sounds may be preferred.

It is best if this rite is led by a Godia in addition to the Godi. If a woman of the folk is not available, place flowers before her image and the Godi or other may speak her words.

When all is in readiness, the folk assemble and proceed in Procession of Honor led by the Godi and Godia, to end before the altar. One of the folk appointed by the Godi will light two candles or torches, one at either side of the altar.

At this time the Godi says:

> *O Great Odin, Azure-Cloaked Wanderer*
> *From the far, ancient lands of our people,*
> *Lord of the Shining Ones*
> *Who do protect our land, our folk and our families.*
> *We call to thee to be with us here.*
> *We call to thee across all of time*
> *And all the worlds of the Gods.*
> *Thy people are still here, O wise One,*
> *Come to us again, and give us to drink of thy*
> *Horn of life and of inspiration*
> *That we may prosper once again.*
> *Come to us now and be with us here.*
> *Great Odin!*

Then the Godia lights two candles or torches, one more at either side of the altar, and says:

> *O Noble Freya, Lady of the far Shining Realms,*
> *Goddess of Power,*
> *Leader of those who come for*

> *The spirits of the noble dead,*
> *Thou who takes away to thy realms*
> *When day is done,*
> *Beauteous Lady with thy necklace of enchantment,*
> *Co-ruler with our great Chief Odin*
> *Of the shining Lands of the Gods.*
> *We call on thee, O blessed Freya*
> *Be with us here, in this rite.*

If rune banners are carried, place them in stands to either side of the altar at this time. Then the Godia or Godi lights a candle or torch, saying:

> *The skies are blue and open, and*
> *The winds blow free and fair*
> *Over the lands of our people.*
> *Great Ones, keep us free as the winds*
> *Which are thy servants.*
> *Hail Odin!*

All: *Hail Odin!*

Give the candle or torch to one of those present, to be placed at the far eastern edge of the ritual area. When this is done, the Godia or Godi lights the next candle or torch, saying:

> *The Sun shines warm and bright*
> *Over the lands of our people.*
> *O Great One, may we have*
> *Lives that are warm and rich.*
> *May we prosper, and honor thee more*
> *As our people wox strong.*
> *Hail Odin!*

All: *Hail Odin!*

Give the candle or torch to one of those present, to be placed at the far southern edge of the ritual area. When this is done, the Vala or Priest lights the next candle or torch, saying:

> *The waters of our ancient lands*
> *Flow eternally clear and fresh,*

> *And the blue seas wash our far shores.*
> *Grant thy followers, O Great One,*
> *A renewal and cleansing spirit*
> *Ever as new as the streams of life*
> *That flow from far Valhalla.*
> *Hail Odin!*

All: *Hail Odin!*

Give the candle or torch to one of those present, to be placed at the far western edge of the ritual area. When this is done, the Godia or Godi lights the next candle or torch, saying:

> *The forests and the mountains*
> *Give sustenance of the soul and spirit*
> *To our folk, and the green and golden fields*
> *Provide sustenance to our bodies.*
> *Grant those who follow thee*
> *A healing and a strength*
> *As deep and rich as the Earth herself.*
> *Hail Odin!*

All: *Hail Odin!*

Give the candle or torch to one of those present, to be placed at the far northern edge of the ritual area or beyond the altar.

The Godia then takes up the sword and gives a salute to the rune banner(s), saying:

> *Since the first dawn we have been*
> *Children of the good Earth.*
> *Giver of life, giver of home*
> *Giver of mysteries and magics*
> *That echo in our legends.*
> *Care for us, O lands of our people*
> *As we do love and care for thee.*
> *Hail Earth, Mother of All!*

All: *Hail Earth, Mother of All!*

Then the Godi takes the sword and gives a salute to the rune banner(s), saying:

> *Although we are gathered here*
> *To give salutation to great Valfather,*
> *Let us also speak in honor*
> *And in reverence*
> *Of the Goddesses and Gods, great ones all,*
> *Whose home is beyond the Rainbow Bridge.*
> *You also do we know as our friends.*
> *Hail ye shining ones of Valhalla!*

All: *Hail ye shining ones of Valhalla!*

If desired, salutes may be given here to the individual Goddesses and Gods of the Shining Land, and to the great or notable ones of our own people.

Then the Godia fills the ceremonial drinking horn with the mead or ale which has been set beside the altar, and holds it aloft before the banner(s), saying:

> *O great and powerful Valfather,*
> *O Fair and Eternal Goddess*
> *Who does ride with him,*
> *O Noble Ones of the Rainbow Land,*
> *We share this drink in honor of thee!*
> *Place thy blessings powerfully within it,*
> *Granting strength of spirit, of soul,*
> *And of body to we who are thy followers.*
> *May ye share with us as we partake.*
> *Hail Odin!*   (All repeat)
> *Hail Freya!*   (All repeat)
> *Hail Gods of Valhalla!*   (All repeat)

The Godia drinks, and gives to the Godi to do likewise. Then the horns or tankards of all those in attendance are filled, usually by the Godi or Godia. Then a horn or toast is given by the Godi or Godia, as they raise their horns on high:

> *May we all have sufficiency.*   (Drink)
> *May we all have long life.*   (Drink)

> *May our lust for life be strong.* (Drink)
> *And may Odin grant us all wisdom.* (Drink)

Other horns may be offered by any of the folk at this time. Now is the time for discussion and for any speaking that any may desire. When the meeting has ended the Godia or Godi has all stand and silently meditate for a moment. Then one holds the sword out in salute before the rune banner(s) saying:

> *The time for our rite is ended.*
> *Let us give thanks for this time*
> *When we may be with the Gods.*
> *As we go our ways, may the spirit*
> *Of far Valhalla,*
> *And the noble Ones of the shining land,*
> *Go ever with us,*
> *With our children,*
> *And with our people.*
> *Hail Odin!*

All: *Hail Odin!*

Then the Godia or Godi puts out the candle or torch at the East, saying:

> *Winds, pure and free,*
> *Be ever with us,*
> *With our children,*
> *And with our people.*
> *Hail Odin!*

All: *Hail Odin!*

Then the Godia or Godi puts out the candle or torch at the South, saying:

> *Warm sun that gives life,*
> *Be ever with us,*
> *With our children,*
> *And with our people.*
> *Hail Odin!*

All: *Hail Odin!*

Then the Godia or Godi puts out the candle or torch at the West, saying:

> *Springs, streams, and lakes, cool and fresh,*
> *Be ever with us*
> *With our children,*
> *And with our people.*
> *Hail Odin!*

All: *Hail Odin!*

Then the Godia or Godi puts out the candle or torch at the North, saying:

> *Forests, mountains, fields,*
> *Be ever with us*
> *With our children,*
> *And with our people.*
> *Hail Odin!*

All: *Hail Odin!*

The sword is replaced upon the altar, and the Godia or Godi says:

> *This rite is ended.*
> *Go ye ever in the Way of the Gods*
> *And live their blessing.*
> *Hail Odin!*

All: *Hail Odin!*

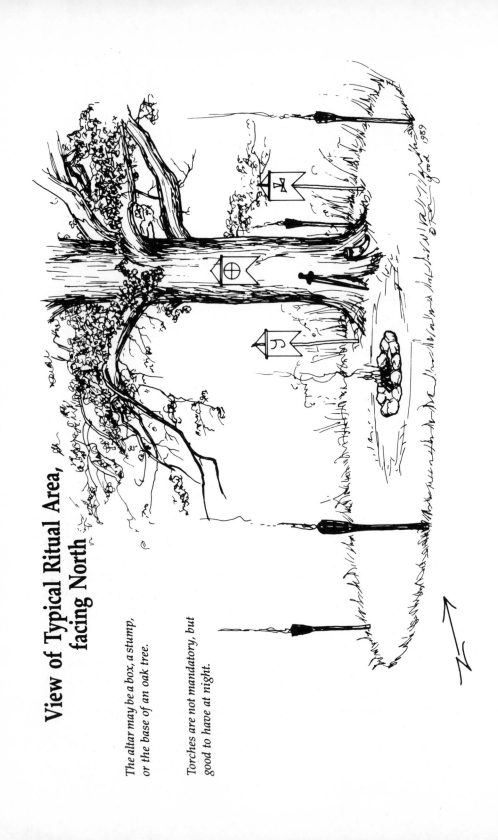

View of Typical Ritual Area, facing North

The altar may be a box, a stump, or the base of an oak tree.

Torches are not mandatory, but good to have at night.

Torch Processional and Ceremony

(This rite may be held when there is need,
or at any time the celebrants desire.)

Prior to this nighttime rite, hang rune banners of Odin, Freya and Thor in the place of the ritual. The Odin banner should be at the center and, if possible, all banners should be before a large tree; an oak is preferable, though most important is the impressiveness of the ritual area. If it is desired and possible, a bonfire should be started before the rune banners, in front of where the followers stand.

Odin Rune

Freya Rune

Thor Rune

If either the Godi or Godia is not present, then a woman or a man is chosen from the worshippers to take that role. If all the celebrants are either men or women, then all the lines of the Godia may be spoken by others. It is good if each person in attendance is given a portion of the liturgy to speak during the ceremony. Salutation to each God should, if possible, be given by one who feels closest to that particular deity. Have available a sufficient number of copies of this rite, marked for easier reading.

The Godi and Godia should (if possible) have oaken Odin pendants (i.e., wooden pendants upon which the Odin Rune has been inscribed or painted) with leather neck thongs for the devotees who do not have their own pendants. Torches should be prepared, one for each in the ceremony, plus one to be planted before each banner. Have booklets of songs and chants relating to the folk and to the Gods (if available) available to be handed out prior to the rite, and beer or ale with sufficient drinking horns should be made ready at the ritual area. Have musical instruments or rhythm instruments ready and distributed, and carry a horn for summoning. The assembly area should be at a distance from the place of banners, so that a roundabout torchlight procession can be made. (The Godi should verify the procession route in advance.)

Just prior to the ceremony, light the torches before the banners, with a short salutation of the Godia's own creation, while the worshippers are gathering at the assembly area. While this is taking place, the Godi should hand out pendants to those who do not have them, explaining the ceremony, and then lead the devotees in singing some of the songs of the evening rite.

When all is in readiness, the Godi and Godia light torches and hand one to each person in attendance (the Godi giving torches to the women and the Godia to the men), saying:

> *May thou be blessed with the living flame*
> *Of Odin, Freya, Thor,*
> *And all the High Gods of Valhalla.*

When all have the flaring torches, the Godi and Godia sound the horn and lead the procession. If an appropriate song is not available, the worshippers chant:

> *We tread the path to the Rainbow Bridge*
> *With joy in heart and flame in hand.*
> *Call to the Gods and spread the word,*
> *The Old Ways return across the land!*

The route to the place of the rite shall be a roundabout one, allowing time for all to gain the spirit of the procession. When finally all have come into the ritual area, the Godi and Godia stand before the banners, facing the worshippers, and the Godi calls:

> *We are here, as in times of old,*
> *Before our Gods,*
> *Our friends of times long past.*
> *O wise Odin hear our calls*
> *And be with us here.*
> *Hail Odin Valfather!*

All: *Hail Odin Valfather!*

> *O strong and hearty Thor,*
> *Hear our calls*
> *And be with us here.*
> *Hail Thor, Mighty Thunderer!*

All: *Hail Thor, Mighty Thunderer!*

Then the Godia calls:

> *We are here, as in times of old,*
> *Before our Gods,*
> *Our friends of times long past.*
> *Valkyrie Freya, hear our calls*
> *And be with us here.*
> *Hail Freya, Queen of Beauty!*

All: *Hail Freya, Queen of Beauty!*

Another of the celebrants calls:

> *O Ancient One, Hulda, hear our calls*
> *And be with us here.*
> *Hail Earth, Mother of All!*

All: *Hail Earth, Mother of All!*

Another: *O good Frigga, guardian of the home,*
> *Hear our calls*
> *And be with us here.*

Another: *We salute ye all, O Gods of far Valhalla.*
> *Hail Tyr, Great Warrior!*

All: *Hail Tyr, Great Warrior!*

Another: *Hail Balder the Bright!*
All: *Hail Balder the Bright!*

Another: *Hail Queen Sif of the Golden Hair!*
All: *Hail Queen Sif of the Golden Hair!*

Another: *Hail Freyr, Lord of the Land!*
All: *Hail Freyr, Lord of the Land!*

Another: *Hail Lady Saga, Mistress of the Arts!*
All: *Hail Lady Saga, Mistress of the Arts!*

Another: *Hail Loki the Trickster!*
All: *Hail Loki the Trickster!*

Another: *Hail Ran, Queen of the Sea!*
All: *Hail Ran, Queen of the Sea!*

Another: *Hail Bragi, Lord of Minstrels!*
All: *Hail Bragi, Lord of Minstrels!*

Another: *Hail Iduna, Giver of Immortality!*
All: *Hail Iduna, Giver of Immortality!*

Another: *Hail Aegir, Fearsome Water King!*
All: *Hail Aegir, Fearsome Water King!*

Another: *Hail to Hella, Queen of the World Below!*
All: *Hail to Hella, Queen of the World Below!*

Another: *Hail Heimdall, Guardian of Heaven's Bridge!*
All: *Hail Heimdall, Guardian of Heaven's Bridge!*

Godia: *All ye Gods of whom we have called,*
And those we have not.
All hail!
All: *All hail!*

Godi: *We ask the Gods to be with us here,*
To grant their strength and wisdom
To us, to our families and to our people
That we may all prosper
In times to come.
Odin hear us!
Ye Gods, hear us!
As we stand here before thee
Thou art with us, and in us,
And of us.
We are thy people, thy folk,

> *Be with us always, we do ask,*
> *Now and forever more.*
> *Hail Odin!*

All: *Hail Odin!*

Then the Godia says:

> *And now, ye followers of the ancient way,*
> *I bid thee plant thy torches about the edge*
> *Of this holy place, and come forth that we*
> *May share our drink of honor before the Gods.*

All place their torches about the edge of the ceremonial area. The Godi and Godia pour beer or ale into their drinking horns, and do the same for all in the rite as they return from planting their torches. Then one in the Grove leads the salutation to the Banners of the Gods, raising his or her horn and calling:

> *All hail to thee, Odin the Wise.*
> *All hail to thee Great Thor.*
> *All hail to thee, O beautiful Freya.*
> *We drink in honor of thee,*
> *And of the Gods of high Valhalla.*
> *As we do honor thee,*
> *May thou also honor us,*
> *And our bonding together be sealed*
> *For ourselves, our folk and our lands.*
> *Hail Odin!*

All: *Hail Odin!*

All then drink. Next the Godi or Godia says:

> *Now friends, let us rest here,*
> *To speak of the Great Ones*
> *Who guide and protect our people.*

All can now relax. If there is provision for a bonfire, it should be lit. Further horns may be drunk in honor of the Gods, and singing or other music for the Gods is appropriate at this time, as well as instruction by those who know the sagas or other useful lore. Although live music is prefereble, recorded music is acceptable. Circle dances or group polka dancing are traditional.

After some time it will be felt that the ceremony should end. All stand, and the Godi says:

> *Friends all, this rite honoring of the Gods*
> *Is now at an end. As each of us*
> *Goes our separate ways,*
> *May the Great Ones of High Valhalla*
> *Be ever with us.*
> *This rite is ended.*
> *Hail Odin!*

All: *Hail Odin!*

The Blot Rite

(Usually this ritual is performed as a part of seasonal rites,
though in this or in modified form it may be held when there is need
or at any time the celebrants desire.)

In ancient times it was common to offer a sacrifice, or *blot* (pronounced "bloh-t"), to Odin or to the other Gods on a holiday or other special occasion. The sacrifice was usually the animal whose meat was then prepared and roasted for the worshippers' feast afterwards. Such practices are only symbolic in this day and age, with home-brewed mead served in lieu of blood, and the feast being specialty dishes brought by the followers, the Godia, and the Godi for a potluck meal after the rite. (Although it is traditional for the host to provide at least the main course, practicality may dictate that the feast be potluck.)

Odin Rune

Freya Rune

Thor Rune

Light the ritual area with flame only: torches or shielded candles may be used if out-of-doors, or if within a building the ritual area is circled with candles. At the northern edge of the ritual area are the images, symbols, or rune banners of Odin, Freya and Thor, with candles or torches placed before them. On a low altar before them have the jug of clear mead, a brazier of burning incense, a dagger, the Blot bowl, and an aspergillis or small bundle of leaves to dip and sprinkle the mead. If a bull's horn is used to start the rite, it should be set at either side of the altar.

When all is in readiness, the Godi or Godia should sound the summoning horn and all gather in a semicircle before the altar. The Godi then calls for a period of silence of at least 13 heartbeats, as all place their minds into a calm and meditative state.

Godi: *Great Odin, we do now work this rite*
In thy honor. Be with us here,
We do ask.

Godia: *O Fair and Magical Freya,*
We do now work this rite
In thy honor. Be with us here,
We do ask.

Godi or
other: *Strong and Sturdy Thor,*
We do now work this rite
In thy honor. Be with us here,
We do ask.

The Godia, or other so chosen, turns briefly to the East and gives salute, saying:

O winds of the East,
Blow soft, cool, and sweet
Upon our people.
Hail Odin!
All: *Hail Odin!*

The Godi, or other so chosen, turns briefly to the South and gives salute, saying:

O warm Sun of the South,
Shine brightly
Upon our people.
Hail Odin!
All: *Hail Odin!*

The Godia, or other so chosen, turns briefly to the West and gives salute, saying:

O blue waters of the West,
Flow cool and giving of life
For our people.
Hail Odin!
All: *Hail Odin!*

The Godi, or other so chosen, turns briefly to the North and gives salute, saying:

> *O lands of the North,*
> *Give rich crops and calm souls*
> *For our people.*
> *Hail Odin!*

All: *Hail Odin!*

Then the Godia takes the jug of mead and holds it for the Godi, who takes the dagger and touches the point to the jug, saying:

> *Great Odin, accept this as sacrifice*
> *In honor of thee, in honor of our Gods,*
> *And in honor of ourselves.*
> *Place thy blessing within,*
> *So that we may draw upon thy wisdom,*
> *And gain victory in all that we shall do.*
> *Hail Odin!*

All: *Hail Odin!*

He puts down the dagger, takes the jug, opens it, and half fills the Blot bowl. He takes the bowl and the aspergillis or bundle of leaves, dipping them into the mead, and sprinkles each of the worshippers briefly, saying:

> *You are blessed*
> *In the Name of Odin.*

When all have been blessed, the Godia takes the bowl and leaves, and similarly blesses the Godi. Then she replaces all upon the altar and turns to those present, saying:

> *At this time, as in times far past,*
> *Are those of us who follow the Old Ones*
> *Blessed and consecrated in their sacred presence.*
> *May the strength, power, magic, and wisdom,*

> *The courage and the steadfastness*
> *Of the Gods themselves*
> *Remain forever within each of us.*
> *Hail Odin!*

All: *Hail Odin!*

The rite may be ended at this time, or may be followed by the Sumul Rite or other observance, as desired.

The Sumul Celebration

*(Usually this ritual is performed as a part of seasonal rites,
though in this or in modified form it may be held when there is need
or at any time the celebrants desire.)*

This rite celebrates the legend of Odin's flight down into the lower realms in the form of a great eagle to steal the cauldron of Inspiration from where it was watched by the dragon Nidhogg. Odin swept up into the skies and poured the contents out over the lands, so that the entire world might benefit from it. One interpretation of this legend (and there are others) is that one's wisdom and intellect, along with a soaring and free-reaching spirit, can raise the contents of the deeply hidden parts of the mind out into the real world so that it transmutes into new, creative, stimulating and valuable works of art, literature and science.

Odin Rune   **Freya Rune**   **Thor Rune**

This rite may be done by itself or as a part of another ritual, always at twilight or night. It is best done outdoors about a campfire or bonfire, though if indoors an eight-spoked Sun wheel should be set at the center of the group with eight or nine candles set on it. If a fireplace is available, the followers may gather before it, and proceed as if outdoors. The area of the ceremony must only be lit by flame. To the north of the fire, just outside of the circle of followers, place either the symbols, appropriate images, or rune banners of Odin, Freya and Thor. (For an indoor fireplace, the rune banners may be hung above the mantle.)

Although the ceremony is intended to be conducted by a Godia, a Godi can preside if no woman of the folk is present or able to take the role. Traditionally, home-brewed mead is used, though some special beer or ale can be substituted. If children are a part of the rite, or adults who do not indulge in alcoholic drink, then it may be advisable to have a second horn available which would be filled with fruit drink, punch or a soft drink. The Godia and Godi should use their judgment on this when preparing for the ritual.

Before the rite, all should be told that they must pace their drinking carefully, for while enough mead should be taken to make inspiration more easy, it would be a serious affront to the Gods to drink too much. All should be told that once they feel they have had enough mead, either simply sniff of the horn or quietly withdraw from the rite.

After the fire has been lit and is burning well, the people should gather about it, with men and women alternating insofar as is possible. The Godia should pour the ceremonial drinking horn full and, standing to the east of the fire circle, hold the horn up toward the rune banners and say:

> *Hail to thee Great Ones of the Shining Lands!*
> *We are gathered here in thy honor,*
> *And in our own, to celebrate*
> *This great gift of the Gods.*
> *We ask that thou place thy blessings*
> *Upon this mead of inspiration,*
> *So that some of thy noble powers*
> *May thus pass into we who salute thee.*
> *And remain.*
> *Grant thy blessings, and be with us.*

Another may say: *Odin give us Wisdom!*
Another may say: *Freya give us Power and Seid!*
Another may say: *Thor, give us Strength!*
Godia: *Accept this libation as our offering.*
               Hail Odin!
All: *Hail Odin!*

She pours a small bit of the mead in the fire (or in a special libation bowl, if indoors, later to be poured beneath a tree), and says to those gathered for the rite:

In ancient times our people would gather
On a night such as this to seek
The inspiration of the Gods,
To speak holy words, or words of joy,
And then to drink in honor of the Great Ones.
I bid thee each to speak, to give salutations,
Or to give laughter.
Then to honor the High Gods with a small drink.
Now, ye blessed of Valhalla,
Let us all do the same, as do I first.

The Godia holds the horn aloft, speaks briefly in honor of her patron deity in words of her own composing, and ends with "Hail Odin!" before drinking.

She then steps before the first person to her left, holds out the drinking horn and says:

I give thee the wisdom of Odin,
The beauty and magic of Freya,
The strength of Thor.

The follower takes the horn, holds it aloft, and either gives a salutation to a God or Goddess, recites an appropriate poem, speaks in remembrance of fallen heroes, folk, blood kin, or whatever else is deemed appropriate. When finished he or she calls:

Hail Odin!

S/he drinks, and hands the horn back to the Godia, who then takes it to the woman or man on her left to repeat the process. (Others of the Grove may also pass the horn, if it is so desired.). Then the next, and the next, thus working deosil (clockwise) about the circle. Each time that the horn has come back to the starting place, the Godia herself speaks and then drinks in honor of Odin.

As the drinking horn empties it is refilled. When the Godia determines that it is time for the rite to end, she will take one final drink and pour any remainder as a libation, saying:

We thank thee, O Great Odin,
Bringer of God strength to humankind.

> *We thank thee, beauteous and magical Freya,*
> *Strong and sturdy Thor,*
> *For being with us on this night.*
> *May some of thy powers*
> *Remain within us all*
> *In times to come.*
> *This rite of Sumul is ended.*
> *Hail Odin!*

All: *Hail Odin!*

Seasonal Festivals
for the Gathered Folk

The Vala's Vision (Maiden's Day)
(February 2)

The place where the ritual is held should have an altar near the north of the ritual area. Beyond it hang a banner of the Odin Rune done in black cloth with silver or gold rune markings, with a rune banner for Freya placed to one side of the Odin Rune and one for Thor placed to the other side of the Odin Rune. (If available, suitable images representing the three Deities may be hung instead of the banners.) A banner with the *lagu* rune (symbolizing both the Dark Goddess Hulda

| Odin | Freya | Thor | Hulda |

and the Brigid, or maiden, aspect) should be hung either just behind the altar or draped over it. Place an incense brazier on the altar, lit shortly before the rite. A sword or dagger should be placed on the altar. If the incense brazier is narrow-mouthed, then a plate should be set on the altar for the burning of parchment, and a copy of the invocation to be read by each as he or she burns their "Parchment of Guilt." Parchment and pens should be set on the altar. Have a drinking horn at the center of the altar.

Mead or ale should be available, and a horn, cup or tankard for each person in attendance; place this beneath or beside the altar. Copies of this rite should be available, suitably marked for easy reading, one for each of the celebrants who has a part in the ceremony.

The ritual area may be lit only by flame. Also, there should be candles or torches on or immediately beside the altar, to be lit during the ceremony. (If candles are on the altar, the left should be white and the right, a dark blue.) Four will be set at the far quarters (directions) of the ritual area while one will be placed before each rune banner.

Additionally, burn a small taper on the altar (set in a central location) from before the start of the ceremony in order to light the other candles or torches, and which the Godia and Godi may use during any readings.

If hand-held banners or standards of the Odin Rune are available symbolizing the Gods and Goddesses of Valhalla or heroes of the people, these may be carried by the devotees. Appropriate music should be played if it is available. Grieg's "Peer Gynt Suite," followed by "Siegfried's Rhine Journey" are ideal, though other music or even nature sounds may be preferred.

It is best if this rite is led by a Godia in addition to the Godi. If a woman of the folk is not available, place flowers before the banner of Freya, and the Godi may speak the words of the Godia. If possible, everyone in the rite should have a part.

When all is in readiness, the folk should assemble. (If there is available room, there may be a Procession of Honor led by the Godi and Godia and with the others following, to end before the altar.) Candles or torches beside the altar should be lit by the Godi or other so appointed.

(If it is desired, the Blot Rite may be performed at this point.)

At this time the Godi lights the candle or torch before the Odin banner and says:

> *O Great Odin, Sky-Cloaked Wanderer*
> *From the far, ancient lands of our people,*
> *Chief of the Shining Ones*
> *Who protect our land, our folk and our families.*
> *We call to thee to be with us here.*
> *We call to thee across all of time*
> *And all the worlds of the Gods.*
> *Thy people are still here, O wise One,*

Come to us again, and us give to drink of thy
Cauldron of life and of inspiration
That we may prosper once again.
Come to us now and be with us here.
Odin the wise.
Hail Odin!

All: *Hail Odin!*

Then the Godia lights candles or torches in front of the Freya banner and says:

O Leader of the Wind Riders,
Thou who weavest fates and destinies
And before whose magics
Men and Gods do bow,
Co-ruler with the Great Odin
Of the shining Lands of the Gods.
We call on thee, O Freya the Fair One!
Be with us here, in this rite.
Hail Freya!

All: *Hail Freya!*

The Godi or other lights the candle or torch before the Thor banner and says:

O red-bearded thunderer,
Friend and protector of our people,
Before whose mighty hammer
Neither God nor man can stand,
We call on thee, O mighty Thor!
Be with us here, in this rite.
Hail Thor!

All: *Hail Thor!*

Then the Godia says to all:

It is at this time that we do perform
A cleansing and a renewal of ourselves,
As Freya became virgin again after giving birth, and
As Thor became purified after slaying the Giants.

With our souls made clear again,
We may see and do much more,
As even the Vala was able to foresee
The future for Great Odin.

She indicates the parchment sheets and pens which are next to the incense brazier.

Take now the parchment from the altar,
And writing implements.
In silence, put on thereon the symbolic runes
Of all within yourself which hinders,

Harms and makes guilty.
Think upon it, yet let it be known
Only to the Gods, and then burn it before
The Ancient One.
And afterward look into the flames,
And search for the future.

Each is given a pen and a sheet of parchment (or paper). As long a time as necessary is allotted for all to perform their own portions of the rite individually; to write or draw that which symbolizes their weaknesses and guilts, then to read aloud the petition to Hulda for remission, forgiveness and destruction of these factors. The Godi and Godia endeavor to be the first and set an example for all others. (If there are many celebrants attending the ceremony, the writing is done by all simultaneously.)

Each reads aloud, as he or she puts the folded parchment sheet into the brazier and sets it aflame (or all say after the Godi if there are many in the ceremony, all the celebrants burning their parchments at the same time):

Hear me, O Hulda,
Dark Goddess of times far distant.
I place before thee the runes
Of all which hinders,
Harms, and makes guilty
Within my own soul.
As this flame burns, O Ancient Norn,

I ask thee to consume all which weakens me,
That it be gone forever, and leave me
Cleansed and strong
In thy holy Name.
I swear by the Sun, O Dark One,
That I shall do all within my power
To build myself stronger, better,
And more noble
In the year to come.
And I thank thee,
O Goddess before the Gods.
Hail Hulda!

Each watches the flames of the torches (or candles) after finishing. After the last has completed, the Godi says:

Look now into the flames
To see the patterns
And the runes
Of that which may be,
Shall be,
Or must be!

After a space of time of about three minutes he informally asks what any might have seen, or what impressions that anyone might have. Again, the Godia and Godi give their own impressions first, to set the example for the others. (This is optional.)

Other prayers or petitions to the Gods may be done next. A Sumul Celebration may follow.

When it has been determined that the meeting is ended the Godia or Godi has all stand and silently meditate for a moment. The Godia or Godi then holds the sword out in salute before the rune banner(s) saying:

The time for our rite is ended.
Let us give thanks for this time
When we may be with the Gods.
As we go our ways, may the spirit
Of far Valhalla, of the High Gods
Of the shining land,

Go ever with us,
With our children,
And with our people.
Hail Odin! (salute)

All: *Hail Odin!* (salute)

The sword is replaced upon the altar, and the Godia or Godi says:

This rite is ended.
Go ye ever in the Way of the Gods
And live their blessing.
All hail the Gods of Valhalla!

All: *All hail the Gods of Valhalla!*

After the ceremony the drink remaining in the drinking horn is poured at the base of a tree with an improvised salutation to the Azure-Cloaked One.

Spring Evenight
(March 21)

Ostara Rune

The place where the ritual is held should have an altar near the north of the ritual area. Beyond it hang a banner of the Odin Rune done in black cloth with silver or gold rune markings, with a rune banner for Freya placed to one side of the Odin Rune and one for Thor placed to the other side of the Odin Rune. (If available, suitable images representing the three Deities may be hung instead of the banners.) Immediately behind the altar should be a smaller banner with the rune symbolizing Ostara, patroness of this festival. Place an incense brazier on the altar, lit shortly before the rite. Place a sword or dagger on the altar. A drinking horn should be placed at the center of the altar, and the entire area decorated with flowers. Have mead or ale available. Include a copy of this rite, suitably marked for easy reading, for each who has a portion of the ceremony. Ideally all the celebrants should be involved.

The ritual area may be lit only by flame. Also, have candles or torches on or immediately beside the altar, to be lit during the ceremony. If candles are used on the altar, they should both be light green in color. Four will be set at the far quarters (directions) of the ritual area while one will be placed before each rune banner.

Additionally, burn a small taper on the altar from before the start of the ceremony in order to light the other candles or torches, which the Godia, the Godi and others may use during any readings.

If a bull's horn or other appropriate musical instrument is available, use it to signal the start of the rite, announce the coming of Spring during the ritual and finally sound it the end of the ceremony.

If hand-held banners or standards of the Odin Rune are available symbolizing the Gods and Goddesses of Valhalla or heroes of the people, these may be carried by the devotees. Play appropriate soft music if it is available. Continually repeating Halvorsen's "Rustle of Spring," or Grieg's "Wedding Day at Troldhagen" is ideal, though other music such as "Spring," from Walter Carlos' "Sonic Seasonings," may be used. Nature sounds may be preferred.

It is best if this rite is led by a Godia in addition to the Godi. If a woman of the folk is not available, flowers should be placed before the banner of Freya and the Godi, or any other may speak the words of the Godia.

Decorate a tree next to the ritual area with fruits with ribbons of many colors.

When all is in readiness, the horn is sounded and the folk assemble. (If there is available room, there may be a Procession of Honor led by the Godi and Godia and with the others following, to end before the altar.) Candles or torches beside the altar are lit by the Godi or other so appointed.

If desired, the Blot Rite may be performed next.

Then the Godi lights the candle or torch before the Odin banner and says:

> *O Great Odin, Sky-Cloaked Wanderer*
> *From the far, ancient lands of our people,*
> *Lord of the Shining Ones*
> *Who do protect our land, our folk, and our families.*
> *We call to thee to be with us here.*

> We call to thee across all of time
> And all the worlds of the Gods.
> Thy people are still here, O wise One,
> Come to us again, and us give to drink of thy
> Cauldron of life and of inspiration
> That we may prosper once again.
> Come to us now and be with us here.
> Odin the wise.
> Hail Odin!

All: *Hail Odin!*

Then the Godia lights candles or torches in front of the Freya banner and says:

> O Leader of the Wind Riders,
> Thou who weavest fates and destinies
> And before whose magics
> Men and Gods do bow,
> Co-ruler with the Great Odin
> Of the shining Lands of the Gods.
> We call on thee, O Freya the Fair One!
> Be with us here, in this rite.
> Hail Freya!

All: *Hail Freya!*

The Godi or other so designated lights the candle or torch before the Thor banner and says:

> O red-bearded Thunderer,
> Friend and protector of our people,
> Before whose mighty hammer
> Neither God nor man can stand,
> We call on thee, O mighty Thor!
> Be with us here, in this rite.
> Hail Thor!

All: *Hail Thor!*

If a bull's horn or other appropriate musical instrument is available, it is sounded to announce the coming of Spring. Then the Godi says:

> *Let us now fill our drinking horn*
> *Before the Gods,*
> *And drink in honor of the season.*

The drinking horn on the altar is filled, and the Godia (or other so chosen) takes it first to the Godi, then to all in the ritual, saying to each as the horn is given:

> *The messengers of Spring*
> *Are all about us.*
> *Drink now to Lady Ostara,*
> *Goddess of Spring!*

After drinking, the celebrant says:

> *Hail Ostara!*

and hands the drinking horn back to the Godia (or other), who then takes it to the next celebrant and repeats the process.

If there are sufficient women available in the rite, they take their men (or vice versa) for a faster and faster circle dance about the decorated tree until all are tired. More horns may be offered (i.e., toasts may be drunk) to the Gods and to those present.

Afterwards other workings may be done, as desired by the Godi, the Godia, or those in the rite.

When it is determined that the ceremony is ended, the Godia or Godi has all stand and silently meditate for a moment. The Godia or Godi then holds the sword out in salute before the rune banner(s) saying:

> *The time for our rite is ended.*
> *Let us give thanks for this time*
> *When we may be with the Gods.*
> *As we go our ways, may the spirit*
> *Of far Valhalla, the High Gods*
> *Of the shining land,*
> *Go ever with us,*
> *With our children,*
> *And with our people.*
> *Hail Odin!*   (salute)
All: *Hail Odin!*   (salute)

The sword is replaced upon the altar and the Godia or Godi says:

> This rite is ended.
> Go ye ever in the Way of the Gods
> And live their blessing.

After the ceremony the drink remaining in the drinking horn is poured at the base of a tree with an improvised salutation to the Sky-Cloaked One.

Walpurgia Feast (May Eve)
(May 1)

The place where the ritual is held should have an altar near the north of the ritual area. Beyond it hang a banner of the Odin Rune done in black cloth with silver or gold rune markings, with a rune banner for Freya placed to one side of the Odin Rune and one for Thor placed to the other side of the Odin Rune. (If available, suitable images representing the three Deities may be hung instead of the banners.) Immediately behind

Freyr Rune

the altar should be a smaller banner bearing the rune of Freyr. Have an incense brazier on the altar, lit shortly before the rite with the scent of flowers. Place a sword or dagger on the altar. A drinking horn is placed at the center of the altar. Include a copy of this rite, suitably marked for easy reading, for each who has a part in the ceremony. If at all possible, every celebrant should speak or perform a portion of the rite.

Decorate the ritual area with flowers, and all who celebrate the rite should bring food dishes for the banquet to follow. It is traditional to erect a maypole with many-colored ribbons in the ritual area. Two garlands of flowers are prepared for use during the rite. Any women in the ceremony are decked with flowers and ribbons, and may similarly decorate the beards, hair, and clothing of their men. Before the rite, the Godia will hand out staffs tied with many-colored ribbons to carry during the ceremony.

The ritual area may be lit only by flame. Also, have candles or torches on or immediately beside the altar, to be lit during the ceremony. Four will be set at the far quarters (directions) of the ritual area while one will be placed before each rune banner. If candles are used on the altar, place a light green candle at the left and a gold one at the right.

Additionally, burn a small taper on the altar from before the start of the ceremony in order to light the other candles or torches, which the Godia and Godi may use during any readings.

If hand-held banners or standards of the Odin Rune symbolizing the Gods and Goddesses of Valhalla or heroes of the people are available, these may be carried by the devotees. Play appropriate music if it is available. Continuous replays of Grieg's "Midsommervalka" or the "Peer Gynt Suite" are ideal, though other music or nature sounds may be preferred.

It is best if this rite is led by a Godia in addition to the Godi. If a woman of the folk is not available, place flowers before the banner of Freya and the Godi, or another may speak the words of the Godia.

When all is in readiness, the folk assemble. Staffs with ribbons should be handed out to all by Godia. (If there is available room, there may be a Procession of Honor led by the Godi and Godia and with the others following, to end before the altar.) Candles or torches beside the altar are lit by the Godi as the celebrants plant their ribboned staffs about the edge of the ritual area.

Then the Godi lights the candle or torch before the Odin banner and says:

> *O Great Odin, Sky-Cloaked Wanderer*
> *From the far, ancient lands of our people,*
> *Chief of the Shining Ones*
> *Who do protect our land, our folk, and our families.*
> *We call to thee to be with us here.*
> *We call to thee across all of time*
> *And all the worlds of the Gods.*
> *Thy people are still here, O wise One,*
> *Come to us again, and us give to drink of thy*
> *Cauldron of life and of inspiration*
> *That we may prosper once again.*

Come to us now and be with us here.
Odin the wise.
Hail Odin!
All: *Hail Odin!*

Then the Godia lights candles or torches in front of the Freya banner and says:

O Leader of the Wind Riders,
Thou who weavest fates and destinies
And before whose magics
Men and Gods do bow,
Co-ruler with the Great Odin
Of the shining Lands of the Gods.
We call on thee, O Freya the Fair One!
Be with us here, in this rite.
Hail Freya!
All: *Hail Freya!*

The Godi or other so chosen lights the candle or torch before the Thor banner and says:

O red-bearded thunderer,
Friend and protector of our people,
Before whose mighty hammer
Neither God nor man can stand,
We call on thee, O mighty Thor!
Be with us here, in this rite.
Hail Thor!
All: *Hail Thor!*

Then the Godia or other so chosen says:

Patron of this good season,
Friend of land and farmstead
And of all things which grow,
We welcome thee, noble Freyr!
Be with us here, in this rite.
Hail Freyr!
All: *Hail Freyr!*

A Blot is next performed as Victory Sacrifice in honor of High Odin.

After the Blot, the Godi says:

> *The summer is now with us,*
> *And at this time is the*
> *Celebration of the triumph of Freyr the Good.*
> *Let us honor him with laughter,*
> *Feasting, and mead.*

Godi and Godia crown the man and woman of the folk who are most in love, or most sensually attracted to each other, with flower garlands (as the May-Grave and his Lady), and ask them to lead in the maypole dance. They are served first at the feast and asked to lead at least some of the dances, either round dances, polkas, or other dances which the folk may wish to perform.

Then the Godia or Godi holds the sword out in salute before the rune banner(s) saying:

> *The time for our rite is ended.*
> *And the time for celebration has begun!*
> *Let us give thanks to the Gods.*
> *May they ever*
> *Go ever with us,*
> *With our children,*
> *And with our people.*
> *Hail Odin!*   (salute)

All: *Hail Odin!*   (salute)

The sword is replaced upon the altar, and the Godia or Godi says:

> *Let us now wind about the maypole*
> *And celebrate with feasting*
> *With drinking, and with dance*
> *In honor of the High Ones.*
> *This rite is ended.*
> *Let the festival begin!*

Now is the time for the maypole dance, for feasting, and for dance of all kinds. Later on in the evening, the drink remaining in the drinking horn is poured at the base of a tree with an improvised salutation to the Azure-Cloaked One.

Summer Sunstead
(June 21)

The place where the ritual is held should be ringed about with eight standing stones (as large as is practical) and have an altar near the north of the ritual area. Beyond the altar hang a banner of the Odin Rune done in black cloth with silver or gold rune markings, with a rune banner for Freya placed to one side of the Odin Rune and one for Thor placed to the other side of the Odin Rune. (If available, suitable images representing the three Deities may be placed instead of the banners.) Place an incense brazier on the altar, lit shortly before the rite.

Balder Rune

Nanna Rune

The patron Gods of this season are Balder and Nanna, who are husband and wife. If it is possible, make up rune banners for each, copying from the runes given in this book, and place them immediately behind the altar.

Place a sword or dagger on the altar, and a drinking horn at the center of the altar. Have mead or ale available beneath or beside the altar. Include copies of this rite, suitably marked for easy reading, for all who are performing parts of the ceremony. Ideally, include all celebrants.

At the center of the ritual area, or beside the bonfire, have a wheel of wood or straw or some other simple, burnable construction, which can be sacrificed to the flames during the rite. If the ritual is to be held indoors, then it should be small enough that it can be burned in the incense brazier. A small model or an eight-spoked wheel scribed on parchment are examples.

The ritual area may be lit only by flame. Also, have candles or torches on or immediately beside the altar, to be lit during the ceremony. Four will be set at the far quarters (directions) of the ritual area while one will be placed before each rune banner. Additionally, burn a small taper on the altar from before the start of the ceremony in order to light the other candles or torches, and which the Godia, the Godi and others may use during any readings. If candles are used on the altar, they should be of yellow color.

If hand-held banners or standards of the Odin Rune are available, symbolizing the Gods and Goddesses of Valhalla or heroes of our own people, these may be carried by the devotees. Play appropriate music if it is available: Wagner's "Entry of the Gods into Valhalla," followed by "Siegfried's Rhine Journey" are ideal. Alternately, "Summer," from Walter Carlos' "Sonic Seasonings" may be played continuously. Depending on the tastes of the Gydia and Godi (as well as those attending the rite), other music or even storm and nature sounds may be preferred.

It is best if this rite is led by a Godia in addition to the Godi. If a woman of the folk is not available, place flowers before the banner of Freya, and the Godi or others may speak the words of the Gydia.

When all is in readiness, the folk assemble. (If there is available room, there may be a Procession of Honor led by the Godi and Godia and with the others following, to end before the altar.). Candles or torches beside the altar are lit by the Godi.

Then the Godi lights the candle or torch before the Odin banner and says:

> *O Great Odin, Sky-Cloaked Wanderer*
> *From the far, ancient lands of our people,*
> *Chief of the Shining Ones*
> *Who do protect our land, our folk and our families.*
> *We call to thee to be with us here.*
> *We call to thee across all of time*
> *And all the worlds of the Gods.*

> *Thy people are still here, O wise One,*
> *Come to us again, and us give to drink of thy*
> *Cauldron of life and of inspiration*
> *That we may prosper once again.*
> *Come to us now and be with us here.*
> *Odin the wise.*
> *Hail Odin!*

All: *Hail Odin!*

Then the Godia lights candles or torches in front of the Freya banner, and says:

> *O Leader of the Wind Riders,*
> *Thou who weavest fates and destinies*
> *And before whose magics*
> *Men and Gods do bow,*
> *Co-ruler with our great Lord Odin*
> *Of the shining Lands of the Gods.*
> *We call on thee, O Freya the Fair One!*
> *Be with us here, in this rite.*
> *Hail Freya!*

All: *Hail Freya!*

The Godi or other so chosen lights the candle or torch before the Thor banner and says:

> *O red-bearded thunderer,*
> *Friend and protector of our people,*
> *Before whose mighty hammer*
> *Neither God nor man can stand,*
> *We call on thee, O mighty Thor!*
> *Be with us here, in this rite.*
> *Hail Thor!*

All: *Hail Thor!*

The Godia or other so chosen then takes up the Sun wheel and holds it aloft, saying:

> *We give greetings to gentle Nanna,*
> *Spirit of the Moon, Consort of Balder,*

> *And patroness of this season.*
> *Her love and devotion shall always*
> *Shine as examples for our people.*
> *Hail Nanna!*

All: *Hail Nanna!*

The Godi or other so chosen then takes the Sun wheel and holds it aloft, saying:

> *We give greetings to high Balder*
> *Giver of life, Husband of Lady Nanna,*
> *And Patron of this season.*
> *Thy brightness and joy and love*
> *Shall always shine*
> *As examples for our people.*
> *Hail Balder!*

All: *Hail Balder!*

Then he throws the Sun wheel on the fire or otherwise burns it. As it burns, the Godia or Godi says:

> *O noble ones,*
> *Accept our offering*
> *Of this ancient symbol*
> *Of the year, of our many lives,*
> *And of Eternity.*
> *Hail to thee both, Nanna and Balder!*

At this time a Blot is held in honor of the season. A Sumul Celebration may also follow.

Next follows any other observances that are desired by the Godia, the Godi, or those in attendance.

When it is time for the meeting to end, the Godia or Godi has all stand silently for the space of 13 heartbeats. Then the Godia says:

> *The first half year has now passed.*
> *The Summer God and Summer Goddess*
> *Have returned, as ever they have*
> *Through the ages.*
> *Like us, their time here will end,*

> But they shall always return again,
> As we shall also.
> Hail Balder!

All: Hail Balder!
> Hail Nanna!

All: Hail Nanna!

Then the Godi holds the sword out in salute before the rune banner(s) saying:

> The time for our rite is ended.
> Let us give thanks for this time
> When we may be with the Gods.
> As we go our ways, may the spirit
> Of far Valhalla, of the High Ones
> Of the shining land,
> Go ever with us,
> With our children,
> And with our people.
> Hail Odin!   (salute)

All: Hail Odin!   (salute)

The sword is replaced upon the altar, and the Godia or Godi says:

> This rite is ended.
> Go ye ever in the Way of the Gods
> And live their blessing.

After the ceremony the drink remaining in the drinking horn is poured at the base of a tree with an improvised salutation to the Azure-Cloaked One.

A feast and the events of the festival follow.

Hloaf Festival (Lammas)
(August 1)

The place where the ritual is held should be ringed about with eight standing stones (as large as is practical) and have an altar near the north of the ritual area. Beyond the altar hang a banner of the Odin Rune done in black cloth with silver or gold rune markings, with a rune banner for Freya placed to one side of the Odin Rune and one for Thor placed to the other side of the Odin Rune. (If available, suitable images representing the three Deities may be hung instead of the banners.) Place an incense brazier on the altar, lit shortly before the rite.

Gerd Rune

The patron Gods of this season are Freyr and Gerd, who are husband and wife. If it is possible, make up rune banners for each, copying from the runes given in this book, and place them immediately behind the altar.

Place a sword or dagger on the altar, and a drinking horn at the center of the altar. Have mead or ale available beneath or beside the altar. Include a copy of this rite, suitably marked for easy reading, for each who has a part of this ceremony. Ideally, everyone in the Grove should have some portion of the rite.

The ritual area may be lit only by flame. Also, have candles or torches on or immediately beside the altar, to be lit during the ceremony. Four are set at the far quarters (directions) of the ritual area while one is placed before each rune banner. Additionally, burn a small taper on the altar from before the start of the ceremony in order to light the other candles or torches, which the Godia, the Godi, and others may use during any readings. If candles are used on the altar, the one to the left of the altar should be yellow, and the one to the right of the altar should be brown in color.

If hand-held banners or standards of the Odin Rune are available, symbolizing the Gods and Goddesses of Valhalla, or heroes of our own people, these may be carried by the devotees. Play appropriate music if it is available. Wagner's "Entry of the Gods into Valhalla" followed by "Siegfried's Rhine Journey" are ideal. Alternately, "Summer" from Walter Carlos' "Sonic Seasonings" may be played continuously. Depending on the tastes of the Godia and Godi (as well as those attending the rite), other music or even storm and nature sounds may be preferred.

It is best if this rite is led by a Godia in addition to the Godi. If a woman of the folk is not available, place flowers before the banner of Freya and the Godi, or others may speak the words of the Godia.

When all is in readiness, the folk assemble. (If there is available room, there may be a Procession of Honor led by the Godi and Godia and with the others following, to end before the altar.) Candles or torches beside the altar are lit by the Godi.

Afterwards the Godi lights the candle or torch before the Odin banner and says:

> *O Great Odin, Sky-Cloaked Wanderer*
> *From the far, ancient lands of our people,*
> *Chief of the Shining Ones*
> *Who do protect our land, our folk, and our families.*
> *We call to thee to be with us here.*
> *We call to thee across all of time*
> *And all the worlds of the Gods.*
> *Thy people are still here, O wise One,*
> *Come to us again, and us give to drink of your*
> *Cauldron of life and of inspiration*
> *That we may prosper once again.*
> *Come to us now and be with us here.*
> *Odin the wise.*
> *Hail Odin!*

All: *Hail Odin!*

Then the Godia lights candles or torches in front of the Freya banner and says:

> *O Leader of the Wind Riders,*
> *Thou who weavest fates and destinies*
> *And before whose magics*
> *Men and Gods do bow,*
> *Co-ruler with the Great Odin*
> *Of the shining Lands of the Gods.*

We call on thee, O Freya the Fair One!
Be with us here in this rite.
Hail Freya!

All: *Hail Freya!*

The Godi or other so chosen lights the candle or torch before the Thor banner and says:

O red-bearded thunderer,
Friend and protector of our people,
Before whose mighty hammer
Neither God nor man can stand,
We call on thee, O mighty Thor!
Be with us here, in this rite.
Hail Thor!

All: *Hail Thor!*

The Godia or other so chosen then says:

We give greetings to the beauteous Gerd,
Of a race more ancient than the Gods,
Consort of Freyr,
And patroness of this season.
Her choice of attaining godhood shall always
Be as an example for our people.
Hail Gerd!

All: *Hail Gerd!*

The Godi or other so chosen then takes the Sun wheel and holds it aloft, saying:

We give greetings to high Freyr,
Spirit of the Earth, Consort of Lady Gerd,
And Patron of this season.
Thy invincible spirit shall always
Be as an example for our people.
Hail Freyr!

All: *Hail Freyr!*

At this time hold a Blot in honor of the season. A Sumul Celebration may also follow.

Next follow any other observances that are desired by the Godia, the Godi, or those in attendance.

When it is time that the meeting ends, the Godia or Godi has all stand silently for the space of 13 heartbeats. Then the Godia says:

> *At this time of the year*
> *Have we we celebrated the decision of Gerd*
> *Of the race of the Giants*
> *To take immortality and godhood,*
> *Rather than remain as she was*
> *And as many have always been.*
> *To go placidly into eventual annihilation.*
> *May we also seek the Higher Paths*
> *And ever move upward*
> *Ever better ourselves,*
> *So that we may in time*
> *Be as the Gods.*

Then the Godi holds the sword out in salute before the rune banner(s) saying:

> *The time for our rite is ended.*
> *Let us give thanks for this time*
> *When we may be with the Gods.*
> *As we go our ways, may the spirit*
> *Of far Valhalla, of the High Ones*
> *Of the shining land,*
> *Go ever with us,*
> *With our children,*
> *And with our people.*
> *Hail Odin!* (salute)

All: *Hail Odin!* (salute)

The sword is replaced upon the altar and the Godia or Godi says:

> *This rite is ended.*
> *Go ye ever in the Way of the Gods*

And live their blessing.

After the ceremony the drink remaining in the drinking horn is poured at the base of a tree with an improvised salutation to the Azure-Cloaked One.

Fall Evenight (Harvest)
(Around September 21st)

Sif Rune

The place where the ritual is held should have an altar near the north of the ritual area. Beyond the altar hang a banner of the Odin Rune done in black cloth with silver or gold rune markings. To one side of the Odin Rune hang a banner with the rune of Thor and to the other side, a rune banner of Freya. If available, place suitable images representing the three Deities instead of the banners. Place an incense brazier on the altar, lit shortly before the rite.

Place many fruits, vegetables, and other foods of the season about the altar and at the base of the rune banners. Scatter autumn leaves on the altar and before the rune banners.

Place a sword or dagger on the altar, and a drinking horn at the center of the altar. Have mead or ale available, beneath or beside the altar. Include a copy of this rite, suitably marked for easy reading, for each who is to perform a portion of this ceremony. If at all possible, all celebrants should have parts of this rite.

The patron deities of this festival are Thor and Sif, who are husband and wife. Make up a rune banner for Lady Sif, copying from runes given in this book, and place it immediately behind the altar.

Light the ritual area only by flame. Also, include candles or torches on or immediately beside the altar, to be lit during the ceremony. Set four at the far quarters (directions) of the ritual area, and place one before each rune banner. Additionally, burn a small taper on the altar from before the start of the ceremony in order to light the other candles or torches, which the Godia and Godi may use during any readings. If candles are used on the altar, both should be red.

If hand-held banners or standards of the Odin Rune are available, symbolizing the Gods and Goddesses of Valhalla, or heroes of the people, the devotees will carry these. Play appropriate music if it is available: Wagner's "Entry of the Gods into Valhalla," followed by "Siegfried's Rhine Journey," are ideal. Alternately, "Autumn," from Walter Carlos' "Sonic Seasonings" may be played continually. Depending on the tastes of the Godia and the Godi (as well as those attending the rite), other music or even storm and nature sounds may be preferred.

It is best if this rite is led by a Godia in addition to the Godi. If a woman of the folk is not available, place flowers before the banner of Freya and the Godi, or others may speak the words of the Godia.

When all is in readiness, assemble the folk. (If there is available room, there may be a Procession of Honor led by the Godi and Godia and with the others following, to end before the altar.) The Godi will light candles or torches beside the altar.

At this time the Godi lights the candle or torch before the Odin banner and says:

> *O Great Odin, Sky-Cloaked Wanderer*
> *From the far, ancient lands of our people,*
> *Chief of the Shining Ones*
> *Who do protect our land, our folk, and our families.*
> *We call to thee to be with us here.*
> *We call to thee across all of time*
> *And all the worlds of the Gods.*
> *Thy people are still here, O wise One,*
> *Come to us again, and us give to drink of thy*
> *Cauldron of life and of inspiration*
> *That we may prosper once again.*
> *Come to us now and be with us here,*
> *Odin the wise!*
> *Hail Odin!*

All: *Hail Odin!*

Then the Godia lights candles or torches in front of the Freya banner and says:

> *O Leader of the Wind Riders,*
> *Thou who weavest fates and destinies*
> *And before whose magics*
> *Men and Gods do bow,*
> *Consort to our great Lord Odin*
> *Of the shining Lands of the Gods.*
> *We call on thee, O Freya the Fair One!*
> *Be with us here, in this rite.*
> *Hail Freya!*

All: *Hail Freya!*

The Godi or other so chosen lights the candle or torch before the Thor banner and says:

> *O red-bearded Thunderer,*
> *Friend and protector of our people,*
> *Before whose mighty hammer*
> *Neither God nor man can stand,*
> *Yet who loves farmstead and*
> *The companionship of those who labor,*
> *We call on thee, O mighty Thor!*
> *Be with us here in this rite.*
> *Hail Thor!*

All: *Hail Thor!*

Then the Godia or other so chosen says:

> *O Patrons of the Harvest Season,*
> *We give thee salutations,*
> *And feast in thy honor.*
> *Thor, protector of farmstead, field and pasture,*
> *And all those who labor for their living.*
> *˙O Sif of the Golden Hair, whose magic tresses*
> *Are as the rich gold of the autumn harvest,*
> *We do ask that thy blessings surround us,*
> *And we thank thee for this bountiful food*
> *Which thou hast given us.*

> *Cast thy blessing upon this bounty,*
> *That it may give strength to our good people,*
> *And lead us further along*
> *The Paths of the Gods.*
> *Hail Thor!*

All: *Hail Thor!*

> *Hail Sif of the Golden Hair!*

All: *Hail Sif of the Golden Hair!*

Godia
or other: *It is at this time*
> *That we must prepare ourselves and our people,*
> *Our homes, our lands, and our families*
> *For the hard seasons which may lie before us.*

Godi
or other: *This is the fetching-in of summer.*
> *As we store up food for the body*
> *Of each and all of our folk,*
> *So also must we put in store*
> *Strength for the spirit and soul*
> *Until the spring, and the fair seasons*
> *Are reborn once again.*

Godi
or other: *This season marks the decline of the year,*
> *Toward the sere seasons to come.*
> *So let us prepare for the lean times,*
> *For ourselves and for our people*

Godi: *Hail Earth,*
> *Mother of all!*   (All repeat)

At this time a Blot is held in honor of the season. A Sumul Celebration may follow.

Next follow any other observances that are desired by the Godia, the Godi, or those in attendance.

When it is time for the meeting to end, the Godia or Godi has all stand silently for the space of 13 heartbeats. Then the Godia or Godi holds the sword out in salute before the rune banner(s) saying:

> *The time for our rite is ended.*
> *Let us give thanks for this time*
> *When we may be with the Gods.*
> *As we go our ways, may the spirit*
> *Of far Valhalla, of the High Ones*
> *Of the shining land,*
> *Go ever with us,*
> *With our children,*
> *And with our people.*
> *Hail Odin!* (salute)

All: *Hail Odin!* (salute)

Replace the sword on the altar, and the Godia or Godi says:

> *This rite is ended.*
> *Go ye ever in the Way of the Gods*
> *And live their blessing.*

After the ceremony, the drink remaining in the drinking horn is poured at the base of a tree with an improvised salutation to the Azure-Cloaked One.

The feast follows.

The Night of Specters
(October 31)

The place where the ritual is held should be encompassed by four trilithon (three-rock) portals, one at East, one at South, one at West and one at North. The structure of each portal should be two posts about one or two feet apart and about five feet high, topped with a lintel or crosspiece which is laid or fastened across the top. Traditionally these would have been actual stones, though in most cases this would be impractical nowadays. If possible, make each of these portals out of rough wood, paint-

Hodur Rune

ed a flat grey or black. Erect some sort of symbolic portals beforehand. Place an altar toward the north of the ritual area. Over the northern portal, hang a banner of the Odin Rune done in black cloth with silver or gold rune markings. At one side hang a rune banner for Freya, and on the other side drape a rune banner for Thor. Place an incense brazier on the altar, and light herbal incense shortly before the rite.

The patron Gods of this season are the Sun God Balder and his blind brother Hodur, both of whom are sons of Odin. If it is possible, make up rune banners for each, (copying from the listing of runes given in this book) and place them immediately to the north of the altar.

Place a sword or dagger on the altar, and a drinking horn at the center of the altar. Mead or ale should be available beneath or behind the altar. Include a copy of this rite, suitably marked for easy reading, for each one who will perform a part of this ceremony. It is best if all celebrants have parts to speak.

Light the ritual area with flame. Also, have candles or torches on or immediately beside the altar to be lit during the ceremony. Each portal has a candle or torch before each post, as if to light the way through. Place one before each rune banner.

Additionally, burn a small taper on the altar from before the start of the ceremony in order to light the other candles or torches, which the Godia, the Godi and any others may use during any readings. If candles are used on the altar, the one to the left should be red and the one to the right should be yellow.

If hand-held banners or standards are available, symbolizing the Gods and Goddesses of Valhalla or heroes of the people, these are carried by the devotees. Play appropriate music if it is available: Wagner's "Entry of the Gods into Valhalla," followed by "Siegfried's Rhine Journey," are ideal. Alternately, "Winter," from Walter Carlos' "Sonic Seasonings," may be played continually. Depending on the tastes of the Godia and Godi (as well as those attending the rite), other music or even storm and nature sounds may be preferred.

It is best if this rite is led by a Godia in addition to the Godi. If a woman of the folk is not available, place flowers before the banner of Freya, and the Godi (or others) speaks the words of the Godia.

When all is in readiness, the folk assemble. (If there is available room, there may be a Procession of Honor led by the Godi and Godia and with the others following, to end before the altar.) Candles or torches beside the altar are lit by the Godi.

At this time the Godi lights the candle or torch before the Odin banner and says:

> *O Great Odin, Sky-Cloaked Wanderer*
> *From the far, ancient lands of our people,*
> *Chief of the Shining Ones*
> *Who do protect our land, our folk and our families.*
> *We call to thee to be with us here.*
> *We call to thee across all of time*
> *And all the worlds of the Gods.*
> *Thy people are still here, O wise One,*
> *Come to us again, and us give to drink of thy*
> *Cauldron of life and of inspiration*
> *That we may prosper once again.*
> *Come to us now and be with us here.*
> *Odin the wise.*
> *Hail Odin!*

All: *Hail Odin!*

Then the Godia lights candles or torches in front of the Freya banner and says:

> *O Leader of the Wind Riders,*
> *Thou who weavest fates and destinies*
> *And before whose magics*
> *Men and Gods do bow,*
> *Consort to our great lord Odin*
> *Of the shining Lands of the Gods.*
> *We call on thee, O Freya the Fair One!*
> *Be with us here, in this rite.*
> *Hail Freya!*

All: *Hail Freya!*

The Godi or other so chosen lights the candle or torch before the Thor banner and says:

> *O red-bearded Thunderer,*
> *Friend and protector of our people,*
> *Before whose mighty hammer*
> *Neither God nor man can stand,*

We call on you, O mighty Thor!
Be with us here, in this rite.
Hail Thor!

All: *Hail Thor!*

The Godia or other so chosen then says:

We give greetings to the shining
Bright One, High Balder, Lord of Light,
And to his somber brother Hodur the Blind,
Fated forever to the darkness of blindness.
Thou teach us, noble ones, that whatever
Destiny and circumstance befalls us in the end,
We shall live beyond death.
Hail Balder!

All: *Hail Balder!*
          Hail Hodur!

All: *Hail Hodur!*

The Godi or other so chosen says:

Ever-present at this time also is the beautiful,
Yet dark and fearsome Ruler of the Realms
of the Dead, known to men as Hellia or Hel.
She gathers in the souls at twilight's end,
And gives to each, what each deserves.
Without hate, without love, without pity.
Hail, Queen of the Dead!

All: *Hail, Queen of the Dead!*

At this time the Godia says:

Let us now place flames before the
Portals of the East and West,
For at this night the veils between
The living and the dead are thin,
And in times long past did the Dark Queen
Lead the spirits and the shades on procession
Through the dark forests, the night,
And the storms

Of this Middle Earth of humankind.
So let us now, in symbol, open the path
That leads between the worlds.

At this time the Godia and Godi place all additional candles or torches to light the way across the ritual area to link the portals of East and West. Then mead is poured into the drinking horn and the Godi holds it aloft toward the God banners saying:

On this night, O Great Ones,
Do we offer thee mead in lieu of blood,
For the times have changed.
Yet our honor and reverence to Thee
Remains as unchanged now
As it was in ages past.
On this night may we drink to welcome
The Gods of High Valhalla, and the ghosts
Of those who were of our people
In times past.

He then gives it to the Godia, saying:

Drink now in honor of the dead.
Those whom we have loved,
And those we knew not, yet
All who were our kindred.

She speaks some words in remembrance of those who have passed on into Hel's realm, and mentions that they are welcome on this night to pass among us. Then she drinks and, with the words above, passes the horn to each within the ceremony, for each to speak of the noble dead and drink before passing the horn back to her. When the horn has been passed to all, it is replaced on the altar and, after a space of 13 heartbeats, the following is said. (Much of this may be spoken by various ones in the rite.):

Listen then, O brethren of Odin, and know ye well.
We come from beyond the stars,
And beyond the stars we shall return,
Ennobled and possessed of great powers,

If we each prove ourselves worthy.
To one who is a hero of our people,
One who has done great things, learned much,
Death is but a portal to the Godhead
Which each of us can attain, in the fullness of time.
It is said that the Great Lords of High Valhalla
Once trod the sacred groves, and were as us,
Saluted the fierce and honorable wolf,
Honored the raven as messengers of the Gods,
And learned wisdom. So shall it be with us.
Know that though we change form and essence
We shall be ever yet the same.
Know that, sooner or later, for each and all of us,
Our own divine and everlasting Sparks of life
Shall go beyond.
Shall range among a million million worlds.
Like great Odin himself, we shall eventually become as Gods,
To be in all times, and in all places.
This, friends, is Odin's message to each and all of us.
Hail Odin!

All: *Hail Odin!*

Other observances may be held at this time if it is desired. A Blot and/or Sumul celebration may also follow.

When it has been determined that the meeting is ended, the Godia or Godi has all silently meditate for a space of 13 heartbeats. Then the Godi holds the sword out in salute before the rune banner(s) saying:

The time for our rite is ended.
Let us give thanks for this time
When we may be with the Gods.
As we go our ways, may the spirit
Of far Valhalla, of the High Ones
Of the shining land,
Go ever with us,
With our children,
And with our people.
Hail Odin!   (salute)

All: *Hail Odin!*   (salute)

Replace the sword upon the altar, and the Godia or Godi says:

> *This rite is ended.*
> *Go ye ever in the Way of the Gods*
> *And live their blessing.*

After the ceremony, the drink remaining in the drinking horn is poured at the base of a tree with an improvised salutation to the Azure-Cloaked One.

Heroes' Day
(November 11)

The place where the ritual is held should be ringed about with standing stones, as large as it is practical to move and erect. Place an altar near the north of the ritual area. Beyond the altar hang a banner of the Odin Rune done in black cloth with silver or gold rune markings. To one side of the Odin rune hang a banner with the rune of Thor, and to the other side, a rune banner of Freya. For this ceremony, place a rune banner of Tyr before the altar. Other rune banners may be similarly set in honor of heroes of our people, their names written in runes. Include an incense brazier on the altar, lit shortly before the rite.

Have a sword or dagger on the altar. Place a drinking horn at the center of the altar. Mead or ale should be available, placed beneath or beside the altar. Include a copy of this rite, and a Roll of Honor to be called forth during the ceremony. Also, the Godi will appoint various of the people in the ceremony to respond when the heroes' names are called.

If this rite is to be held at night, light the ritual area with flame. Have candles or torches on or immediately beside the altar, to be lit during the ceremony. Place one torch or candle before each rune banner. If candles are used on the altar, the left should be red and the right, a light blue.

If hand-held banners or standards of the Odin Rune are available, symbolizing the Gods and Goddesses of Valhalla, or heroes of the people, these may alternately be carried by the devotees and placed to either side of the rune banners of the Gods. Play appropriate music if it is available: Wagner's "Entry of the Gods into Valhalla," followed by Wagner's "Magic Fire Music." "Siegfried's Funeral Music" is appropriate during the ceremony, or other music deemed appropriate by the celebrants. Martial music is also proper.

It is best if this rite is led by a Godia in addition to the Godi. If a woman of the folk is not available, place flowers before the banner of Freya and the Godi, or others may speak the words of the Godia.

When all is in readiness, the folk assemble. (If there is available room, have a Procession of Honor led by the Godi and Godia and with the others following, bearing the rune banners, to end in the ceremonial area.) The Godi or another lights candles or torches beside the altar.

At this time the Godi lights the candle or torch before the Odin banner and says:

> *O Great Odin, Sky-Cloaked Wanderer*
> *From the far, ancient lands of our people,*
> *Chief of the Shining Ones*
> *Who do protect our land, our folk, and our families.*
> *We call to thee to be with us here.*
> *We call to thee across all of time*
> *And all the worlds of the Gods.*
> *Thy people are still here, O wise One,*
> *Come to us again, and us give to drink of thy*
> *Cauldron of life and of inspiration*
> *That we may prosper once again.*
> *Come to us now and be with us here.*
> *Odin the wise!*
> *Hail Odin!*

All: *Hail Odin!*

Then the Godia lights candles or torches in front of the Freya banner, and says:

> *O Leader of the Wind Riders,*
> *Thou who weavest fates and destinies*
> *And before whose magics*
> *Men and Gods do bow,*

> *Co-ruler with the great Odin*
> *Of the shining lands of the Gods.*
> *We call on thee, O Freya the Fair One!*
> *Be with us here, in this rite.*
> *Hail Freya!*

All: *Hail Freya!*

The Godi (or other so chosen) lights the candle or torch before the Thor banner and says:

> *O red-bearded Thunderer,*
> *Friend and protector of our people,*
> *Before whose mighty hammer*
> *Neither God nor man can stand,*
> *Yet who loves farmstead and*
> *The companionship of those who labor,*
> *We call on thee, O mighty Thor!*
> *Be with us here, in this rite.*
> *Hail Thor!*

All: *Hail Thor!*

Then the Godi says:

> *Let us now speak in remembrance of those*
> *Who have done much for our folk.*
> *Those whose names we know,*
> *And also those whose names have been lost.*
> *At this time do we meet to renew our pledge*
> *To our nation, to our homeland,*
> *To the place where each of us was born,*
> *Home of our children, our families, and our friends.*
> *May it ever be a place of honor, of truth,*
> *Of freedom, and of opportunity.*
> *And may each of us work to keep it so.*
> *Hail to this, our homeland!*

All: *Hail to this, our homeland!*

Then the Godia says:

> *At this time do we meet in honor*
> *Of those who have done great*
> *And noble deeds for our families and our people,*
> *In times of peace, and in time of war.*
> *We also here remember those of our own blood*
> *Who have fallen in battle, who have given their lives*
> *For the nations in which our people live,*
> *To defend home and families and friends.*
> *They shall never be forgotten,*
> *Though the Earth turn cold*
> *And the oceans run dry.*
> *Hail to the Noble Ones!*

All: *Hail to the Noble Ones!*

The Godi calls:

> *We call upon the Gods to recognize and to honor*
> *The great heroes of our people.*
> *Soaring Valkyries, hear our call!*
> *Great Tyr, hear our call!*

There shall be a pause of five heartbeats, and then a man calls:

> *Valeda, wise Vala!*

A woman answers: *She is here, and she shall return!*

Another calls: *Eric the Red, great voyager!*
A man answers: *He is here, and he shall return!*

Another calls: *_____, soldier and beloved uncle!*
A relative answers: *He is here and he shall return!*

Another calls: *_____, nurse and beloved niece!*
A woman answers: *She is here and she shall return!*

Another calls: _____, *pilot and good comrade!*
The friend answers: *He is here and he shall return!*

The calling continues until the Roll of Honor is done.
At this time, hold a Blot in honor of the heroes.
Next follow any other appropriate observances.
When the meeting ends, the Godia or Godi holds the sword out in salute before the rune banner(s) saying:

> *The time for our rite is ended.*
> *Let us give thanks for this time*
> *When we may be with the Gods.*
> *As we go our ways, may the spirit*
> *Of far Valhalla, of the High Ones*
> *Of the shining land,*
> *Go ever with us,*
> *With our children,*
> *And with our people.*
> *Hail Odin!* (salute)

All: *Hail Odin!* (salute)

Replace the sword upon the altar, and the Godia or Godi says:

> *This rite is ended.*
> *Go ye ever in the Way of the Gods*
> *And live their blessing.*

After the ceremony, the drink remaining in the drinking horn should be poured at the base of a tree with an improvised salutation to the Azure-Cloaked One.
The feast and other celebrations follow.

Winter Sunstead and Yule
(Dec. 21, 24, 25, 31, Jan. 1, 2)

This ceremony is in several parts, and can be performed in separate parts on several successive evenings (Winter Sunstead on the evening of the Solstice, Frigga's Day or Festival of Light on the evening of the 24th, and the Tribal Yule Feast on the afternoon of the 25th), or can be accomplished all on one evening, depending on the cele brants' desires.

Frigga Rune

The place where the ritual is held should have an altar near the north of the ritual area, and a Yule tree decorated for the season. Beyond it hang a banner of the Odin Rune done in black cloth with silver or gold rune markings. To one side of the Odin banner is the rune banner of Freya, and to the other side is the banner of Thor. Provide a banner for Frigga, the patroness of the season. All banners, as well as the entire ceremonial area, should be decorated festively for Yule. (If available, suitable images representing the four Deities may be placed instead of the banners, and decorated also.) Place an incense brazier on the altar, lit shortly before the rite.

For one who follows the Old Ways, it is often rewarding to decorate the Yule tree so that it reflects Yggdrasill, the mythic World Tree. To do so, trim the tree as normal, but with particularly Norse features such as a bright star at the top (representing the North Star, the Hub of the Sky), an eagle near the top (representing Odin as giver of wisdom and victory). *Below* the base of the tree should be a cave with the Earth Dragon, images of the three Norns, a pool (a mirror will do) and a cauldron. Stags may be in the snow about the base, and squirrels within the branches. A manger scene is also appropriate (placed in straw against the trunk of the tree) with Mother Frigga and her newborn child (the promise of the new year), along with domestic animals. A pair of wolves may guard them. Three male wanderers, representing Odin, Thor and Loki may be shown bringing gifts to Frigga's Sacred Child. If possible, place Valkyries on the backs of winged horses in the higher tree branches, and/or winged female figures (Valkyries and swan maidens, since they are really the same). There should be many stars and lights in and around the tree.

The patron Gods of this season are Heimdall for the Winter Sunstead (Winter Solstice), Mother Frigga and All-father Odin for the Festival of Light (also called Frigga's Day or Yule Eve) December 24, and Thor for the Yule Feast on December 25. If it is possible, make up a rune banner for Heimdall, copying his rune as given in this book, and hang it near the altar.

Heimdall Rune

Place a sword or dagger on the altar, as well as harness bells and decorations of the season, and a drinking horn. Have mead or ale available beneath or beside the altar. Include a copy of this rite, suitably marked for easy reading, for each who is to perform a portion of this ceremony. It is well if every celebrant has spoken words in this rite, if at all possible.

Light the ritual area with flame. Also, have candles or torches on or immediately beside the altar, to be lit during the ceremony. Set four at the far quarters (directions) of the ritual area, and place one before each rune banner. Additionally, burn a small taper from before the start of the ceremony in order to light the other candles or torches, which the Godia and Godi may use during any readings. Candles on the altar should be white when honoring Heimdall on the 21st, white to the left and silver to the right for the Festival of Light on the night of the 24th, and white to the left and red to the right for the Yule Feast on the day of the 25th. In all cases, additional altar candles of green and red are appropriate.

If hand-held banners or standards of the Odin Rune are available, symbolizing the Gods and Goddesses of Valhalla or heroes of the people, the devotees may carry these. Seasonal carols are appropriate background music, particularly those which are particularly Pagan in origin. If it is possible, someone in the Grove should assemble song books of Pagan-oriented Yule carols as well as many of the more modern popular-type songs.

It is best if this rite is led by a Godia, in addition to the Godi. If a woman of the folk is not available, place flowers and a wreath before the banners of Freya and the Godi, or others may speak the words of the Godia.

When all is in readiness, the folk assemble. (If there is available room, have a Procession of Honor led by the Godi and Godia and with the others following, which ends before the altar.) Candles or torches beside the altar are lit by the Godi.

The Godi lights the candle or torch before the Odin banner, rings the harness bells and says:

> *O Great Odin, wise Allfather*
> *From the far, ancient lands of our people,*
> *Chief of the Shining Ones*
> *Who do protect our land, our folk, and our families.*
> *We call to thee to be with us here.*
> *We call to thee across all of time*
> *And all the worlds of the Gods.*
> *Thy people are still here, O wise One,*
> *Come to us again, and give us to drink of thy*
> *Cauldron of life and of inspiration*
> *That we may prosper once again.*
> *Come to us now and be with us here*
> *To celebrate this joyous season.*
> *Hail Odin!*

All: *Hail Odin!*

The Godia lights candles or torches before the Freya banner, rings the harness bells and says:

> *O Leader of the Wind Riders,*
> *Thou who weavest fates and destinies*
> *And before whose magics*
> *Men and Gods do bow,*
> *Consort to our great Lord Odin*
> *Of the shining Lands of the Gods.*
> *We call on thee, O Freya the Fair One!*
> *Be with us here, in this rite*
> *To celebrate this joyous season.*

Hail Freya!
All: *Hail Freya!*

    The Godi or other so chosen lights the candle or torch before the Thor banner, rings the harness bells and says:

O red-bearded Thunderer,
Friend and protector of our people,
Laughing and hearty,
Generous and good.
We call on thee, O mighty Thor!
Be with us here, in this rite.
Hail Thor!
All: *Hail Thor!*

In celebration of "Winter Sunstead" on Solstice Day:

Godi
or other: *The Ring of the Year continues,*
            Without beginning and without end.
            Friends, the second half-year has passed.
            This time of old was called the Wolf Season,
            In our old lands a time of cold and harshness.
            But surely as the warm seasons
            Shall follow this,
            So also shall our Gods be with us.

Godia
or other: *The times that shall come are cold,*
            Yet look to the sky
            And see the promise that the High ones
            Have made to us:
            The stars which we call "Freya's Gown"
            Are high in the winter sky,
            And the winter way winds from her feet
            To mark the path of souls across the sky.
            So also, in the coldest of seasons,
            Is the promise of life and plenty to come.

Godia
or other: *At this time we are at the balance point of the year,*
The days have grown shorter and there is chill;
Thus we remember the distant ages of ice and snow,
And the threat of chaos in the terrible Fimbulwinter
*   Of legend.*
Yet, though the days may be cold and bitter,
There will be the promise of the future, as days
Slowly grow longer.

After a pause of five heartbeats, the Godia or other continues:

At this time do we call on far-seeing Heimdall,
Watcher for the Gods,
To give us vision for the future,
And the steadfastness and patience
To wait for better times.
Hail Heimdall!
All: *Hail Heimdall!*

The Sumul celebration should here be performed in honor of Midwinter.

On the night of Freya's Day, or the Festival of Light,
perform the following:

Various members of the Grove speak parts of this rite, rather than the Godi and Godia:

Godi: *This is the season of the Newborn God,*
And of hope born anew.
The Lady of the Skies is his Mother,
And the One Who Builds the World
Is his father.

Other: *All animals and all magical creatures*
At this time come in pilgrimage
From across this Mid-Earth
To honor the Mother, the Allfather,
And the Sacred Child.

Other:	*At this time and in this place*
	Must we be thankful for family, for friends,
	And for our good people, as well as for
	The fine gifts of the season.
	Hail to the Blessed Mother!
All:	*Hail to the Blessed Mother!*
	Hail to the Allfather!
All:	*Hail to the Allfather!*
	Hail to the God Child of Promise!
All:	*Hail to the God Child of Promise!*

At this time presents are opened, followed by singing of seasonal carols and popular songs of this festive time.

On the Family Day of the Yule Feast, perform the following:

It is not necessary to have a formal ceremony with the usual openings and closings on the day of the Yule Feast, though the celebrants may prefer such a rite anyhow. Whether formal or not, the following are appropriate:

The Godi (or other so chosen) leads with an appropriate prayer to the Allfather.

Pork or ham is served, as if after sacrifice.

Toasts to Odin (victory and power), Thor (strength and power), Njord and Freyr (good harvest and peace), and Bragi (solemn vows for the coming year).

"Father Thor" brings in gifts to children, and to adults. He and his gifts should be humorous and in character. It will be obvious that he is one of the fathers or uncles dressed in Viking garb, carrying a hammer, and a sack of gifts. (As usual on the eve of December 25, the Old King has made his usual secret visit to leave presents.)

Reading seasonal texts should follow, as well as singing Yule carols and light popular seasonal songs.

Perform this as a New Year's Eve celebration:

For the New Year's Eve celebration, all celebrants have their own drinking horns, cups or tankards.

First perform the rite for Winter Sunstead, then the following:

Godi: *The new year will soon be upon us.*
       Thus I call on all who are present here
       To charge their horns with mead,
       And silently to make their solemn vows
       For the coming seasons
       In honor of the Gods' skald, Bragi.
       Hail Bragi!
All: *Hail Bragi!*

At this time the Godi or Godia should lead in toasts to Odin (victory and power), Thor (strength and power), Njord and Frey (good years and peace), and Bragi (solemn vows for the coming year).

CLOSING:

When the meeting has ended, the Godia or Godi has all stand and silently meditate for a moment. Then the Godia or Godi holds the sword out in salute before the rune banner(s) saying:

               The time for our rite is ended.
               Let us give thanks for this time
               When we may be with the Gods.
               As we go our ways, may the spirit
               Of far Valhalla, of the High Ones
               Of the shining land,
               Go ever with us,
               With our children,
               And with our people,
               During this joyous season.
               Hail Odin!   (salute)
All: *Hail Odin!*   (salute)

Replace the sword upon the altar, and the Godia or Godi says:

> *This rite is ended.*
> *Go ye ever in the Way of the Gods*
> *And live their blessing.*
> *Have a joyous Yule,*
> *And a prosperous New Year!*

After the ceremony, pour the drink remaining in the drinking horn at the base of a tree with an improvised salutation to the Azure-Cloaked One.

Household Seasonal Celebrations

The Vala's Vision (Maiden's Day)

This ritual is held on the day of the Vala's Vision, around February 2. It is a time of festival for several families gathered together, each bringing food and drink for the potluck feast.

Prior to the time of the rite, celebrate a day of games and good company for children and parents alike. The area should be set up for candle dipping and decoration of the candles by all family members after the ceremony. The ritual may be held out-of-doors or inside. Place a bare-branched tree at the center of the ritual area, decorated by the children with white cotton or "spray snow," hung with crystals and clear glass ornaments, a string of clear white lights and other decorations of the wintry season. At the base of the tree the children should make a straw bed and a straw lady to put into it. Have pencils, pens and clean paper available, as well as a large incense brazier or iron dish or cauldron in which to burn the "forgiveness petitions." Place banners of Odin and Frigga at the northern edge of the ritual area, or some appropriate other symbols of the female and male in the Divine. Whatever symbols are used, light a candle or torch before each of them.

At the beginning of the rite, the Master of the House summons the celebrants by blowing a horn. When all are gathered, he and the Lady of the House light candles and give them to all of the children present, then lead the children in procession about the perimeter of the ritual area. (Parents should accompany the children for safety.) Upon the return of the slow procession to the starting point, they instruct the small ones to place their lamps about the Lady Tree, saying:

> *Place this light*
> *About the Wise Woman's Tree*
> *So that the Great Ones*
> *May be with us.*

When all are in readiness, the Master of the House raises his hand and says:

> *Friends, I now bid thee*
> *To join in a celebration*
> *Of Lady Day.*
> *We remember the Wise Woman*
> *Who sees into the future,*
> *And the young Lady*
> *Who will bring Spring.*

The Lady of the House then says:

> *We call upon the Wise Woman*
> *To help us see clear the way*
> *To the seasons which shall follow,*
> *And to the Grandmother of All*
> *So that we can forgive ourselves*
> *And each other.*
> *And like the young Maiden* (indicates straw bed and doll)
> *Be fresh and new again.*

The Master of the House hands out paper and writing implements, saying to the assembled folk:

> *Let us all take paper and pencils,*
> *And each write alone and in our own words*
> *The things for which we want forgiveness*
> *Before the Gods*
> *And the Grandmother of All.*
> *What thou hast written, show to no one,*
> *So that only the Gods will know.*
> *Fold thy papers as thou finish,*
> *Come forth, and burn them here.*
>   (indicates brazier or cauldron)

As each finishes, she or he comes forward to burn the folded paper in the brazier or cauldron. The Master of the House sees that each petition is lit and that it burns safely as the lady of the house says to each adult or child:

Say after me:
"Grandmother of All,
Grant me forgiveness
For all that I have done wrong,
As I burn this before thee."

Each will repeat, as the paper burns. The Lady of the House or the Master may give each a cup of milk or of punch after they have finished burning their respective papers.

When all have written and burned their "forgiveness petitions," the Lady of the House says:

Grandmother Hulda, Grandmother of the Gods
And friend of our children, our families, our people,
We put before you all which does hinder, harm,
And make guilty.
Consume and erase all, we do ask,
And make us as fresh and good
As the new snow.
And like the young Maiden (indicates straw bed and doll)
Be fresh and new again.
Blessings be to Hulda,
And to ourselves.

May the Holy Lady bless our homes,
Our families, and all we own.
So mote it be.

All: *So mote it be.*

The Master of the House then says to the assembled family members:

May our Lord and our Blessed Lady
Give blessings upon us.
Let us give joy and good friendship
Before the Great ones,
And in so doing, honor them.
This rite is ended.
The Gods be with thee.

All: *The Gods be with thee.*

The children are then asked to blow out the candles that they have set about the tree.

Afterwards there is family candle dipping and decorating, with the children being helped as necessary by the adults.

If there is a fireplace or an outside fire, weiners and marshmallows are roasted, and the Master and Lady of the House encourage the children to see pictures and visions in the flames and the coals.

Spring Evenight

This ritual is held the day of Spring Equinox, around March 21. It is a time of festival for several families gathered together, each bringing food and drink for the potluck feast.

Prior to the time of the rite, have a day of games and good company for children and parents alike. The ritual may be held out-of-doors or inside. A green tree should be placed at the center of the ritual area, and decorated by the children with many multi-colored ribbons hung with fruits and vegetables in the branches, a string of green lights and other decorations of the spring season. Small ribboned maypoles are made and given to each of the children present. A bowl of seeds and cups of water are available, as well as planting pots for each member of the family. Sections of the household flower bed, garden or yard should have been turned and soaked in advance for the planting rite. Cookies and fruit juice are provided after the planting.

Place banners of Odin and Frigga at the northern edge of the ritual area, or some appropriate other symbols of the female and male in the Divine. Whatever symbols are used, light a candle or torch before each of them.

At the beginning of the rite, the Master of the House summons the celebrants by blowing a horn. When all are gathered, he and the Lady of the House give the small maypoles to all the children, then lead the children in procession about the perimeter of the ritual area and all around the neighboring places as well. (Upon the return of the procession to the starting point, they instruct the small ones to place their ribboned staffs about the ritual area and about the Spring Tree, saying:

> *Place these spring staffs*
> *About the Spring Tree*
> *So that the Great Ones*
> *May be with us.*

When all are in readiness the Master of the House raises his hand and says:

> *Friends, I now bid thee*
> *To join in a celebration*
> *Of the season of Spring.*
> *This is the time for all things new,*
> *And for new life.*
> *The days are good,*
> *And the times to come will be happy*
> *For all of us.*

The Lady of the House then takes the bowl of seeds and holds it on high, saying:

> *Allfather Odin and Good Mother Frigga,*
> *Bless these seeds, and bless us as we plant them,*
> *To make the world greener, better and more alive.*

The Master of the House takes the cups of water and hands them out, along with seeds from the bowl, saying to each member of the family:

> *Take these seeds, and plant them.*
> *Give them this water, and wish them well.*
> *Remember where thou plantest thy seeds,*
> *And care for them in the times to come.*
> *Remember always to make our world*
> *Greener, better and more alive.*

As each finishes planting the seeds, s/he returns to be given cookies and fruit juice by the Lady of the House.

When all have finished planting, the Lady of the House says:

> *May the Holy Lady bless our homes,*

> *Our families, and all we own.*
> *So mote it be.*

All: *So mote it be.*

The Master of the House then says to the assembled family members:

> *May our Lord and our Blessed Lady*
> *Give blessings upon us.*
> *Let us give joy and good friendship*
> *Before the Great Ones,*
> *And in so doing, honor them.*
> *This rite is ended.*
> *The Gods be with thee.*

All: *The Gods be with thee.*

Children's games such as "blind man's bluff," "hide and seek," and others may be played, followed by a marshmallow roast later in the evening.

Walpurgia (or Beltane)

This ritual is to be held on or about the day of May 1. It is a time of festival for several families gathered together, each bringing food and drink for the potluck feast.

Prior to the time of the rite, have a day of games and good company for children and parents alike. The ritual may be held out-of-doors or inside. Place a green tree in the ritual area, decorated by the children with many green and gold ribbons, a string of gold and green lights and other decorations of this season. Set up a maypole in the middle of the yard, with a colored ribbon for each in the ceremony (it is best if the children can have a major role in setting up the maypole). Make candles available, to be given to the children as the ceremony starts. Ribbons and garlands are worn by all present. Set a wheel of straw where it can be burned by the family members during the ceremony.

Place banners of Odin and Freya at the northern edge of the ritual area, or some appropriate other symbols of the female and male in the Divine. Whatever symbols are used, light a candle or torch before each of them.

At the beginning of the rite, the Master of the House summons the celebrants by blowing a horn. When all are gathered, he and the Lady of the House light the candles and give them to the children, telling them to place the candles at the edge of the ritual area:

> *Place these candles*
> *About the edge of our ritual area,*
> *So that the Great Ones*
> *May be with us.*

When all are in readiness the Master of the House raises his hand and says:

> *Friends, I now bid thee*
> *To join in a celebration*
> *Of the season of May Eve.*
> *This is the time to begin enjoying*
> *The warm seasons ahead.*
> *The days are good,*
> *And the times to come will be happy*
> *For all of us.*

The Lady of the House then leads the children to the maypole, saying:

> *The wheel of the year turns again.*
> *Let us take the colored ribbons*
> *Of this festive maypole,*
> *And bring in the Season of Life.*

All take ribbons and, led by the Master and Lady of the house, weave in and out clockwise about the circle until they are at the center and can go no further, chanting over and over:

> *Victory time,*
> *Bright and shining King,*

Be with us
As we dance the Ring.

When they are all at the center, the Master or the Lady calls:

Summer has won!
Everyone, run for your candles,
And set the straw wheel afire!

All go for their candles and set the straw wheel on fire. The Master and Lady judge which boy and which girl have lit the first fire, and call each of them "King of the May" and "Queen of the May," with crowns or garlands, and a small treat, given to each of them.
When all is finished, the Lady of the House says:

May the Holy Lady bless our homes,
Our families, and all we own.
So mote it be.
All: *So mote it be.*

The Master of the House then says to the assembled family members:

May our Lord and our Blessed Lady
Give blessings upon us.
Let us give joy and good friendship
Before the Great ones,
And in so doing, honor them.
This rite is ended.
The Gods be with you.
All: *The Gods be with you.*

Children's games such as "wolf and the hunters" (otherwise known as "tag") and others may be played, and ring dances around the maypole, followed by the potluck feast and a marshmallow roast later in the evening.

Summer Sunstead

This ritual is to be held about the time of the Summer Solstice, near June 21. It is a time of festival for several families gathered together, each bringing food and drink for the potluck feast.

Prior to the time of the rite, have a day of games and good company for children and parents alike. The ritual may be held out-of-doors or inside. Place a green tree at the center of the ritual area, decorated by the children with many yellow and orange ribbons, a string of orange and yellow lights, and other decorations of this season. Have candles available to give to the children as the ceremony starts.

Place banners of Odin and Freya at the northern edge of the ritual area, or some appropriate other symbols of the female and male in the Divine. Light a candle or torch before each symbol.

At the beginning of the rite, the Master of the House summons the celebrants by blowing a horn. When all are gathered, he and the Lady of the House light the candles and give them to the children, telling them to place the candles at the edge of the ritual area:

> *Place these candles*
> *About the edge of our ritual area,*
> *So that the Great Ones*
> *May be with us.*

When all are in readiness, the Master of the House raises his hand and says:

> *Friends, I now bid thee*
> *To join in a celebration*
> *Of the season of Midsummer.*
> *This is the time to celebrate*
> *The life that the Gods give to us,*
> *And the victory of life for the whole world.*
> *The days are good,*
> *And the times to come will be happy*
> *For all of us.*

The Lady of the House then says:

> *Let us now remember the Earth,*
> *Mother of All*
> *Her love and devotion shall always*
> *Bring forth life anew.*
> *And so also, shall our family prosper.*

Then the Master of the House says:

> *Let us now remember the Father,*
> *King of wild things, fields and farms,*
> *Giver of life, and protector of all.*
> *Thy brightness and joy and love*
> *Shall always shine*
> *As example for our people.*

The eldest child should place a wreath or ribbons over the banner of Odin, and the Master of the House serves cake and punch to all of the children.

When all is finished, the Lady of the House says:

> *May the Holy Lady bless our homes,*
> *Our families, and all we own.*
> *So mote it be.*

All: *So mote it be.*

The Master of the House then says to the assembled family members:

> *May our Lord and our Blessed Lady*
> *Give blessings upon us.*
> *Let us give joy and good friendship*
> *Before the Great Ones,*
> *And in so doing, honor them.*
> *This rite is ended.*
> *The Gods be with thee.*

All: *The Gods be with thee.*

Give several soft "boffers" of foam rubber (the type sold in hardware stores for water-pipe insulation) to the children to use in harmless swordplay, with the victor in each match being given a kiss by a child of the opposite sex. Later have a barbeque or weiner roast, and a potluck dinner for all.

Hloaf-Festival (Lammas)

This ritual is held on or about the time of the Lammas: August 1. It is a time of festival for several families gathered together, each bringing food and drink for the potluck feast.

Prior to the time of the rite, have a day of games and good company for children and parents alike. The ritual may be held out-of-doors or inside. Place a leafy tree at the center of the ritual area, decorated by the children with many yellow and brown ribbons, a string of yellow lights, little straw figures and other decorations of this season. Have candles available, and give them to the children as the ceremony starts.

Place banners of Odin and Freya at the northern edge of the ritual area, or some appropriate other symbols of the female and male in the Divine. Light a candle or torch before each symbol.

At the beginning of the rite, the Master of the House summons the celebrants by blowing a horn. When all are gathered, he and the Lady of the House light the candles and give them to the children, telling them to place the candles at the edge of the ritual area:

> *Place these candles*
> *About the edge of our ritual area,*
> *So that the Great Ones*
> *May be with us.*

When all are in readiness, the Master of the House raises his hand and says:

> *Friends, I now bid thee*
> *To join in a celebration*

> *Of the season of Lammas, August Eve.*
> *This is the time to remember*
> *The warmth of Summer.*
> *The days are good,*
> *And the times to come will be happy*
> *For all of us.*

The Lady of the House then says:

> *Let us now remember that we must*
> *Search for the treasure of life,*
> *And search for beauty,*
> *So that each of us, and our family,*
> *Shall be happy apart and together.*

Then the Master of the House says:

> *Let us now remember that*
> *Nothing is beyond each of us.*
> *If we wish enough,*
> *And work for it enough,*
> *We can do anything,*
> *And be whatever we resolve to be,*
> *For ourselves and for our family.*

The eldest child places a wreath or ribbons at the base of the leafy tree, lights a candle there, and pours water at the base of the tree.

When all is finished, the Lady of the House says:

> *May the Holy Lady bless our homes,*
> *Our families, and all we own.*
> *So mote it be.*

All: *So mote it be.*

The Master of the House then says to the assembled family members:

> *May our Lord and our Blessed Lady*
> *Give blessings upon us.*

> *Let us give joy and good friendship*
> *Before the Great Ones,*
> *And in so doing, honor them.*
> *This rite is ended.*
> *The Gods be with thee.*

All: *The Gods be with thee.*

Children's games such as "London Bridge is Falling Down," or "Race for the Star" can be played, as well as others. Later in the evening enjoy a potluck dinner. If stories are told, some early versions of the Cinderella myth (it is one of the oldest stories of which we have record) should be discussed.

The Week of the Spirits (Halloween)

The family should begin observances on the evening of October 24, the week prior to Halloween, also known as November Eve or Winter Fire. This is a special time for remembering our ancestors and our departed loved ones, and is a solemn time set aside for contemplating the mystery of life and death as taught by the Ancient Ways.

On the evening of the 24th it is proper to begin a period of light fasting, meaning simple (often meatless, sweetless, and/or fatless) meals. The fast comes to an end with the early supper and Halloween treats on the evening of the 31st. It is well to avoid going out or engaging in too many social activities during this week since this is a time during which the family should be together, sharing memories of the past.

A family shrine should be set up, with small banners or other representations of Odin and Freya, set with pictures of well-loved but departed friends and relatives, and a simple white candle as a symbol of the Divine. The candle should be replaced and re-lit each day by one of the children.

The family should keep its own chest of ancestor relics; personal belongings of now-departed family members (such as Grandpa's scarf or Grandma's fan). During Winter Fire Week we bring out all the various photos and relics, as well as old family albums. We look over all the various photos and relics, recounting the life histories of those represented.

Each night of this festival is dedicated to a special subject: one night we may dedicate to ghost stories (which can be instructive in dealing with theories of life and death), another to heroic myths of ancient times, another evening to legends of the fairy folk and wood sprites, and so on. It may be of value to focus on different ancestors each night—perhaps one evening recounting the lives of ancestors who heroically served their people and their countries, another telling about those of our people who have been martyred for their faith, their convictions or freedom, and perhaps another evening set aside for those ancestors who were dedicated to the various arts, as well as even a night dedicated to remembering family pets.

A Family Fire Festival is held on November Eve. On the big night of October 31st, after routine trick-or-treat festivities are completed, have a ceremonial and important re-kindling by the children of the hearthfire (and also of any pilot lights), in honor of this ancient season of renewal. Emphasize that November Eve, the Night of the Spirits, is the Herald of Winter. After the fire kindling and as midnight approaches, the children should set candles in the windows and leave the doors unlocked. Serve the meal at midnight, when the dead are invited to join the family. (A plate of food is set out for the dead; the physical food is given to family pets afterward.) Prayers are said to Odin, Freya, Ran (Queen of the Oceans) and Hellia (Queen of the Realms of the Dead) for the recent dead. Insofar as is known, serve the favorite foods of departed relatives. (If other Odinist or other Pagan families are visiting, this meal may be a big potluck.) Prayers are offered, especially for the martyrs and souls which must undergo their own purgatories.

The Nights of the Halloween Festival

October 24 — Festival prelude. The children put up seasonal decorations, and parents set up the family shrine.

October 25 — *The Night of the Heroes.* Remembering those of the family who have done much in war and in peace, and recounting their deeds.

October 26 — *The Night of the Seers.* Remembering ancestors who have dealt with the supernatural, who have foreseen the future, and telling stories of their adventures.

October 27 — *The Night of the Martyrs.* Those of our people who have died for their faith, their convictions, their freedom or for our people.

October 28 — *The Night of the Bards.* Artists, musicians and others who have spoken of or pictured the Old Ways, and those others whose work evokes magic.

October 29 — *The Night of the Recent Dead.* Remembering relatives and friends, and telling about their lives.

October 30 — *The Night of Remembrance for Family Pets.* Pets are family members; they must be recalled and their memories cherished.

October 31 — *Family Fire Festival.* After the mundane celebration of the night, conduct a prayer ceremony for souls still undergoing purification. Children relight the hearth and pilot lights. A commemorative midnight dinner is held, at which the dead are welcomed.

Evening Meal Format for the Week of the Spirits

- The whole family sets the table. Seasonal plates, cups and napkins are used.
- A bell is placed on the table to be rung by one of the children.
- Each child picks out a favorite Halloween candle, places it on the table and lights it.
- All artificial lights are put out.
- A member of the family gives the prayer for that night.
- The fireplace (if the family has one) is lit as food is served.
- A child rings the bell to banish all unwelcome spirits and to welcome the good.
- Adults will alternate in reading instructive stories and legends, or telling useful tales according to the subject for the nights, or appropriate selections from the Eddas and other mythology as the meal is eaten. The children's questions and requests are answered.

- Finally, the lights are turned on again and the whole family clears the table.

Practical Suggestions

Children always enjoy decorating the house for Halloween.

In family readings and narrations, discuss the meaning of the season from an Odinist or other Pagan point of view.

Children and parents can make lanterns (Jack-O-Lanterns and similar) to put in windows and to hang in trees.

The family can visit cemeteries and decorate groves.

The vigil can be kept in the seasonal shrine, burning day and night, for the festival.

This is an appropriate time for house cleaning and closet cleaning, to get rid of that which is outworn.

Festival of Odin

This ritual is to be held during the celebration held on or about the day of St. Martin, a Catholic saint who was given many of Odin's original attributes. There is strong evidence that this day (November 12) was originally a festival time devoted to Odin and to Cernunnos, who has many similarities to the Wanderer.

This is a time of festival for several families gathered together, each bringing food and drink for the potluck feast. Prior to the time of the rites, have a day of games and feasting. The ritual should be held out-of-doors if possible, with the area appropriately decorated for the season with grain, fruits, maize, vegetables, nuts, leaves and flowers. Some of the last remaining Halloween decorations may be used for a final time on this day. Place banners of Odin and Freya at the northern edge of the ritual area, or some appropriate other symbols of the female and male in the Divine. Whatever symbols are used, light a candle or torch before each of them.

At the beginning of the rites, the Master of the House summons the celebrants by the blowing of a horn. When all are gathered, he and the Lady of the House light candles and give them to all of the children present; then they lead the children in procession about the perimeter of the ritual area. (Parents should accompany the children for safety.) Upon the return of the slow procession to the starting point, they instruct the small ones to place their lamps at the edge of the ceremonial area, saying:

> *Place this light*
> *At the edge of our festival*
> *So that the Great Ones*
> *May be with us.*

When all are in readiness, the Master of the House raises his hand and says:

> *Friends, I now bid thee*
> *To join in a celebration*
> *To our patron, the wise Odin,*
> *Known also by his other names*
> *Of Cernunnos and St. Martin*

The Lady of the House then says:

> *We call too upon Our Blessed Lady,*
> *The good Freya*
> *Queen of the Harvests, giver of life*
> *And of plenty*
> *Since before time began.*

The Master of the House calls to the assembled family members:

> *Let us all give thanks*
> *For the foods of the harvest, and*
> *For the challenge of the hunt.*
> *May the wise Allfather bless our homes*
> *And bless our animals, one and all.*
> *So mote it be.*

All: *So mote it be.*

The Lady of the House then calls:

> *Let us all give thanks*
> *For the fullness of this time,*
> *For the rich promise of the harvest time,*
> *And for the love which binds our families*
> *And our people.*
> *May the Holy Lady bless our homes,*
> *Our families, and all we own.*
> *So mote it be.*

All: *So mote it be.*

Both then link hands and call to the assembled family members:

> *May our Lord and Blessed Lady*
> *Give blessings upon us.*
> *Let us give joy and reveling*
> *Before the Great Ones,*
> *And in so doing, honor them.*
> *This rite is ended.*
> *The Gods be with thee.*

All: *The Gods be with thee.*

The children are then asked to blow out the candles that they have set about the area of the ceremony.

Yule
(December 21, 24, 25, and 31)

Parents should obtain Scandinavian or German Advent Calendars for the children, choosing calendars which are magical and somewhat pagan in their illustrations, and have the children begin using them on December 1. These charming holiday calendars are typically each a holiday picture, either in a fantasy forest scene or in an old-fashioned town. Various bushes, logs, windows, doors and so on have the numbers 1 through 24 on them. On each evening of December a child opens the number of that particular day, to find a small "surprise," or a scene-within-a-scene inside the door. Some advent calendars will have candies within each numbered door or window. Advent calendars are usually available at shops that specialize in Scandinavian or German imports and, surprisingly, are rather low in cost.

Also, a festive Yule Calendar, a Danish-style cloth scroll with seasonal decorations, should be embroidered or fabric painted with the number one at the top, two below it, and so on to 24 at the bottom. After the children are asleep, clothespin a small toy or magazine to the number for the next day, as a surprise for each child upon arising in the morning. (Again, these are often on sale at shops that carry Scandinavian goods.)

Decorate the house on what is currently called St. Nicholas' Day (otherwise known as "The Old God's Day"), December 6. Set up the tree soon thereafter. The children should do as much of the decoration as possible, with the parents supervising. During the season, have traditional Yule carols in the background. Assemble a family songbook, compiling Pagan-oriented carols for frequent family singing before the tree.

Modern Yule tree decorations are acceptable for this season, of course, though parents may wish to decorate the Yule tree so that it reflects Yggdrasill, the mythic World-Tree. To do so, the tree should be trimmed as is normal, but with particularly Norse features such as a bright star at the top (representing the North Star, the Hub of the Sky) and an eagle near the top (representing Odin as giver of wisdom and victory). A little *below* the base of the tree should be a cave with the

Earth Dragon, images of the three Norns, a pool (a mirror will do) and a cauldron. Stags may be in the snow about the base, and a squirrel within the branches. A manger scene is also appropriate (placed in straw against the trunk of the tree) with Mother Frigga and her newborn child (the promise of the new year), along with domestic animals. A pair of wolves may guard them. Three male wanderers, representing Odin, Thor, and Loki, may be shown bringing gifts to Frigga's Sacred Child. If possible, Valkyries on the backs of winged horses may be in the higher tree branches, and/or winged female figures (Valkyries and swan maidens, since they are really the same). There should be many stars and lights in and around the tree.

It is fully in line with Odinism to have a creche with the Sacred Child, the Mother Goddess, the God, animals, plus wise men (and wise women) all giving honor to the Child of Promise. Even a Viking ship and (if they can be obtained) statuettes representing the Gods and Goddesses of Valhalla may be added.

Hang a wreath with candles and mistletoe over the family dinner table, with a child lighting the candles before each meal and letting them burn for awhile after all are finished.

Hold a family ceremony to mark the Winter Solstice (about December 21), where families of our people (Odinists and/or other Pagans) can gather for a potluck banquet and to exchange gifts (drawing names is recommended if the group is large), followed by singing of carols before the tree.

On the evening of December 24, have a gathering and simple ceremony in which each child sets out a candle, lays a wreath about it and lights the candle. Then each family member opens one gift. Carols are sung, the Master and Lady of the House give brief salutations to the Gods and to the season, then the children make their own wishes and blow out their candles.

The morning of December 25 is of course one for opening gifts and trying them out. Later in the day it is proper to visit friends and relatives to give them gifts, and neighbors to give them your own family food specialty and wish them well for the season. If practicable, offer invocations to Odin and Freya before the festive banquet of the 25th.

It is recommended that seasonal music be kept in the household until the New Year.

Hold a family rite late on December 31 for all to affirm their vows for the coming year.

On January 6 the children should awaken to find, on the hearth, one final seasonal gift apiece from the Old Woman, the Crone Goddess, whom the Italians call Bufana and who in northern Europe is called Mother Holle. Most decorations traditionally come down after Twelfth Night (January 6), though a few may be kept in place until Lady Day (February 2).

Family Day (Mothernight)
(December 21)

This ritual is to be held on or about the time of the Winter Sunstead, near December 21. It is a time of festival for several families gathered together, each bringing food and drink for the potluck feast, and gifts to be exchanged. (If the number of people is large, names should be drawn—though each child should get two or more gifts anyhow!)

Prior to the time of the rite, have a day of good company for children and parents alike, with the group meal being held for all. Have the Yule tree already placed in the ritual area, though with a few additional decorations placed this evening by the children. Place the gifts about the tree. Provide candles for the children to place during the ceremony.

At the beginning of the rite the Master of the House summons the celebrants. When all are gathered, he and the Lady of the House light the candles and give them to the children, telling them to place the candles at the edge of the ritual area:

> *Place these candles*
> *About the edge of our ritual area,*
> *So that the Great Ones*
> *May be with us.*

When all are in readiness, the Master of the House raises his hand and says:

> *Friends and family members, I now bid thee*

> To join in a celebration
> Of the balance point of the seasons,
> And, before we open the gifts,
> A thanks to the Mothers here,
> As to the Mother above.
> Thou hast all our love,
> All our devotion.
> All hail to the Mothers!

All: *All hail to the Mothers!*

A special gift and embraces by the children should be given to each mother.

When all is finished, the Lady of the House says:

> May the Holy Lady bless our homes,
> Our families, and all we own.
> So mote it be!

All: *So mote it be!*

The Master of the House then says to the assembled family members:

> May our Lord and our Blessed Lady
> Give blessings upon us.
> Let us give joy and good friendship
> Before the Great Ones,
> And in so doing, honor them.
> This rite is ended.
> The Gods be with thee
> And let the gifts be opened!

Open the gifts then, and hold a caroling session before the tree.

The Festival of Light (Christmas)
(December 24)

This ritual is to be held on the evening of December 24. Hold the ritual before the family Yule tree, decorated for the season. Have candles and wreaths available to give to the children as the ceremony starts.

At the beginning of the rite, the Master of the House summons the family and has the children light all candles in the house, and put out all artificial lights. When all are gathered, he and the Lady of the House give a candle and a wreath to the children, telling them to place the candles within the wreaths and to light them there.

> *Light thy candle in honor*
> *Of the Child of Promise,*
> *Of a magical time,*
> *And a magical night.*

Then the Master and Lady of the House lead the family in singing at least three carols. Appropriate music should be in the background as each member of the house selects and opens one gift.

Finally, the Master of the House says:

> *This is the time for wonder,*
> *For living again the time of beauty*
> *And of joy.*
> *On this beautiful night we again*
> *Renew, within us all,*
> *The promise of hope and joy*
> *For the seasons to come.*

The Lady of the House says:

> *This is the time for wonder,*
> *For magic, for enchantment,*
> *And for love.*

> *On this beautiful night we who are grown*
> *Can once more remember a child's joy,*
> *And children can touch the sky!*

If it is so desired, more can be said or done at this time.
When all is finished, the Lady of the House says:

> *May the Holy Lady bless our homes,*
> *Our families, and all we own.*
> *So mote it be!*

All: *So mote it be!*

The Master of the House then says to the assembled family members:

> *May our Lord and our Blessed Lady*
> *Give blessings upon us.*
> *Let us give joy and good friendship*
> *Before the Great Ones,*
> *And in so doing, honor them.*
> *This rite is ended.*
> *The Gods be with thee!*

All: *The Gods be with thee!*

Solitary Rites

Solitary Celebration of the Vala's Vision (Maiden's Day)
(February 2)

If a follower of the Old Way cannot find others of like mind to share a ritual in honor of High Valhalla, this rite may be performed by the solitary individual. If possible, perform the rite either in some out-of-the-way outdoor spot, or in some place within one's dwelling that is set aside for the honoring of Odin.

Before dressing for the ceremony one should bathe, bearing strongly in mind that the water is cleansing the soul and spirit, as well as the body, for one should be purified in all ways before calling on the Great Ones.

The clothing worn for this ceremony should be what one would feel proper wearing before Thor, Odin and Freya. It should have a special cut and feel to symbolize the strength and power due to one of the Old Ways, different enough to "set the mind apart" from the ordinary world of men when it is worn. Leather, metal, fur-trimmed garments, and perhaps a cloak would be appropriate. The archaic guideline is: "For battle, for love or magic, and for speaking with Gods." For the Maiden's Festival observance, wear some garment of pure and unstained white.

Using the illustrations included on page 269, carefully prepare drawings—on clean, new paper or cloth—of the runes for Odin ⊕ , Thor ⊥ and Freya ß . (Additional runes may be set below these as you so desire, symbolizing your own highest ideals and those of your own folk, the people you feel are closest to you spiritually). If it is possible, in advance, make up cloth banners, or even small wood/stone plaques, to be kept for such rites. It may be preferable to draw them anew above or before the altar for each ceremony, or even to scribe them on the ground before the rite is begun. In short, prepare the runes in the way which *feels* best!

Take with you a bag of runestones, or consult the section in this book which summarizes them, and draw or paint on pebbles or small tiles the runes which seem appropriate for the season. Memorize the rune which best symbolizes that what you want to accomplish during the coming season.

Go alone to the place of solitude which you have chosen, or go to the room which you have prepared, carrying with you the implements needed for the rite, plus a drinking horn and mead.

Set up the ritual so that you face North. If outdoors, then a tree or large stone should point in that direction. Take eight stones of convenient size (about as large as a man's head for an outdoor ceremony, or smaller rocks if indoors) and lay the stones down at equal intervals starting from the north and working sunwise (clockwise) about an eight-foot circle. Place additional stones at the North to support a small simple altar, or to serve as an altar.

Between the altar and the stone marking the north-point of the circle place or draw the runes of our Gods: Odin at the center, Freya to one side and Thor at the other. On the altar place a burner of incense and a drinking horn or tankard with some beer or ale in it. Place a copy of this ritual where it can be easily seen.

If the ritual is held outdoors and there are no other persons about, light torches (or candles in glass jars for smaller flames shielded from the wind). If indoors, ordinary candles may be used. If two of them are placed on the altar, the left should be white and the right, a dark blue.

If music is used for meditation prior to the rite, pieces such as Grieg's "Peer Gynt Suite," followed by "Siegfried's Rhine Journey" would be ideal, though other music or even nature sounds may be preferred.

When all is prepared, light the candles or torches at the four quarters, saying for each:

> *I light here a flame*
> *In honor of the coming season*
> *Of chill, and of solitude.*
> *Be with me now Odin, Freya, Thor!*

Then light a candle or torch at the altar, saying:

O Great Ones, I dedicate this place
In thy honor and for thy magics.
Be with me, and in me, and of me,
Odin the Wise,
Freya the Beautiful,
Thor the Mighty.

Sit before the altar and pour mead into your horn, then raise it to the banners and to the tree, saying:

I drink to thee, O Great Ones.
Though I am the only one of our people
Here in this place, it is still
A place of the Gods.
So long as thy magical flame
Burns in my heart.
Hail Odin!   (drink)
Hail Freya!   (drink)
Hail Thor!   (drink)
Hail Hulda!   (drink)
I salute also the spirit of the Vala,
The far-seeing prophetess
Who sought out the patterns
Of the future for Great Odin.
Grant me thy clear vision,
O Wise Woman! (drink)

Lay out the runestones which are symbolic of the coming season. Then take up pen and parchment or clean paper and write the runes which best summarize why you feel guilty, and all that you feel you have done wrong in the past. Scribe the runes, and write plainly all that bothers you the most about yourself. Spend a lengthy time looking at the runes and meditating on them all, looking for the link between the symbols of the season and what you wish to accomplish. Finally, fold your parchment or paper with your own personal desires runed on it, and burn it in the incense brazier, saying:

Hear me, O Hulda,

> *Dark Goddess of times far distant.*
> *I place before thee the symbols*
> *Of all which hinders,*
> *Harms, and makes guilty*
> *Within my own soul.*
> *As this flame burns, O Ancient Norn,*
> *I ask thee to consume all my guilt, all my pain,*
> *That it be gone forever.*
> *And leave me pure*
> *In thy holy Name.*
> *I swear by the Sun, O Dark One,*
> *That I shall do all within my power*
> *To build myself stronger, better,*
> *And more noble*
> *In the year to come.*
> *And I thank thee,*
> *O Goddess before the Gods.*
> *Hail Hulda!*

Then gaze into the flames for a long while to see if you can perceive impressions, images or patterns which might give some hint of the future. If so, write them down.

Next this time you may perform any other observances or meditations which you feel are appropriate.

When you feel that the rite should end, face the runes of the Gods and take up the drinking horn or tankard one last time, saying:

> *O Great Ones of High Valhalla,*
> *I give honor to thee*
> *For being with me here.*
> *May some of thy sacred presences*
> *Remain within me as I leave.*
> *And be ever near me, as well as with*
> *Those who are my true people.*
> *To thee I drink this toast,*
> *And pour this libation.*
> *Hail Hulda!*   (salute)
> *Hail Freya!*   (salute)
> *Hail Thor!*   (salute)
> *Hail Odin!*   (salute)

Pour some of the drink out before the altar, and drink what remains. Then put out the torches at the North, East, South and West, followed by those before the rune banners. Then stand before the altar with your arms out, saying:

> *I thank thee, O Great Ones.*
> *This rite is ended.*

Solitary Spring Evenight

(March 21)

If a follower of the Old Way cannot find others of like mind to share a ritual in honor of High Valhalla, this rite may be performed by the solitary individual. Conduct the ceremony either in some out-of-the-way outdoor spot, or in some place within one's dwelling that is set aside for the honoring of Odin and the Old Gods.

Bathe before dressing for the ceremony, bearing strongly in mind that the water is cleansing the soul and spirit, as well as the body, for one should be purified in all ways before calling on the Great Ones.

The clothing for this ceremony should be what you would feel proper wearing before Thor, Odin, Freya and the patroness of the season, Ostara. It should have a special cut and feel to symbolize the strength and power which should be due to one of the Old Ways, and should be different enough to "set the mind apart" from the ordinary world of men when it is worn. One should dress for this rite as seems appropriate for a meeting with the Gods of the North—leather, metal, fur-trimmed garments and perhaps a cloak. The archaic guideline is: "For battle, for love or magic, and for speaking with Gods." Colored ribbons, green leaves and flowers should be worked into one's ritual garments. Some ribbons and fruit should be taken to decorate a small tree at your ritual site.

Using the illustrations included on page 269, carefully prepare drawings—on clean, new paper or cloth—of the runes for Odin ⊕ , Thor  , Freya ᛒ and Ostara ⊙ .

(Additional runes may be set below these as you so desire, symbolizing your own highest ideals and those of your own folk, the people you feel are closest to you spiritually.) If possible, in advance make up cloth banners or (even small) wood or stone plaques to be kept for such rites. It may be preferable to draw them anew above or before the altar for each ceremony, or even to scribe them on the ground before the rite is begun. In short, prepare the runes in the way which feels best!

Take with you a bag of runestones, or consult the section in this book which summarizes them, and draw or paint on pebbles or small tiles the runes which seem appropriate for the season. Memorize the rune which best symbolizes what you want to accomplish during the coming season.

Play appropriate soft music for meditation if it is available. Continuously repeating Halvorsen's "Rustle of Spring," or Grieg's "Wedding Day at Troldhagen" is ideal, though other music such as "Spring," from Walter Carlos' "Sonic Seasonings," may be used, or nature sounds may be preferred.

Go alone to the place of solitude which you have chosen, or go to the room which you have prepared, carrying with you the implements needed for the rite.

Set up the ritual so that you face North. If outdoors, then a tree or large stone should point in that direction. Take eight stones of convenient size (about as large as a man's head for an outdoor ceremony or smaller rocks if indoors) and lay the stones down at equal intervals starting from the north and working sunwise (clockwise) about an eight-foot circle. Place additional stones at the North to support a small simple altar, or to serve as an altar.

Between the altar and the stone marking the north-point of the circle place or draw the runes of our Gods—Odin at the center, Freya to one side and Thor at the other. Next to the altar itself should be the rune of Ostara. On the altar place a burner of incense and a drinking horn or tankard with some beer or ale in it. Place a copy of this ritual where it can be easily seen.

If the ritual is held outdoors and there are no other persons about, light torches (or candles in glass jars for smaller flames shielded from the wind). If indoors, use ordinary light green candles.

Set the ritual area up before a tree, with the tree at the North.

When all is prepared, light the candles or torches at the four quarters, saying for each:

I light here a flame
In remembrance of the coming season
Of warmth, joy and life.
Be with me now Odin, Freya, Thor
And Ostara, bringer of new life!

Then light a candle or torch at the altar, saying:

O Great Ones, I dedicate
This area in thy honor
And for thy magics.
Be with me, and in me,
And of me,
Odin the Wise,
Freya the Beautiful,
Thor the Mighty,
Ostara the Fruitful!

Pause for the space of 13 heartbeats or more, and say:

O High Ones, in thy honor,
And in honor of Earth

Do I decorate this symbolic tree
And, in symbol, become one with Nature.

Decorate the tree with ribbons and fruit, taking your time. Then walk in a dance-like step (or in the mock battle-steps of a martial arts form, as you prefer) eight times about the tree which you have trimmed with the ribbons and fruits, saying over and again:

The messengers of Spring
Are all about me.
All hail to Lady Ostara,
Goddess of Spring!
As the season blossoms,
May my strength grow as the tree.
Hail Odin!

Sit before the altar and pour mead into your horn, then raise it to the banners and to the tree, saying:

> I drink to thee, O Great Ones.
> Though I am the only one of our people
> Here in this place, it is still
> A place of the Gods,
> So long as thy magical flame
> Burns in my heart.
> Hail Odin!   (drink)
> Hail Freya!   (drink)
> Hail Thor!   (drink)
> Hail Ostara!   (drink)

Then relax for a while.

Lay out the runestones which are symbolic of the coming season. Next take up pen and parchment or clean paper and write the runes which best summarize what you wish to accomplish during the coming season. Spend a lengthy time looking at the runes and meditating on them all, looking for the link between the symbols of the season and what you wish to accomplish. Finally, fold your parchment or paper with your own personal desires written in runes upon it and burn it in the incense brazier, saying:

> The Power goes forth
> Before the Great Gods of Valhalla.
> I swear by the Sun, O mighty Ones,
> That I shall do all within my power
> To become that which I desire,
> And I call upon thee
> To aid me.
> Hail ye Gods!
> Hail Odin!

At this time you may perform any other observances or meditations which you feel are appropriate.

When you feel that the rite should end, face the runes of the Gods and take up the drinking horn or tankard one last time, saying:

> O Great Ones of High Valhalla,

I give honor to thee
For being with me here.
May some of thy sacred presence
Remain within me as I leave.
And be ever near me, as well as with
Those who are my true people.
To thee do I drink this toast,
And pour this libation.
Hail Freya! (salute)
Hail Thor! (salute)
Hail Odin! (salute)
Hail Ostara, Lady of Spring! (salute)

Pour some of the drink out before the altar, and drink what remains. Then put out the torches at the North, East, South and West, followed by those before the rune banners. Finally, stand before the altar with your arms out, saying:

I thank thee, O Great Ones.
This rite is ended.

Intermediate Festivals

The same rites as for Spring Evenight may be performed for the Tree Planting, or Charming of the Plow. Easter-type decorations may be used in addition to those specified above. At this time Ostara's patronage of the season has been yielded to Erda (also known as Berchta or Hulda in their Earth Goddess personae), and to Odin. Altar candles should be light green to the left, and dark blue to the right.

Solitary Walpurgia (May Eve)
(April 30—May 1)

If a follower of the Old Way cannot find others of like mind to share a ritual in honor of High Valhalla, this rite may be performed by the solitary individual. Conduct the ceremony either in some out-of-the-way outdoor spot, or in some place within one's dwelling that is set aside for the honoring of Odin.

Bathe before dressing for the ceremony, bearing strongly in mind that the water is cleansing the soul and spirit, as well as the body, for one should be purified in all ways before calling on the Great Ones.

The clothing worn for this ceremony should be what you would feel proper wearing before Thor, Odin, Freya, and before Freyr, the patron of this season. It should have a special cut and feel to symbolize the strength and power which should be due to one of the Old Ways, and should be different enough to "set the mind apart" from the ordinary world of men when it is worn—leather, metal, fur-trimmed garments, and/or perhaps a cloak; the archaic guideline is: "For battle, for love or magic, and for speaking with Gods." Colored ribbons, green leaves and flowers should be worked into one's ritual garments.

Food should be carried along for a symbolic meal "with the Gods."

Using the illustrations included on page 269, carefully prepare drawings—on clean, new paper or cloth—of the runes for Odin $\oplus$, Thor $\perp$, Freya β and Freyr $\Join$. (Additional runes may be set below these as you so desire, symbolizing your own highest ideals and those of the your own folk, the people you feel are closest to you spiritually). If possible, in advance make up cloth banners or (even small) wood or stone plaques to be kept for such rites. It may be preferable to draw them anew above or before the altar for each ceremony, or even to scribe them on the ground before the rite is begun. In short, prepare the runes in the way which feels best!

Go alone to the place of solitude which you have chosen, or go to the room which you have prepared, carrying with you the implements needed for the rite.

The ritual should be set up so that you face North. If outdoors, then a tree or large stone should point in that direction. Be certain that for this rite that a small bush or young tree is near the altar, and have ribbons and fruit available to decorate it. Take eight stones of convenient size (about as large as a man's head for an outdoor ceremony or smaller rocks if indoors) and lay the stones down at equal intervals starting from the north and working sunwise (clockwise) about an eight-foot circle. Place additional at the North to support a small simple altar, or to serve as an altar.

Between the altar and the stone marking the north point of the circle, place or draw the runes of our Gods—Odin at the center, Freya to one side and Thor at the other. The rune of Freyr should be just behind the altar. Flowers should be spread over the altar and about the ritual area. On the altar place a burner of flower-scented incense and a drinking horn or tankard with some beer or ale in it. Place a copy of this ritual where it can be easily seen.

If the ritual is held outdoors and there are no other persons about, light torches (or candles in glass jars for smaller flames shielded from the wind). If indoors, use ordinary candles. Altar candles should be light green to the left, and gold to the right.

Take with you a bag of runestones, or consult the section in this book which summarizes them, and draw or paint on pebbles or small tiles the runes which seem appropriate for the season. Memorize the runes which best symbolize what you want to accomplish during the coming season.

Play appropriate soft music for meditation if it is available; continually repeating Grieg's "Midsommervalka" or the "Peer Gynt Suite" is ideal, though other music or nature sounds may be preferred.

When all is prepared, light the candles or torches at the four quarters, saying for each:

> *I light here a flame*
> *In remembrance of the coming season*
> *Of warmth, joy, and life.*
> *Be with me now Odin, Freya, Thor,*
> *And Freyr, friend of fields and pastures!*

Then light a candle or torch at the altar, saying:

> *O Great Ones, I dedicate*
> *This area in thy honor*
> *And for thy magics.*
> *Be with me, and in me,*
> *And of me,*
> *Odin the Wise,*
> *Freya the Beautiful,*
> *Thor the Mighty,*
> *Freyr the Good!*

Pause for the space of 13 heartbeats or more and say:

> *O High Ones, in thy honor,*
> *And in honor of Earth*
> *Do I decorate this symbolic tree,*
> *And, in symbol, become one with Nature.*

Decorate the tree with ribbons and fruit, taking your time. Then walk in a dance-like step (or in the mock-battle steps of a martial arts form, as you prefer) eight times about the tree which you have trimmed with the ribbons and fruits, saying over and again:

> *With others in ages far past*
> *Do I thread the ancient way*
> *With my Gods again!*

Sit before the altar and pour mead into your horn, then raise it to the banners and to the tree, saying:

> *I drink to thee, O Great Ones.*
> *Though I am the only one of our people*
> *Here in this place, it is still*
> *A place of the Gods,*
> *So long as thy magical flame*
> *Burns in my heart.*
> *Hail Odin!* (drink)
> *Hail Freya!* (drink)
> *Hail Thor!* (drink)
> *Hail Freyr!* (drink)

Then relax for a while before beginning your rune spell.

Lay out the runestones which are symbolic of the coming season. Then take up pen and parchment or clean paper and write the runes which best summarize what you wish to accomplish during the coming season. Spend a lengthy time looking at the runes and meditating on them all, looking for the link between the symbols of the season and what you wish to accomplish. Finally, fold your parchment or paper with your own personal desires written in runes upon it, and burn it in the incense brazier, saying:

> *The power goes forth*
> *Before the Great Gods of Valhalla.*
> *I swear by the Sun, O mighty ones,*
> *That I shall do all within my power*
> *To become that which I desire,*
> *And I call upon thee*
> *To aid me.*
> *Hail ye Gods!*
> *Hail Odin!*

At this time you may partake of the food and drink you have brought along, and afterward perform any other observances or meditations which you feel are appropriate.

When you feel that the rite should end, face the runes of the Gods and take up the drinking horn or tankard one last time, saying:

> *O Great Ones of High Valhalla,*
> *I give honor to thee*
> *For being with me here.*
> *May some of thy sacred presences*
> *Remain within me as I leave.*
> *And be ever near me, as well as with*
> *Those who are my true people.*
> *To thee do I drink this toast,*
> *And pour this libation.*
> *Hail Freya!*   (salute)
> *Hail Thor!*   (salute)
> *Hail Odin!*   (salute)
> *Hail Freyr!*   (salute)
> *Hail Gerd!*   (salute)

Pour some of the drink out before the altar, and drink what remains. Then put out the torches at the North, East, South and West, followed by those before the rune banners. Finally, stand before the altar with your arms out, saying:

> *I thank thee, O Great Ones.*
> *This rite is ended.*

Solitary Summer Sunstead
(June 21)

If a follower of the Old Way cannot find others of like mind to share a ritual in honor of High Valhalla, this rite may be performed by the solitary individual. Conduct the ceremony either in some out-of-the-way outdoor spot, or in some place within one's dwelling that is set aside for the honoring of Odin.

Bathe before dressing for the ceremony, bearing strongly in mind that the water is cleansing the soul and spirit, as well as the body, for one should be purified in all ways before calling on the Great Ones.

Ritual garb should have a special cut and feel to symbolize the strength and power due to one of the Old Ways, different enough to "set the mind apart" from the ordinary world of men when it is worn. Dress for this rite as seems appropriate for a meeting with the Gods of the North: leather, metal, fur-trimmed garments, and perhaps a cloak. The archaic guideline is: "For battle, for love or magic, and for speaking with Gods." Traditionally, ivy sprigs should be worked into one's ritual clothes.

Using the illustrations included on page 269, carefully prepare drawings—on clean, new paper or cloth—of the runes for Odin ᛜ , Thor ᛚ and Freya ᛒ , as well as for the patrons of this season, Balder ᚼ and Nanna ᚺ . (Additional runes may be set below these as you so desire, symbolizing your own highest ideals and those of the your own folk—the people you feel are closest to you spiritually).

If possible, in advance make up cloth banners or wood or stone plaques (even small ones) to be kept for such rites. It may be preferable to draw them anew above or before the altar for each ceremony, or even to scribe them on the ground before the rite is begun. In short, prepare the runes in the way which feels best!

Take a bag of runestones, or consult the section in this book which summarizes them, and draw or paint on pebbles or small tiles the runes which seem appropriate for the season. Memorize the runes which best symbolizes what you want to accomplish during the coming season.

Go alone to the place of solitude which you have chosen, or go to the room which you have prepared, carrying with you the implements needed for the rite, plus a drinking horn and mead.

If music is available for meditation, Wagner's "Entry of the Gods into Valhalla," followed by "Siegfried's Rhine Journey" are ideal. Alternately, "Summer" from Walter Carlos' "Sonic Seasonings" may be played continuously. Depending on your tastes, other music or even storm and nature sounds may be preferred.

Set up the ritual so that you face North. If outdoors, then a tree or large stone should be pointed in that direction. Take eight stones of convenient size (about as large as a man's head for an outdoor ceremony or smaller rocks if indoors) and lay the stones down at equal intervals starting from the north and working sunwise (clockwise) about an eight-foot circle. Place additional stones at the north to support a small simple altar, or to serve as an altar.

Between the altar and the stone marking the north point of the circle, place or draw the runes of our Gods: Odin at the center, Freya to one side and Thor at the other. The runes of Balder and Nanna should be just behind the altar. On the altar place a burner of flower-scented incense and a drinking horn or tankard with some beer or ale in it. Place a copy of this ritual where it can be easily seen.

If the ritual is held outdoors and there are no other persons about, light torches (or candles in glass jars for smaller flames shielded from the wind). If indoors, use ordinary candles. Yellow candles are traditional for this season.

Lean against the altar a wheel of wood or straw or some other simple, burnable construction, which can be sacrificed to the flames during the rite. If the ritual is to be held indoors, then it should be small, little enough that it can be burned in the incense brazier. A small wooden or straw model, or even an eight-spoked wheel drawn on parchment, are examples.

When all is prepared, light the candles or torches at the four quarters, saying for each:

> *I light here a flame*
> *In remembrance of the coming season*
> *Of warmth, joy, and life.*
> *Be with me now Odin, Freya, Thor!*

Then light a candle or torch at the altar, saying:

> *O Great Ones, I dedicate*
> *This area in thy honor*
> *And for thy magics.*
> *Be with me, and in me,*
> *And of me,*
> *Odin the Wise,*
> *Freya the Beautiful,*
> *Thor the Mighty,*
> *Freyr the Good!*
> *Be with me now also,*
> *Noble patrons of this season,*
> *Balder, giver of life,*
> *And Nanna, giver of love.*

Take up the Sun wheel, hold it aloft, and after the space of 13 heartbeats say:

> *I give greetings to gentle Nanna,*
> *Friend of my magical and spiritual people,*
> *Spirit of the Moon, Consort of Balder,*
> *And patroness of this season.*
> *Her love and devotion shall always*
> *Shine as examples for my people*
> *And for me.*
> *Hail Nanna!*

Pause for the space of 13 heartbeats and then say:

> *I give greetings to high Balder,*

Friend of my magical and spiritual people,
Giver of life, Consort of Lady Nanna,
And Patron of this season.
Thy brightness and joy and love
Shall always shine
As examples for our people
And for me.
Hail Balder!

Then burn the Sun wheel, saying:

O noble ones,
Accept my offering
Of this ancient symbol
Of the year, of the many lives I have known,
And of eternity.
Hail to thee both, Nanna and Balder!

Sit before the altar and pour mead into your horn, then raise it to
the banners, saying:

I drink to thee, O Great Ones.
Though I am the only one of our people
Here in this place, it is still
A place of the Gods,
So long as thy magical flame
Burns in my heart.

Hail Odin!	(drink)
Hail Freya!	(drink)
Hail Thor!	(drink)
Hail Balder!	(drink)
Hail Nanna!	(drink)

Then relax for a while before beginning your rune spell.

Lay out the runestones which are symbolic of the coming season.
Then take up pen and parchment or clean paper and write the runes
which best summarize what you wish to accomplish during the coming season. Spend a lengthy time looking at the runes and meditating
on them all, looking for the link between the symbols of the season
and what you wish to accomplish. Finally, fold your parchment or

paper with your own personal desires written in runes upon it, and burn it in the incense brazier, saying:

> The power goes forth
> Before the Great Gods of Valhalla.
> I swear by the Sun, O mighty ones,
> That I shall do all within my power
> To become that which I desire,
> And I call upon thee
> To aid me.
> Hail ye Gods!
> Hail Odin!

At this time, perform any other observances or meditations which you feel are appropriate.

When you feel that the rite should end, face the runes of the Gods and take up the drinking horn or tankard one last time, saying:

> O Great Ones of High Valhalla,
> I give honor to thee
> For being with me here.
> May some of thy sacred presences
> Remain within me as I leave.
> And be ever near me, as well as with
> Those who are my true people.
> To thee do I drink this toast,
> And pour this libation.
> Hail Freya!   (salute)
> Hail Thor!   (salute)
> Hail Odin!   (salute)
> Hail Balder!   (salute)
> Hail Nanna!   (salute)

Pour some of the mead out before the altar, and drink what remains. Then put out the torches at the North, East, South and West, followed by those before the rune banners. Finally, stand before the altar with your arms out, saying:

> I thank thee, Great Ones
> This rite is ended.

Solitary Hloaf-Rite (Lammas)
(August 1)

If a follower of the Old Way cannot find others of like mind to share a ritual in honor of High Valhalla, this rite may be performed by the solitary individual. Conduct the ceremony either in some out-of-the-way outdoor spot, or in some place within one's dwelling that is set aside for the honoring of Odin.

Bathe before dressing for the ceremony, bearing strongly in mind that the water is cleansing the soul and spirit, as well as the body. One should be purified in all ways before calling on the Great Ones.

Ritual garb should have a special cut and feel to symbolize the strength and power due to one of the Old Ways, different enough to "set the mind apart" from the ordinary world when it is worn. Dress for this rite as seems appropriate for a meeting with the Gods of the North—leather, metal, fur-trimmed garments and perhaps a cloak. The archaic guideline is: "For battle, for love or magic, and for speaking with Gods." Traditionally, ivy sprigs should be worked into the ritual clothes.

Using the illustrations included on page 269, carefully prepare drawings—on clean, new paper or cloth—of the runes for Odin ᛟ , Thor ᛏ and Freya ᛒ , as well as for the patrons of this season, Frey ᛦ and Gerd ᚼ . (Additional runes may be set below these as you so desire, symbolizing your own highest ideals and those of the your own folk, the people you feel are closest to you spiritually). If possible, make up in advance cloth banners or wood or stone plaques (even small ones) to be kept for such rites. It may be preferable to draw them anew above or before the altar for each ceremony, or even to scribe them on the ground before the rite is begun. In short, prepare the runes in the way which feels best!

Use a bag of runestones, or consult the section in this book which summarizes them, and draw or paint on pebbles or small tiles the runes which seem appropriate for the season. Memorize the runes which best symbolize what you want to accomplish during the coming season.

Go alone to the place of solitude which you have chosen, or go to the room which you have prepared, carrying with you the implements needed for the rite, plus a drinking horn and mead.

If music is available for meditation, Wagner's "Entry of the Gods into Valhalla," followed by "Siegfried's Rhine Journey" are ideal. Alternately, "Summer," from Walter Carlos' "Sonic Seasonings" may be played continuously. Depending on your tastes, other music or even storm and nature sounds may be preferred.

Set up the ritual so that you face North. If outdoors, then a tree or large stone should point in that direction. Take eight stones of convenient size (about as large as a man's head for an outdoor ceremony or smaller rocks if indoors) and lay the stones down at equal intervals starting from the north and working sunwise (clockwise) about an eight-foot circle. Place additional stones at the North to support a small simple altar, or to serve as an altar.

Between the altar and the stone marking the north-point of the circle place or draw the runes of our Gods: Odin at the center, Freya to one side and Thor at the other. The runes of Freyr and Gerd should be just behind the altar. On the altar place a burner of flower-scented incense and a drinking horn or tankard with some beer or ale in it. Include a copy of this ritual be placed where it can be easily seen.

If the ritual is held outdoors and there are no other persons about, light torches (or candles in glass jars for smaller flames shielded from the wind). If indoors, use ordinary candles. Place a yellow candle at the left of the altar, and a brown candle to the right.

When all is prepared, light the candles or torches at the four quarters, saying for each:

> *I light here a flame*
> *In remembrance of the coming season*
> *Of warmth, joy and life.*
> *Be with me now Odin, Freya, Thor!*

Then light a candle or torch at the altar, saying:

> *O Great Ones, I dedicate*
> *This area in thy honor*
> *And for thy magics.*
> *Be with me, and in me,*
> *And of me,*

Odin the Wise,
Freya the Beautiful,
Thor the Mighty,
Be with me now also,
Noble patrons of this season,
Valiant Freyr of the Earth,
And beauteous Gerd of the Ancient Ones!

Meditate in silence for the space of at least 25 heartbeats, and then beat thrice on the ground and say:

Freyr the brave, of the magical sword,
Spirit of the Earth,
I give thee greetings now,
And ask thy power and magic
To be ever with me.

Meditate in silence for the space of at least 25 heartbeats, and then beat thrice on the ground and say:

O noble and most beautiful Lady Gerd,
The light of whose loveliness
Glistened in the clear air.
I salute thy pride, and strength, O Lady.
I salute thy decision to go forward
Into Godhood and into Eternity.
Grant me of thy wisdom, thy magic,
And, in time, of thy high destiny,
O Blessed One of the Gods

Sit before the altar and pour mead into your horn, then raise it to the banners, saying:

I drink to thee, O Great Ones.
Though I am the only one of our people
Here in this place, it is still
A place of the Gods,
So long as thy magical flame
Burns in my heart.
Hail Odin!

(drink)

> *Hail Freya!*   (drink)
> *Hail Thor!*   (drink)
> *Hail Frey!*   (drink)
> *Hail Gerd!*   (drink)

Then relax for a while before beginning your rune spell.

Lay out the runestones which are symbolic of the coming season. Then take up pen and parchment or clean paper and write the runes which best summarize what you wish to accomplish during the coming season. Spend a lengthy time looking at the runes and meditating on them all, looking for the link between the symbols of the season and what you wish to accomplish. Finally, fold your parchment or paper with your own personal desires written in runes upon it, and burn it in the incense brazier, saying:

> *The power goes forth*
> *Before the Great Gods of Valhalla.*
> *I swear by the Sun, O mighty ones,*
> *That I shall do all within my power*
> *To become that which I desire,*
> *And I call upon thee*
> *To aid me.*
> *Hail ye Gods!*
> *Hail Odin!*

At this time perform any other observances or meditations which you feel are appropriate.

When you feel that the rite should end, face the runes of the Gods and take up the drinking horn or tankard one last time, saying:

> *O Great Ones of High Valhalla,*
> *I give honor to thee*
> *For being with me here.*
> *May some of thy sacred presences*
> *Remain within me as I leave.*
> *And be ever near me, as well as with*
> *Those who are my true people.*
> *To thee do I drink this toast,*
> *And pour this libation.*
> *Hail Freya!*   (salute)
> *Hail Thor!*   (salute)

Hail Odin!   (salute)
Hail Frey!   (salute)
Hail Gerd!   (salute)

Pour some of the mead out before the altar, and drink what remains. Then put out the torches at the North, East, South and West, followed by those before the rune banners. Stand before the altar with your arms out, saying:

I thank thee, O Great Ones.
This rite is ended.

Solitary Fall Evenight (Autumn)
(September 21)

If a follower of the Old Way cannot find others of like mind to share a ritual in honor of High Valhalla, this rite may be performed by the solitary individual. Conduct the ceremony either in some out-of-the-way outdoor spot, or in some place within one's dwelling that is set aside for the honoring of Odin.

Bathe before dressing for the ceremony, bearing strongly in mind that the water is cleansing the soul and spirit, as well as the body, for one should be purified in all ways before calling on the Great Ones.

Ceremonial clothing should be what you would feel proper wearing before Thor, Odin and Freya. It should have a special cut to symbolize the strength and power due to one of the Old Ways, different enough to "set the mind apart" from the ordinary world when it is worn. Dress for this rite as seems appropriate for a meeting with the Gods of the North—leather, metal, fur-trimmed garments, and perhaps a cloak. The archaic guideline is: "For battle, for love or magic, and for speaking with Gods."

Using the illustrations included on page 269, carefully prepare drawings—on clean, new paper or cloth—of the runes for Odin ᛦ , Thor ᛚ and Freya ᛒ , as well as for the other patrons of this season, Sif ᚾ who rules with Thor ᛏ . (Additional runes may be set below these as you so desire, symbolizing your own highest ideals and those of your own folk, the people you feel are closest to you spiritually). If possible, make up in advance cloth banners or wood or stone plaques (even small ones) to be kept for such rites. It may be preferable to draw them anew above or before the altar for each ceremony, or even to scribe them on the ground before the rite is begun. In short, prepare the runes in the way which feels best!

Use a bag of runestones, or consult the section in this book which summarizes them, and draw or paint on pebbles or small tiles the runes which seem appropriate for the season. Memorize the runes which best symbolize what you want to accomplish during the coming season.

Go alone to the place of solitude which you have chosen, or go to the room which you have prepared, carrying with you the implements needed for the rite, plus a drinking horn and mead.

If music is available for meditation, Wagner's "Entry of the Gods into Valhalla," followed by "Siegfried's Rhine Journey" are ideal. Alternately, "Autumn," from Walter Carlos' "Sonic Seasonings" may be played continuously. Other music, or even storm and nature sounds, may be preferred.

Set up the ritual so that you face North. If outdoors, then a tree or large stone should point in that direction. Take eight stones of convenient size (about as large as a man's head for an outdoor ceremony or smaller rocks if indoors) and lay the stones down at equal intervals starting from the North and working sunwise (clockwise) about an eight-foot circle. Place additional stones at the North to support a small simple altar, or to serve as an altar.

Between the altar and the stone marking the north-point of the circle, place or draw the runes of our Gods: Odin at the center, Freya to one side and Thor at the other. Position the rune of Lady Sif just before the others. On the altar place a burner of flower-scented incense and a drinking horn or tankard with some beer or ale in it. Include a copy of this ritual where it can be easily seen. Bring some food along for a ceremonial meal with the Gods.

If the ritual is held outdoors and there are no other persons about, light torches (or candles in glass jars for smaller flames shielded from the wind). If indoors, use ordinary candles. Red candles are traditional at this season.

A period of meditation should take place prior to ritual. Place your mind into a calm and receptive state, think of the season and the times far past. Consider the golden autumn not only of the year, but of the lives of men and women, of nations, of whole civilizations—the bright and warm flame that "flares impossibly bright" before guttering away into darkness—to someday return again. Think of how this season was in the far past, with your own folk that you may have known in that distant time. When you are ready to begin the rite, say:

> *As it was at the beginning of time*
> *So it is now!*

When you are ready to begin, light the candles or torches at the four quarters, saying for each:

> *I light here a flame*
> *In remembrance of the coming season*
> *Where the harvests are gathered in.*
> *Be with me now Odin, Freya, Thor!*

Then light a candle or torch at the altar, saying:

> *O Great Ones, I dedicate*
> *This area in thy honor*
> *And for thy magics.*
> *Be with me, and in me,*
> *And of me,*
> *Odin the Wise,*
> *Freya the Beautiful,*
> *Thor the Mighty,*
> *Be with me now also,*
> *Noble patroness of this season,*
> *Beautiful Sif, consort to great Thor.*

Sit before the altar and pour mead into your horn, then raise it to the banners, saying:

> *I drink to thee, O Great Ones.*
> *Though I am the only one of our people*

Here in this place, it is still
A place of the Gods,
So long as thy magical flame
Burns in my heart.
Hail Odin! (drink)
Hail Freya! (drink)
Hail Thor! (drink)
Hail Sif! (drink)

Meditate in silence for the space of 25 heartbeats, and then say:

O Patrons of the Harvest Season,
I give thee salutations,
Thor, protector of farmstead, field, and pasture,
And all those who labor for their living.
Lady Sif of the Golden Hair, whose magic tresses
Are as the rich gold of the autumn harvest,
I do ask that thy blessings surround me,
And be about my kindred
Whom I have not yet found.
I thank thee for the bounty of the season
Which thou hast given to thy people.
Cast thy blessing upon this food I have brought here,
That it may give strength to body, spirit, and soul,
And lead me further along the Paths of the Gods.
Hail Thor!
Hail Sif of the Golden Hair!
And beyond all that shall happen,
Hail Earth,
Mother of all!

Then relax for a while before beginning your rune-spell.

Lay out the runestones which are symbolic of the coming season. Then take up pen and parchment or clean paper and write the runes which best summarize what you wish to accomplish during the coming season. Spend a lengthy time looking at the runes and meditating on them all, looking for the link between the symbols of the season and what you wish to accomplish. Finally, fold your parchment or paper with your own personal desires written in runes upon it, and burn it in the incense brazier, saying:

> *The power goes forth*
> *Before the Great Gods of Valhalla.*
> *I swear by the Sun, O mighty ones,*
> *That I shall do all within my power*
> *To become that which I desire,*
> *And I call upon thee*
> *To aid me.*
> *Hail ye Gods!*
> *Hail Odin!*

At this time you may perform any other observances or meditations which you feel are appropriate.

When you feel that the rite should end, face the runes of the Gods and take up the drinking horn or tankard one last time, saying:

> *O Great Ones of High Valhalla,*
> *I give honor to thee*
> *For being with me here.*
> *May some of thy sacred presences*
> *Remain within me as I leave.*
> *And be ever near me, as well as with*
> *Those who are my true people.*
> *To thee do I drink this toast,*
> *And pour this libation.*
> *Hail Freya!*   (salute)
> *Hail Thor!*   (salute)
> *Hail Odin!*   (salute)
> *Hail Sif!*   (salute)

Pour some of the mead out before the altar, and drink what remains. Then put out the torches at the North, East, South and West, followed by those before the rune banners. Stand before the altar with your arms out, saying:

> *I thank thee, O Great Ones.*
> *This rite is ended.*

Sweep away the leaves from around the altar.

Solitary Night of the Specters
(October 31)

If a follower of the Old Way cannot find others of like mind to share a ritual in honor of High Valhalla, this rite may be performed by the solitary individual. Conduct the ceremony either in some out-of-the-way outdoor spot, or in some place within one's dwelling that is set aside for the honoring of Odin.

Bathe before dressing for the ceremony, bearing strongly in mind that the water is cleansing the soul and spirit, as well as the body—for one should be purified in all ways before calling on the Great Ones.

Ceremonial clothing should be what you feel proper wearing before Thor, Odin and Freya. It should have a special cut and feel to symbolize the strength and power due to one of the Old Ways, and should be different enough to "set the mind apart" from the ordinary world when it is worn. One should dress for this rite as seems appropriate for a meeting with the Gods of the North—leather, metal, fur-trimmed garments, and perhaps a cloak. The archaic guideline is: "For battle, for love or magic, and for speaking with Gods."

Using the illustrations included on page 269, carefully prepare drawings—on clean, new paper or cloth—of the runes for Odin ⊕ , Thor ⊥ and Freya ß , as well as for the patrons of this season, Frey ⌐ and Gerd ⅄ . (Additional runes may be set below these as you so desire, symbolizing your own highest ideals and those of the your own folk, the people you feel are closest to you spiritually). If possible, make up in advance cloth banners or (even small) wood or stone plaques to be kept for such rites. It may be preferable to draw them anew above or before the altar for each ceremony, or even to scribe them on the ground before the rite is begun. In short, prepare the runes in the way which feels best!

Use a bag of runestones, or consult the section in this book which summarizes them, and draw or paint on pebbles or small tiles the runes which seem appropriate for the season. Memorize the runes which best symbolize what you want to accomplish during the coming season.

Go alone to the place of solitude which you have chosen, or go to the room which you have prepared, carrying with you the implements needed for the rite, plus a drinking horn and mead.

If music is available for meditation, Wagner's "Entry of the Gods into Valhalla," followed by "Siegfried's Rhine Journey" are ideal. Alternately, "Winter," from Walter Carlos' "Sonic Seasonings" may be played continuously. Other music, or even storm and nature sounds may be preferred.

Set up the ritual so that you face North. If outdoors, then a tree or large stone should point in that direction. Fashion "portals" of stone or wood at North, East, South and West, at each quarter placing two vertical posts with a horizontal lintel across them to make a sort of open doorway. Place additional stones at the North to support a small simple altar, or to serve as an altar.

Between the altar and the stone marking the north-point of the circle place or draw the runes of our Gods: Odin at the center, Freya to one side and Thor at the other. The runes of Balder and Hodur should be just before the others. On the altar place a burner of herbal incense and a drinking horn or tankard with some beer or ale in it. Place a copy of this ritual where it can be easily seen.

If the ritual is held outdoors and there are no other persons about, torches should be lit (or candles in glass jars for smaller flames shielded from the wind). Indoors, ordinary candles may be used. Each portal should have two candles or torches before it, as if to "light the way" for the specters. If candles are to be placed on the altar, the left one should be red and the right should be yellow.

A period of meditation should take place prior to ritual. Place your mind into a calm and receptive state, think of the season and the times far past. Consider that at this time the Dark Lady, in some places with Odin himself, would ride through the wilderness night, through the storm, and through the snow leading a procession of ghosts, of wolves, of the strange elvish folk and those Valas or high Godis who would sometimes join. Consider that on this night the veils are thin between the worlds of the living and the realms of the dead. Those whom you have known, now long departed, can return on this night to whisper their greetings in your mind. And on this night you should speak your greetings to them, and perhaps ask for their advice and guidance. Think of how this season was in the far past with your own folk that you may have known in that distant time.

When you are ready to begin, light the candles or torches at the four quarters, saying for each:

> *I light here a flame*
> *In remembrance of the coming season*
> *On this night of dim shadows.*
> *Be with me now Odin, Freya, Thor!*

Then light a candle or torch at the altar, saying:

> *O Great Ones, I dedicate*
> *This place in thy honor*
> *And for thy magics.*
> *Be with me, and in me,*
> *And of me,*
> *Odin the Wise,*
> *Freya the Beautiful,*
> *Thor the Mighty,*
> *Be with me now also,*
> *Noble patrons of this season,*
> *Balder the Bright,*
> *And Hodur the Blind.*

Sit before the altar and pour mead into your horn, then raise it to the banners, saying:

> *I drink to thee, O Great Ones.*
> *Though I am the only one of our people*
> *Here in this place, it is still*
> *A place of the Gods*
> *So long as thy magical flame*
> *Burns in my heart.*
> *Hail Odin!*   (drink)
> *Hail Freya!*   (drink)
> *Hail Thor!*   (drink)
> *Hail Balder!*   (drink)
> *Hail Hodur!*   (drink)
> *And at this season alone,*
> *Do I also drink on honor*

To the Chieftess of the Lands of the Dead.
Hail, Lady Hellia!   (drink)

Meditate in silence for the space of 25 heartbeats, and then say:

O Patrons of this Night of Thin Veils
I give thee salutations and greetings to the shining
Bright One, High Balder, Lord of Light,
And to his somber brother Hodur the Blind,
Fated forever to the darkness of blindness.
Teach me, noble ones, that whatever
Destiny and circumstance befalls me in the end,
I shall live beyond death.
Hail Balder!
Hail Hodur!

Remain silent for the space of 25 heartbeats, and then continue:

Ever-present at this time also is the beautiful,
Yet dark and fearsome Ruler of the Realms
Of the Dead, known to men as Hellia or Hel.
She gathers in the souls at twilight's end,
And gives to each, what each deserves.
Without hate, without love, without pity.
Hail, Queen of the Dead!

Again observe silence for the space of 25 heartbeats, and then say:

I now place flames before the
Portals of the East and West,
For at this night the veils between
The living and the dead are thin,
And in times long past did the Dark Queen
Lead the spirits and the shades on procession
Through the dark forests, the night,
And the storms
Of this Middle Earth of humankind.
Now, in symbol, I open the path

> *That leads between the worlds.*

Place all additional candles or torches placed to light the way across the ritual area to link the portals of East and West. Then shall more mead be poured into the drinking horn and hold it aloft toward the God runes, saying:

> *On this night, O Great Ones,*
> *I offer thee mead in lieu of blood,*
> *For the times have changed.*
> *Yet my honor and reverence to thee*
> *Remains as unchanged now*
> *As it was in ages past.*
> *On this night may I drink to welcome*
> *The Gods of High Valhalla, and the ghosts*
> *Of those who were of my people*
> *In times past.*
>
> *I drink now in honor of the dead.*
> *Those whom I have loved,*
> *And those whom I have not know, yet*
> *All who were my kindred.*

After a brief pause, say the following, and think upon it as you do speak:

> *My folk come from beyond the stars,*
> *And beyond the stars I shall return in time,*
> *Ennobled and possessed of great powers.*
> *If I am worthy,*
> *Death is but a portal to Godhead*
> *Which can be attained, in the fullness of time.*
> *It is said that the Great Lords of High Valhalla*
> *Once trod the sacred groves, and were as I,*
> *Saluted the fierce and honorable wolf,*
> *Honored the raven as messengers of the Gods,*
> *And learned wisdom. So shall it be with me, I here resolve.*
> *Even though I may change form and essence*
> *And pass from life to life,*
> *I shall be ever yet the same.*

Sooner or later my own divine and everlasting spark of life
Shall go beyond.
I myself shall range among a million million worlds.
Like Great Odin himself, I shall eventually
Attain to the power of Godhood,
To be in all times, and in all places.
Hail Odin! (salute)

Remain silent for a long time, and meditate upon what you have just read, and spoken.

Next, you may perform any other observances or meditations which you feel are appropriate.

When you feel that the rite should end, face the runes of the Gods and take up the drinking horn or tankard one last time, saying:

O Great Ones of High Valhalla,
I give honor to thee
For being with me here.
May some of thy sacred presences
Remain within me as I leave.
And be ever near me, as well as with
Those who are my true people.
To thee do I drink this toast,
And pour this libation.
Hail Freya! (salute)
Hail Thor! (salute)
Hail Odin! (salute)
Hail Balder! (salute)
Hail Hodur! (salute)
Hail, Queen of the Dead! (salute)

Pour some of the mead out before the altar, and drink what remains. Then put out the torches at the North, East, South and West, followed by those before the rune banners. Stand before the altar with your arms out, saying:

I thank thee, O Great Ones.
This rite is ended.

Put out the candles or torches, and pour whatever mead remains

at the base of a tree, speaking some words of your own heart to the
Gods and to the noble dead.

Solitary Salutations to the Heroes
(November 11)

If a follower of the Old Way cannot find others of like mind to
share a ritual in honor of High Valhalla, this rite may be performed by
the solitary individual. Conduct the ceremony either in some out-of-
the-way outdoor spot, or in some place within one's dwelling that is
set aside for the honoring of Odin, and of the Old Ways.

Bathe before dressing for the ceremony, bearing strongly in
mind that the water is cleansing the soul and spirit, as well as the body.
One should be purified in all ways before calling on the Great Ones.

One's ceremonial clothing should be that in which you would
feel proper wearing before Thor, Odin, Freya and Tyr, the patron of
this memorial celebration. It should have a special cut and feel to symbolize the strength and power due to one of the Old Ways, different
enough to "set the mind apart" from the ordinary world when it is
worn. Dress for this rite as seems appropriate for a meeting with the
Gods of the North—leather, metal, fur-trimmed garments, and perhaps a cloak. The archaic guideline is: "For battle, for love or magic,
and for speaking with Gods."

Using the illustrations included on page 269, carefully prepare
drawings—on clean, new paper or cloth—of the runes for Odin ᛟ ,
Thor ᛚ and Freya ᛒ , as well as for the patron of this season, Tyr
the Warrior ᛏ . Additional runes may be scribed and placed next to
these as you so desire, symbolizing those who have done much for
your spiritual people in war and in peace. The names may be written
in the runic alphabet as found in this book.

Go alone to the place of solitude which you have chosen, or go to
the room which you have prepared, carrying with you the implements
needed for the rite, plus a drinking horn and mead.

If music is available for meditation, it should be played, such as

Wagner's "Entry of the Gods into Valhalla," followed by Wagner's "Magic Fire Music." "Siegfried's Funeral Music" is appropriate during the ceremony, or other music that you deem suitable.

Set up the ritual so that you face North. If outdoors, then a tree or large stone should point in that direction. Take eight stones of convenient size (about as large as a man's head for an outdoor ceremony or smaller rocks if indoors) and lay the stones down at equal intervals starting from the north and working sunwise (clockwise) about an eight-foot circle. Place additional stones at the north to support a small simple altar, or to serve as an altar.

Between the altar and the stone marking the north-point of the circle place or draw the runes of our Gods: Odin at the center, Freya to one side and Thor at the other. The rune of Tyr should be placed adjacent, as well as the runes of all those whom you wish to remember. On the altar place a burner of incense and a drinking horn or tankard with some beer or ale in it. Include a copy of this ritual where it can be easily seen, and an Honor Roll.

If the ritual is held outdoors and there are no other persons about, light torches (or candles in glass jars for smaller flames shielded from the wind). If indoors, use ordinary candles. Red and light blue candles are traditional at this season.

Meditate prior to the ritual. Consider our heroes, and the high ideals which guided them. Remember that they will live as long as any remembers them, and their echoes will remain when the mountains have worn to dust.

When you are ready to begin, light the candles or torches at the four quarters, saying for each:

> *I light here a flame*
> *In remembrance of the great heroes*
> *Of my brethren, my people.*
> *Be with me now Odin, Freya, Thor and Tyr!*

Then light a candle or torch at the altar, saying:

> *O Great Ones, I dedicate*
> *This area in thy honor*
> *And for thy magics.*
> *Be with me, and in me,*
> *And of me,*

Odin the Wise,
Freya the Beautiful,
Thor the Mighty,
Be with me now also,
Invincible Tyr, Great Warrior.

Sit before the altar and pour mead into your horn, then raise it to the banners, saying:

I drink to thee, O Great Ones.
Though I am the only one of our people
Here in this place, it is still
A place of the Gods.
So long as thy magical flame
Burns in my heart.
Hail Odin!   (drink)
Hail Freya!   (drink)
Hail Thor!   (drink)
Hail Tyr!   (drink)

Meditate in silence for the space of 25 heartbeats, and then say:

I now speak in remembrance of those
Who have done much for my folk.
Those whose names I know,
And also those whose names have been lost.
I salute thee all!   (drink)

At this time do I renew my pledge
To my nation, to my homeland,
To the place where I was born,
And to the places I knew and loved
As a child.
May this land ever be a place of honor, of truth,
Of freedom and of opportunity.
And may I work always to keep it so.
Hail to this, my homeland,
Blessed before the Gods!

After the space of 25 heartbeats, say:

> *At this time do I honor*
> *Those who have done great*
> *And noble deeds for my family, my people,*
> *By blood and in spirit*
> *In times of peace, and in time of war.*
> *I remember those of my own blood*
> *Who have fallen in battle, who have given their lives.*
> *They shall never be forgotten,*
> *Though the Earth turn cold*
> *And the oceans run dry.*
> *Hail to the Noble Ones!*

After the space of 25 heartbeats, say:

> *I call upon the Gods to recognize and to honor*
> *The great heroes of my people.*
> *Soaring Valkyries, hear my call!*
> *Great Tyr, hear my call!*

There shall be a pause of five heartbeats, then say:

> *Valeda, wise Vala.*
> *May the Gods honor thee!*

> *Eric the Red, great voyager.*
> *May the Gods honor thee!*

> *_____, soldier and beloved uncle.*
> *May the Gods honor thee!*

Continue through the Honor Roll which you have before you.
  At this time you may perform any other observances or meditations which you feel are appropriate.
  When you feel that the rite should end, face the runes of the Gods and take up the drinking horn or tankard one last time, saying:

> *O Great Ones of High Valhalla,*
> *I give honor to thee*

For being with me here.
May some of thy sacred presences
Remain within me as I leave.
And be ever near me, as well as with
Those who are my true people.
To thee do I drink this toast,
And pour this libation.

Hail Freya!	(salute)
Hail Thor!	(salute)
Hail Odin!	(salute)
Hail Tyr!	(salute)
Hail, beloved Heroes of my people!	(salute)

Pour some of the mead out before the altar, and drink what remains. Then put out the torches at the North, East, South and West, followed by those before the rune banners. Then stand before the altar with your arms out, saying:

I thank thee, O Great Ones.
This rite is ended.

Solitary Winter Sunstead and Yule
(December 21)

If a follower of the Old Way cannot find others of like mind to share a seasonal ritual in honor of High Valhalla, this rite may be performed by the solitary individual. Conduct the ceremony either in some out-of-the-way outdoor spot, or in some place within one's dwelling that is set aside for the honoring of Odin.

This ceremony is in several parts, and can be performed in separate parts on several successive evenings (Winter Sunstead on the evening of the Solstice, Frigga's day or Festival of Light on the evening of the 24th, and the Tribal Yule Feast on the afternoon of the 25th), or can be accomplished all on one evening, depending on your desires.

The place where the ritual is held should have an altar near the north of the ritual area, and a Yule-tree decorated for the season. For one who follows the Old Ways, it is often rewarding to decorate the Yule-tree so that it reflects Yggdrasill, the mythic World-Tree. To do so, the tree should be trimmed as is normal, but with particularly Norse features such as a bright star at the top (representing the North Star, the Hub of the Sky), an eagle near the top (representing Odin as giver of wisdom and victory). A little *below* the base of the tree should be a cave with the Earth Dragon, images of the three Norns, a pool (a mirror will do), and a cauldron. Stags may be in the snow about the base, and squirrels within the branches. A manger scene is also appropriate (placed in straw against the trunk of the tree) with Mother Frigga and her newborn child (the promise of the new year), along with domestic animals. A pair of wolves may guard them. Three male wanderers, representing Odin, Thor and Loki, may be shown bringing gifts to Frigga's Sacred Child. If possible, Valkyries on the backs of winged horses may be in the higher branches, and/or winged female figures (Valkyries and swan maidens, since they are really the same). There should be many stars and lights in and around the tree.

The patron Gods of this season are Heimdall for the Winter Sunstead (Winter Solstice), Mother Frigga and Allfather Odin for The Festival of Light (also called Frigga's Day or Yule Eve) December 24, and Thor for the Yule Feast on December 25. If it is possible, make up a rune banner for Heimdall, copying his rune as given in this book, to be hung near the altar.

Bathe before dressing for the ceremony, bearing strongly in mind that the water is cleansing the soul and spirit, as well as the body. One should be purified in all ways before calling on the Great Ones.

Ceremonial garb should be what you would feel proper wearing before Thor, Odin and Freya. It should have a special cut and feel to symbolize the strength and power due to one of the Old Ways, and should be different enough to "set the mind apart" from the ordinary world of men when it is worn. Dress for this rite as seems appropriate for a meeting with the Gods of the North—leather, metal, fur-trimmed garments, and/or perhaps a cloak. The archaic guideline is: "For battle, for love or magic, and for speaking with Gods." The decorations of this festive season should be worked into your clothing.

Using the illustrations included on page 269, carefully prepare drawings—on clean, new paper or cloth—of the runes for Odin ᛟ , Thor ᛏ and Freya ᛒ , as well as for the other patrons of this season, Heimdall ⊕ , the Watcher of the Rainbow Bridge. (Additional runes may be set below these as you so desire, symbolizing your own highest ideals and those of the your own folk, the people you feel are closest to you spiritually). If possible, make up in advance cloth banners or wood or stone plaques (even small ones) to be kept for such rites. It may be preferable to draw them anew above or before the altar for each ceremony, or even to scribe them on the ground before the rite is begun. In short, prepare the runes in the way which feels best!

Use a bag of runestones, or consult the section in this book which summarizes them, and draw or paint on pebbles or small tiles the runes which seem appropriate for the season. Memorize the runes which best symbolize what you want to accomplish during the coming season.

Go alone to the place of solitude which you have chosen, or go to the room which you have prepared, carrying with you the implements needed for the rite, plus a drinking horn and mead.

If music is available, it should be carols of the season—particularly the older ones which originally were Pagan in origin.

The ritual should be set up so that one faces to the North. Indoors, a Yule tree should be placed near the altar. If outdoors, then a tree near the altar should be at least partially decorated before the rite. Decorate the area festively according to the season.

Take eight stones of convenient size (about as large as a man's head for an outdoor ceremony or smaller rocks if indoors) and lay the stones down at equal intervals starting from the north and working sunwise (clockwise) about an eight-foot circle. Place additional stones at the North to support a small simple altar, or to serve as an altar.

Between the altar and the stone marking the north-point of the circle should placed or drawn the runes of our Gods: Odin at the center, Freya to one side and Thor at the other. The rune of Heimdall should be just before the altar. On the altar should be placed a burner of sweet incense and the drinking horn or tankard with some beer or ale in it. A copy of this ritual also may be placed where it can be easily seen.

If the ritual is held outdoors and there are no other persons about, torches should be lit (or candles in glass jars for smaller flames shielded from the wind). Indoors, ordinary candles may be used. Candles on the altar should be white when honoring Heimdall on the

21st, white to the left and silver to the right for the Festival of Light on the night of the 24th, and white to the left and red to the right for the Yule Feast on the day of the 25th. In all cases, additional altar candles of green and red are appropriate, as well as additional colored candles in the ritual area about you.

A period of meditation should take place prior to the ritual.

When you are ready to begin, light the candles or torches at the four quarters, saying for each:

> *I light here a flame*
> *In honor of this joyous season*
> *Of promise.*
> *Be with me now Odin, Freya, Thor!*

Then light a candle or torch at the altar, saying:

> *O Great Ones, at this happy season*
> *I dedicate this place in thy honor*
> *And for thy magics.*
> *Be with me, and in me,*
> *And of me,*
> *Odin the Wise,*
> *Freya the Beautiful,*
> *Thor the Mighty,*
> *And Heimdall,*
> *Watcher of the Rainbow Bridge.*

Sit before the altar and pour mead into your horn, then raise it to the banners, saying:

> *I drink to thee, O Great Ones.*
> *Though I am the only one of our people*
> *Here in this place, it is still*
> *A place of the Gods.*
> *So long as thy magical flame*
> *Burns in my heart.*
> *Hail Odin!* (drink)
> *Hail Freya!* (drink)
> *Hail Thor!* (drink)
> *Hail Frigga!* (drink)
> *Hail Heimdall!* (drink)

In Celebration of "Winter Sunstead" on Solstice Day:

After the space of 25 heartbeats, say:

> The Ring of the Year continues,
> Without beginning and without end.
> And the second half-year has passed.
> This time of old was called the Wolf Season,
> In the old lands of my spiritual folk,
> A time of cold and harshness.
> But surely as the seasons of warmth
> Shall follow this,
> So also shall my Gods be with me.
>
> The times that shall come are cold,
> Yet I look to the sky
> And see the promise of the High Ones:
> The stars of Freya's Gown, Girdle and Distaff
> Are high in the winter sky,
> And the Winter Way winds from her feet
> To mark the path of souls across the sky.
> So also, in the coldest of seasons,
> Is there promise of life and plenty to come.
>
> At this time is the balance point of the year,
> The days have grown shorter and there is chill;
> I remember the distant ages of ice and snow,
> And the threat of chaos in the terrible Fimbulwinter
>   Of legend.
> Yet, though the days may be cold and bitter,
> There will be the promise of the future, as days
> Slowly grow longer.
>
> At this time do I call on far-seeing Heimdall,
> Watcher for the Gods,
> To give me, and those who are close,
> The gift of vision for the future,
> And the steadfastness and patience
> To wait for better times.
> Hail Heimdall!

On the night of Freya's Day, or the Festival of Light, the following should be performed:

(Three symbolic presents should have been wrapped and set on the altar by you.)

After the space of 25 heartbeats, say:

> *This is the season of the newborn God,*
> *And of hope born anew.*
> *The Lady of the Skies is his Mother,*
> *And the One Who Builds the World*
> *Is his father.*
> *All animals and all magical creatures*
> *At this time come in pilgrimage*
> *From across this Mid-Earth*
> *To honor the Mother, the Allfather,*
> *And the Sacred Child.*
>
> *At this time and in this place*
> *I am thankful for that which I have.*
> *My blessings go forth for others whom I know,*
> *And for those whom I do not yet know:*
> *And for the fine gifts of the season.*
> *Hail to the Blessed Mother!*
> *Hail to the Allfather!*
> *Hail to the God Child of Promise!*

At this time presents should be opened, followed by singing of seasonal carols and popular songs of this festive time.

On the family day of the Yule Feast, the following should be performed:

(It is not necessary to have a formal ceremony, with the usual openings and closings, on the day of the Yule Feast, though you may prefer such a rite anyhow. Whether formal or not, the following are appropriate:)

Read or compose an appropriate prayer to the Allfather.

Pork or ham may be eaten, as if after sacrifice.

Offer toasts to Odin (victory and power), Thor (strength and power), Njord and Frey (good harvest and peace), and Bragi (solemn vows for the coming year).

Reading of "Yule Journey" should follow, or other seasonal texts.

Singing of Yule carols and light popular seasonal songs should follow.

This should be performed as a New Year's Eve celebration:

First perform the rite for Winter Sunstead, then recite the following:

> The new year will soon be here.
> Thus I charge my horn with mead,
> And make my solemn vows
> For the coming seasons
> In honor of the Gods' skald, Bragi.
> Hail Bragi!

Repeat to yourself the resolutions and vows which you have made for the coming year, and drink to seal the proclamation you have made with the Gods and with yourself.

At this time the you should make your own toasts to Odin (victory and power), Thor (strength and power), Njord and Frey (good harvest and peace), and Bragi (solemn vows for the coming year).

Next, you may perform any other observances or meditations which you feel are appropriate.

Closing:

When you feel that the rite should end, face the runes of the Gods and take up the drinking horn or tankard one last time, saying:

O Great Ones of High Valhalla,
I give honor to thee
For being with me here
During this joyous season.
May some of thy sacred presences
Remain within me as I leave.
And be ever near me, as well as with
Those who are my true people.
To thee do I drink this toast,
And pour this libation.
Hail Freya! (salute)
Hail Thor! (salute)
Hail Odin! (salute)
Hail Heimdall! (salute)

Pour some of the mead out before the altar, and drink what remains. Then put out the torches at the North, East, South, and West, followed by those before the rune banners. Stand before the altar with your arms out, saying:

I thank thee, O Great Ones.
May this joyous season
Be a blessing of magic.
This rite is ended.

Put out the candles or torches, and pour whatever mead remains at the base of a tree.

Then, if it is at all possible, visit someone and present them with a gift, or do them a favor and wish them well for the season.

Solitary Affirmation Ritual

If a follower of the Old Way cannot find others of like mind to share a ritual in honor of High Valhalla, this rite may be performed by the solitary individual. The ceremony should be performed at the New Moon or when the Moon is waxing, though need and not season determines the performance.

If possible, perform the rite near midnight, or late in the evening. Hold it either in some out-of-the-way outdoor spot, or within one's dwelling set aside for the honoring of Odin.

Bathe before dressing for the ceremony, bearing strongly in mind that the water is cleansing the soul and spirit, as well as the body, for one should be purified in all ways before calling on the Great Ones.

Wear clothing for this ceremony that you would feel proper wearing before Thor, Odin and Freya. It should have a special cut and feel to symbolize the strength and power which should be due to one of the Old Ways, and should be different enough to "set the mind apart" from the ordinary world of men when it is worn.

Using the illustrations included on page 269, carefully prepare

drawings—on clean, new paper or cloth—of the runes for Odin ⊕ ,

Thor ⚎ , and Freya ᛒ . (Additional runes may be set below these

as you so desire, symbolizing your own highest ideals and those of your own folk, the people you feel are closest to you spiritually). If possible, in advance make up cloth banners or (even small) wood or stone plaques to be kept for such rites. It may be preferable to draw them anew above or before the altar for each ceremony, or even to scribe them on the ground before the rite is begun. In short, prepare the runes in the way which feels best.

Go alone to the place of solitude which you have chosen, or go to the room which you have prepared, carrying with you the implements needed for the rite.

Set up the ritual should be set up so you face North. If outdoors, have a tree or large stone pointed in that direction. Take eight stones of convenient size (about as large as a man's head for an outdoor ceremony or smaller rocks if indoors) and lay the stones down at equal intervals starting from the north and working sunwise (clockwise) about an eight-foot circle. Additional stones should be placed at the North to support a small simple altar, or to serve as an altar.

Between the altar and the stone marking the north-point of the circle place or draw the runes of our Gods: Odin at the center, Freya to one side and Thor at the other. On the altar place a burner of incense and a drinking horn or tankard with some beer or ale in it. Include a copy of this ritual where it can be easily seen.

If the ritual is held outdoors and there are no other persons about, light torches (or candles in glass jars for smaller flames shielded from the wind). If indoors, use ordinary candles.

Place a flame at the north point of the stone circle, saying,

> *I give honor to the Lands of my Gods,*
> *Ancient and good,*
> *And the power that is within them.*
> *Hail Odin!* (salute)

Put a flame at the east point of the stone circle, saying:

> *I give honor to the Winds of my Gods*
> *Ever fresh and new,*
> *And the power that is within them.*
> *Hail Odin!* (salute)

Put a flame at the south point of the stone circle, saying:

> *I give honor to the warm Sun of my Gods,*
> *Ever giving of new life,*
> *And the power that is within.*
> *Hail Odin!* (salute)

Put a flame at the west point of the stone circle, saying:

> *I give honor to the seas and lakes*
> *And rivers of my Gods,*
> *And the power that is within them.*
> *Hail Odin!* (salute)

Stand before the altar and place a light before the Rune of Odin, saluting and saying:

> *Hail Odinsheiti, giver of victory,*
> *Thou who knowest the runes of wisdom,*
> *And of power.*
> *Bring me again to be with thy people.*
> *Those who know the strength of thy*
> *Ancient ways.*
> *Give me of thy wisdom.*
> *That I may better honor thee*
> *As I prosper in thy name.*
> *Hail Odin!*

Add any other items which you might wish to mention to Odin, and then drink in his honor. Next place a light before the Rune of Thor, saluting and saying:

> *Hail Thor, laughing, red-bearded*
> *Thunderer and guardian.*
> *Bring me again to be with thy people.*
> *Those who know the joy and robust power of thine*
> *Ancient Ways.*
> *Give me of thy might, and of thy laughter*
> *That I may better honor thee*
> *As I prosper in thy name.*
> *Hail Thor!*

Add any other items which you might wish to mention before Thor, and then drink in his honor. Next place a light before the Rune of Freya, saluting and saying:

> *Hail Freya the Fair One,*
> *Beautiful enchantress, jewel of the Gods*
> *And chooser of the mortals who are most honored.*
> *Bring me again to be with thy people.*
> *Those who know the magic and beauty*
> *And triumph of thine Ancient Ways.*
> *Give me of thy pride and persuasion*
> *That I may better honor thee*

As I prosper in thy name.
Hail Freya!

Add any other items which you might wish to mention before
Freya, and then drink in her honor.

Stand silently for a long while, meditating on the presences of the
Old Ones, the Gods of our folk who are eternally young, eternally
powerful, and returning again here and now to cast their sacred presences about you. Sense their power about you. Now is the time to add
any words which you would deem appropriate, for yourself or for
others.

When you feel that the rite should end, face the runes of the Gods
and take up the drinking horn or tankard one last time, saying:

O Great Ones of High Valhalla,
I give honor to thee
For being with me here.
May some of thy sacred presences
Remain within me as I leave.
And be ever near me, as well as with
Those who are my true people.
To thee do I drink this toast,
And pour this libation.
Hail Freya! (salute)
Hail Thor! (salute)
Hail Odin! (salute)

Pour some of the drink out before the altar, and drink what
remains. Then put out the torches at the north, east, south and west,
followed by those before the rune banners, Next, stand before the
altar with your arms out, saying:

I thank thee, O Great Ones.
The rite is ended.

Protection in Travel

When just setting out on a journey by land, it is comforting to the mind and useful for one's security to do a spell for protection of car or truck, and of yourself. The simple rite given below can be modified and done in your own words, since as in all such rituals it is the thought and the intent that counts. (It can be adapted to boats or planes also, although in a passenger airliner you will have to do the whole thing from where you sit as the engines are started. Use your imagination, improvise and visualize as best you can!)

Place yourself next to your vehicle with your hands on it, and breathe in deeply. Imagine as vividly as you are able that you are pulling pure, white light into your body from the Sun and the deep, volcanic energy from the Earth itself. Imagine with each breath that you are drawing it in, not only through your lungs, but through every pore in your body. Hold it within your body, feeling the slight pressure of power accumulated within yourself even as you let out your physical breath. Do this three times, then point the index and middle fingers of your right hand at one wheel, saying quietly:

> *Power within, and power so stay*
> *To work the protection I desire,*
> *And to remain for this journey.*

Slowly inhale physically and exhale the three breaths you have drawn, imaging with your mind as clearly as possible that you are radiating the power in a clear, white beam into the wheel where it will remain. (More mundanely, glance at the tire to make certain that it is properly inflated, with good treads and no damage.). Step to your left to the next wheel or corner of your vehicle and repeat the drawing and fixing of power as above. Continue until all wheels are so charged.

Stand before the engine. Open the hood and, as above, draw five breaths of white light and, in your imagination, "stream" it into the engine. Imagine as clearly as possible that the entire engine and all fittings upon it are glowing with the light that you have imbued within it. (This might also be a good opportunity to check your coolant and oil.) Then close the hood.

Draw within yourself three more breaths of the white light through every pore, and say quietly:

> *Protection and power*
> *I do call forth,*
> *That it may be wrapped about*
> *My conveyance and about*
> *Myself and any of my family,*
> *Or any of my friends.*

Starting from the front of your vehicle, walk clockwise about it, with the forefinger and middle finger of your right hand directing three slow breaths of light into it, saying quietly:

> *I do send forth this power*
> *Which I have drawn from*
> *The sky and the Earth,*
> *To be fixed within this vehicle*
> *To remain and to grow strong*
> *As I travel on this journey.*

Stop before the front of your vehicle and on its nose casually draw the Hammer of Thor with your finger. Pause for a moment and then say quietly:

> *Hearty Thor, friend of travelers,*
> *I have placed on my vehicle*
> *Your sign of strength and protection.*
> *Use the power which I have breathed into my vehicle*
> *So that wherever I go, no harm may*
> *Come to my conveyance or to me.*
> *Hail Thor!*

With your finger, casually draw an eye just to the right front of the hood, saying quietly:

Beautiful and magical Freya, far traveler,
Use the power which I have breathed into my vehicle
So that all who travel herein will be within
Thy circle of serenity, safety and security.
May no danger threaten,
And no harm be done to anyone
By this vehicle.
Hail Freya!

Glance at your lights to be certain that they are clean with no chips or cracks, and briefly look under the car to be certain there is no leaking oil or coolant. To an outsider this entire rite should look as if you were simply doing a last walkaround check of your vehicle before starting it.

You should depart immediately. (Of course, you can help the spell by driving safely!)

Bonding of Brotherhood

When a bond is to be sealed between two true friends, let them go to a sacred grove, or to a wilderness place of special imporance to the both of them, at a time when the Sun is at its zenith. They should go after a recent rain so that the ground is soft and wet. (If this is not possible, they should bring water from a nearby spring or stream to soften the soil where the pledging takes place.) Carry a pin or sharp knife, plus a few mementos which the friends have in common. These could be symbols of their land, items of remembrance from their duty in wartime (and perhaps in remembrance of comrades who died), symbols of their ideals, etc. Also, they should carry a drink to be taken in honor of their friendship.

(This ceremony can be altered and the words modified as the friends feel is best, since of course it is the intent and the feeling which is important, rather than the specific form of the rite.)

Both remain silent for a few moments at the place they have chosen, thinking on their friendship and on the many things that the two have shared in common. Then they face the East, and one raises his/her hand in salute, calling:

> *Strong winds and high clouds,*
> *Soft breezes and raging storms,*
> *Hearken well to what is said here,*
> *And write our words*
> *Upon the winds.*

Next they face South, and the other raises a hand in salute, calling:

> *O bright face of the Sun*
> *Of this world and of all others*
> *Hearken well to what is said here,*

And burn our words
Across the bright skies.

Then to the West, and the first raises a hand in salute, calling:

Deep lakes and rushing rivers,
And the eternal sea who is mother to all things,
Hearken well to what is said here.
May our words be spoken
By the very waters.

Lastly to the North, and the second raises a hand in salute, calling:

Lands that are fruitful and lands that are barren,
Tall forest and open heath,
Hearken well to what is said here.
May our words be graven
Upon the stones themselves.

If there are other things to be said, or other good friends to be remembered, now is the time to speak of them, each in his or her own words.

If the ground is dry, soak a spot with water from a nearby stream, spring or well.

One then makes a footprint in the ground, and then the other superimposes his or her own footprint in that just made by the friend. Next each person takes their own personal, sterilized knife or pin and draws blood from the thumb, and both persons let a drop of blood fall into these footprints to thus seal their kinship before Mother Earth. The two shall assume a tight handclasp, each with his right hand holding the friend's right wrist, as each says:

As long as the tree is in the ground
And the acorn thereon,
Do I pledge to you true friendship
And kinship,
Bonded to you as my brother, (or sister)
To aid you and to protect you
Through all the worlds
And all the ages.

I thus swear before the Earth, Mother of All,
I thus swear before the Sun,
Before the mighty Gods,
And high heaven itself,
That I will be your true friend
As long as oak and Earth do stand.

At this time it is appropriate to share a drink together in honor of their friendship, and they speak any other words that might be proper.

They turn to the East, and the second friend raises a hand in salute, calling:

Winds and storms,
Mark well what has been pledged here.

Next to the South, and the first friend raises a hand in salute, calling:

Sun and sky,
Mark well what has been pledged here.

To the West, the second raising a hand in salute, calling:

Lakes, rivers, and sea,
Mark well what has been pledged here.

Lastly to the North, the first raising a hand in salute, calling:

Land, forest, and heath,
Mark well what has been pledged here.

Then the two should leave. If possible, they should soon find occasion to share a meal together and drink together, giving toasts to their friendship.

Betrothal Ceremony

Traditionally, the father or the best friend of the male suitor should go to see the father of the prospective bride, to ask him for her hand. The reason for this archaic custom is that now, as in times long past, such a spokesman is able to enumerate the suitor's good qualities. If the discussion goes well, then the conditions of the marriage, such as home, jobs, and schooling should be discussed.

Although the father or other close relative of a young maiden will speak for her and make arrangements for her, a widow or divorcee may betroth herself, as may a woman who is of age.

Traditionally, good birth should be considered, as well as the power, wealth and influence of the families and of prominent relatives. It has always been good practice for the families to be fairly closely matched in rank, wealth, intellect, personal interests and so on. Now as in the distant past a marriage has a better chance for success if both man and woman have much in common, both materially and mentally.

Still, every betrothal, every marriage, is different. In the final analysis, the feelings of the man and the woman for each other will, in the present era, usually be the determining factor.

If it is so desired by them, the man and the woman may exchange private vows before or after this ceremony.

When it has been determined that a betrothal will be announced, guests are invited for the festivities. Each friend brings food and drink for a potluck banquet, though the families of the bride- and groom-to-be may wish to host the affair. Although not the custom in ancient times, a ring of betrothal may be supplied by the groom-to-be. (Money for a symbolic dowry may be in the groom's possession, to be given, if so desired. If so, make mention of it when the betrothal-ring is named in the rite.). In addition to the Godi or Godia there will be six witnesses. Before the rite, write an agreement and sign for the property and other agreements that will be a part of the marriage.

When all is in readiness the Godi or Godia asks all to be silent for
a moment, and then says:

> We are gathered here at this time
> To mark and to witness the betrothal
> Of two who have chosen
> To live together as husband and as wife.

> This is a declaration of intent,
> And a year and a day may pass
> Ere the two are wedded.
> If either thinks otherwise,
> Or if minds and hearts are changed,
> Then this must be
> Within a year and a day.

> At this time and at this place we call also
> Upon Allfather Odin, Freya of love and desire,
> And Goodfriend Thor
> To witness the words that here shall be spoken.

Then shall the woman say:

> I name the witnesses here, _____, _____,
> _____, _____, _____, _____.
> That you, _____, betrothe yourself to me,
> _____,
> With a lawful betrothal,
> To seal the bargain
> As the fulfillment and performance
> Of the whole agreement
> Which has been duly written and signed,
> Without fraud and without tricks,
> So that this be a complete and legal match.
> And also, thou givest me a ring   (And a dowry)
> To seal the bargain
> Before our friends, before our families,
> And before the high Gods.

Then the man says:

> *I name the witnesses here,* _____, _____,
> _____, _____, _____, _____,
> *That you,* _____, *betrothe yourself to*
> *me,* _____,
> *With a lawful betrothal,*
> *To seal the bargain*
> *As the fulfillment and performance*
> *Of the whole agreement*
> *Which has been duly written and signed,*
> *Without fraud and without tricks,*
> *So that this be a complete and legal match.*
> *And also, that I give to you a ring*   (And a dowry)
> *To seal the bargain*
> *Before our friends, before our familes,*
> *And before the high Gods.*

Then the Godi or Godia says:

> *All have heard and witnessed that which has been said.*
> *Are there any who say nay?*

Pause for five heartbeats.

> *Then, in symbol of your betrothal,*
> *Place the ring upon her finger,*
> *And seal the troth with a kiss.*

The couple will do so, and the Godi or Godia continues:

> *Before those gathered here,*
> *And before the High Gods,*
> *You are betrothed, and*
> *Within a year and a day shall be wed,*
> *If all goes as it should.*

The Godi or Godia pours a horn of ale for the two to share, and
gives each to drink, saying:

> *In the name of our people, and our Gods,*
> *May you know the best of fortune,*
> *And be wed within a year and a day.*

Then the horn is given to each of the guests (or witnesses), saying:

> *I ask you to wish well to the betrothed,*
> *And to drink in their honor.*

When the last guest has so pledged, the Godi or Godia says:

> *This rite is ended*
> *May our Gods be with us always!*

Wedding

A woman of the folk who follows the Ways of Valhalla is always to be highly respected, as she is one who at times can become the presence of a high Goddess of the Golden Lands. Further, she is the link with the past and the future, and when she decides to have her children, remember that any of her offspring may be the ones who will far advance the family, the folk, and indeed be honored by all humankind, one who will do great deeds that will benefit every living being. Upon becoming a wife she is greatly honored, and in any gathering of family or folk her counsels shall have great weight.

Marriage is a means of joining worthy families together, and of linking men and women who have a particular magic between them. If possible (and for young people especially), seek the parents' advice, for parents and good friends can be counted upon to give the honest advice that could perhaps enable one, otherwise blinded by love and passion, to see the flaws in a possible bad match. If it is at all possible, the conditions of the Betrothal Ceremony should be fulfilled, even if that rite is itself not accomplished. In particular, an agreement as to who has the rights to which properties, which will be in common, which separate, and agreement as to the division of belongings and wealth in case the two eventually wish to go their own separate ways, should be duly signed and witnessed well before the wedding rite.

If it is so desired by them, the man and the woman may have a civil ceremony before or after this rite.

The families of the bride and groom, or the bride and groom themselves, should host the wedding and the festivities which follow. Although not the custom in ancient times, rings may be exchanged by the two being married.

The bride should be dressed in white, wearing a long, wide headdress or veil, fastened to the top of her head and hanging down her back. At her breast she wears a jewel or rune ornament in remembrance of Lady Freya's powerful and magical Brisingamen gem. The keys to the new home, or an ornate set of keys on a colored sash, are on the altar to be presented to the bride as symbol of her attaining to the household.

A groomsman carries a sword for the groom, and either wears or carries it.

When all is in readiness the Godi asks all to be silent for a moment, and then says:

> We are gathered here at this time
> To mark and to witness the joining in marriage
> Of two who would be husband and wife.
>
> At this time and at this place we call also
> Upon Allfather Odin, Freya of love and desire,
> And Goodfriend Thor
> To witness the words that here shall be spoken.
>
> In the ancient manner do we also invoke
> The Goddess Var, who,
> As told in our ancient legends,
> Hears the vows
> Of men and of women.

After a pause of five heartbeats, the Godia says:

> Carry in the Hammer
> To consecrate the bride, and the groom.
> Lay this symbol of our Gods
> In the lap of each,
> To so wed these two together
> With the hand of Var.

A Hammer of Thor is brought forth, and the Godi says to the groom:

> Kneel now, to receive the ancient blessing.

To the groom as the Hammer is touched to him:

> Before the High Gods, and before our people,

Art thou blessed anew once again.

The Hammer of Thor is handed to the Godia, who says to the bride:

Kneel now to receive the ancient blessing.

To the bride as the Hammer is touched to her:

Before the High Gods, and before our people,
Art thou blessed anew once again.

When both are blessed the Godi bids them to rise. The Godi then says to the Groom:

_____, if you truly desire
To marry this woman,
I ask thee to give, wholeheartedly,
The blade which symbolizes thy strength.
Swear thy weapon to her,
Always to be at her service.

The groom takes the sword and offers it to the bride, saying:

My most beloved,
Accept the oath of love which I offer thee.
I vow this sword, as I vow my soul,
Ever to be at thy service.
Like this blade my heart will be strong,
Like this steel my love will endure.
Accept it, my chosen one,
For all which is mine
Will now be thine.

The bride takes the sword silently in her hands and touches it to her forehead for the time of three heartbeats. She returns it to him, saying:

My most beloved,
I accept this oath, sworn on thy blade.

Thou knowest what is in my heart
As I know what is in thine.

The Godia then says to the bride:

_____, *if thou truly desire*
To marry this man,
I ask thee to give, wholeheartedly,
The jewel of beauty which thou wearest,
In symbol of our Lady's great magic and power.
Swear thy jewel to him,
Always to be at his service.

The bride then takes her jewel and holds it out to the groom, saying:

My most beloved,
Accept the oath of love which I offer thee.
I vow this jewel, as I vow my soul,
Ever to be at thy service.
Like its beauty will my heart will be strong,
Like its value my love will endure.
Accept it, my chosen one,
For all which is mine
Will now be thine.

The groom takes the jewel silently in his hands and touches it to his forehead for the time of three heartbeats. He then returns it to her, saying:

My most beloved,
I accept this oath, sworn on thy jewel.
Thou knowest what is in my heart
As I know what is in thine.

The Godi says:

Thou who shalt be husband and wife,
Listen to what we say, here and now.
Whatever each of thee

May accomplish in future years,
Wherever thou may wander,
Know full well that thou shalt do all
For our people, for thy family and thy kin,
And to be worthy each of the other.

The Godia holds forth the keys to the bride, saying:

If thou would be mistress of the household
And all therein, honored for thy wisdom
In the councils of our people,
And equal partner to thy husband,
I bid thee to take these keys,
Symbol of thy new life.

The keys are handed to the bride, and a bridesmaid sees that they are fastened at her waist as the Godia says:

At this time, and henceforth,
As the keys are given to thee,
Dost thou take over a new household.
Be wise in all thou doest.

The Godi then says to the groom:

With this rite thou gainest a treasure of greatest
    value,
Care for her, and protect her always.
For there is none who is her equal.

Then the Godia says to both:

Above thee are the stars,
Below thee are the stones.
Remember always,
Like a star should thy love be constant,
Like the Earth should thy love be firm.
Possess one another, yet be understanding.
Have patience, for storms may come and go.
Be free always in giving of affection and of warmth,

> *For our Gods and our people*
> *Will always be with thee.*

After a pause of five heartbeats the Godi asks:

> *Dost thou desire, (bride's name)*
> *To have this man as thy husband,*
> *Forsaking all others?* (The answer is given by the bride.)
> *Dost thou desire, (groom's name)*
> *To have this woman as thy wife,*
> *Forsaking all others?* (The answer is given by the groom.)

Then the Godia says:

> *All have heard and witnessed that which has been said.*
> *Are there any who say nay?*

After a pause of five heartbeats the Godi says:

> *Then, in symbol of thy joining, one to the other,*
> *Place each the ring upon the other's finger,*
> *And seal the troth with a kiss.*

The couple will do so, and the Godi or Godia continues:

> *Before those gathered here,*
> *And before the High Gods,*
> *Thou art man and wife,*
> *And henceforth be as one.*

Pause at this time if the bride and groom wish to receive the congratulations and felicitations of those in attendance. After a suitable time the Godia continues.

The Godia pours a horn of ale for the two to share, and gives each to drink, saying:

> *In the name of our people, and our Gods,*
> *May thou knowest the best of fortune,*
> *And thy life henceforth be one*
> *Of joy and prosperity for thee,*

And pride and strength for our people.

Then the horn is given to each of the bridesmaids and grooms-men , saying:

I ask thee to wish well to those now wedded,
And to drink in their honor.

When the last guest has so pledged, the Godi says:

This rite is ended.
May our Gods be with us always!

Birth Pledging of an Infant

When a child is born, as soon as possible after the birth it is proper to dedicate the new one to the Gods of Valhalla. This may be done by the mother or by some close female relative.

The infant should be bundled as warmly as necessary and taken out under the stars. For a short while the one who carries the child is silent and still, meditating to "become one with the Gods." Then she gently places the bundled infant on the Earth, saying these or similar words:

> *Mother of the most ancient times,*
> *Bless this blissful child,*
> *Conceived and birthed in love.*
> *Grant him/her thine own strength,*
> *Thy power and thy eternal magic.*

Then she holds the child up toward the stars, saying these or similar words:

> *Blessed Mother Frigga, bless and protect this tiny one*
> *Who is loved so deeply by us.*
> *Give thy warmth and thy love,*
> *And be with him/her always.*
> *Hail Freya!*
> *Wise Allfather, bless and protect this tiny one*
> *Who is loved so deeply by us.*
> *Give thy wisdom and victory over all,*
> *And be with him/her always.*
> *Hail Odin!*
>
> *Strong and hearty Thor, guard this tiny one*
> *Who is loved so deeply by us.*

207

Give thy protection and thy strength,
And be with him/her always.
Hail Thor!

She who gives the prayer should then clasp the little one close to her and spend awhile longer looking up toward the stars. If she has some talents as a spae-woman she will be able to sense some omens for the infant's future lifetime.

Coming-of-Age Rite

This rite is held when a young person of the people feels that he or she is ready to be accepted as an adult of the folk. It is performed on or after the 13th birthday, though under special circumstances the ritual may be held earlier. The youth must have already proven before the elders and parents an ability to earn a sufficient living by mastering some trade, shown that he or she is able to set up a household and maintain it without help, and meet all monetary and social responsibilities to the outside world and to the people. Above all else, the requirements for this ceremony must be common sense and realistic, and must depend on the real-life status of the youth's people and their place in the world.

Although various groups may have their own prerequisites for this rite of passage, the following are usually chosen:
- Proficiency at a job or trade suitable to earn a living.
- Self-discipline needed to set up and maintain a household.
- Organizing ability to maintain a budget and pay debts properly.
- Good to excellent at some form of self-defense (judo, karate, marksmanship, knife fighting, etc), and good judgment on when and how to use it.
- First aid training.
- Having completed a week's solitary wilderness vigil.
- Good health and a mature, balanced personality.

In return for being henceforth considered an adult, the youth must have made appropriate agreements with his or her parents, including, for example, the completion of education, contributing a certain amount of "room and board" each month, and adherence to household rules. For their part, the parents may agree to make special provisions for housing, or helping to house, the youth (and later for the young one's spouse) for a period of five to eight years. The parents and others of the folk should be ready to render what assistance and advice will be needed until the young one is firmly established.

It is best that this ritual is held during one of the eight main yearly festivals, though need and not formality shall determine the time of the rite.

For the day prior to the ritual the candidate undergoes a partial fast, taking only very light food and clear liquid, and devotes time to prayers and spells in honor of the High Ones of Valhalla. At the time of this morning rite the candidate dresses in fresh, white clothing and comes before the group. On the altar is a sword or knife, symbolic tools of the youth's chosen trade, and a pouch containing symbolic money from the parents and other relatives.

It is preferable that the Godi and Godia (for at least this portion of the rite) be the youth's father and mother, or some selected relatives.

When all is in readiness the Godi says:

> *At this time do we have among us*
> *A youth who now seeks the way*
> *Of those mature in years.*
> *I ask thee, _____, In the Name of the Allfather,*
> *To come forth and stand before us now.*

The Youth comes before the Godi and Godia and gives salute in their honor.

Godia: _____, *we welcome thee before us,*
> *In the Name of High Freya,*
> *And we give praise to thy resolve*
> *To join with the leaders of our people.*

Godi: _____, *we welcome thee before us,*
> *In the Name of Great Thor,*
> *And we salute the strength within thee.*
> *May it grow ever stronger.*

Godia: *Dost thou at this time feel that thou*
> *Art able to assume the full responsibilities*
> *Of adulthood, to do honor to thyself,*
> *To thy parents, and to thy people?*

Youth: *By Odin, Freya and Thor, I am.*

Godi: *Art thou now able and skilled*
To sustain thyself by an honorable trade,
And to make thy living thereby,
To do honor to thyself,
To thy parents, and to thy people?

Youth: *By Odin, Freya and Thor, I am.*

Godi: *Hast thou now attained the training,*
The strong arm, the steady hand,
And the cool head to protect thyself,
Thy parents, and thy people?

Youth: *By Odin, Freya and Thor, I do.*

Then the Godia takes the knife or sword from the altar and holds it aloft, calling:

> *Hear us now, O Gods of High Valhalla!*
> _____ *is now recognized as fit and ready*
> *To sit with the councils of our people,*
> *To defend and to judge.*
> *I ask thee always to guide hand and heart.*
> *Hail Odin!*

Then the sword or knife is handed to the Youth as the Godia says:

> *May thy hand be steady, thy heart strong,*
> *In the service of thyself, thy family,*
> *And thy people.*

Youth: *By Odin, Freya and Thor,*
My hand shall be steady and my heart strong.

Then the Godi takes the tools symbolic of the Youth's trade and holds them aloft, calling:

Hear us now, O Gods of High Valhalla!
_____ *is now recognized as fit and ready*
To earn his/her home and sustenance.
I ask thee always to give strength and wisdom.
Hail Odin!

Then the tools symbolic of the trade are handed to the Youth as the Godi says:

Mayest thou have strength and wisdom,
In working for thyself, thy family,
And thy people.

Youth: *By Odin, Freya and Thor,*
I shall have strength and wisdom.

Then the Godia takes the pouch of money and holds it aloft, calling:

Hear us now, O Gods of High Valhalla!
_____ *is now granted this symbolic gift of gold.*
Mayest thou grant prosperity in times to come.
Hail Odin!

Then the pouch of money is handed to the Youth as the Godi says:

Mayest thou gain prosperity in times to come,
To the benefit of thyself, thy family,
And thy people.

Youth: *By Odin, Freya and Thor,*
I shall prosper.

Then the Godia calls:

Hear and hearken, O High Ones of Valhalla!
_____ *here is recognized as a man (woman)*
Of our people!
Be with him (her) always!

Then the Godi calls:

> *Hear and hearken, good folk!*
> _____ *here is recognized as a man (woman)*
> *Of our people!*
> *Know this now and always!*

The youth faces the people, saying:

> *I give thanks to the eternal Gods*
> *And to thee, my family and folk.*
> *At this time and at this place*
> *I have become a man (woman)!*
> *My life shall from now be changed.*

(Holds high the pouch)

> *I shall always seek wealth for myself*
> *And for my people, and my Gods.*

(Holds high the tools)

> *I shall always earn my way wisely.*
> *For myself, my people, and my Gods.*

(Holds high the knife)

> *I shall always be an indominatable warrior*
> *Honorably protecting myself, my people,*
> *And my Gods. This I swear!*
> *Hail Odin!*

(All)   *Hail Odin!*
> *Hail Freya!*

(All)   *Hail Freya!*
> *Hail Thor!*

(All)   *Hail Thor!*

Then the Godi or Godia shakes hands or embraces the youth and says:

> *Welcome, new friend.*
> *It is good to have thee*
> *As one of our people.*

Led by the Godi or by the parents (or even by friends), all drink horns of mead in honor of the new man (woman) of the people.

If it is so desired, feasting and other celebration follow.

The Rite of Pledging for a Child

Perform this ceremony as the Moon increases, preferably near one of the High Festivals.

The place where the ritual is held should have an altar near the north of the ritual area. Beyond it hang a banner of the Odin Rune done in black cloth with silver or gold rune markings. At the center of the altar place an image of Freya with a raven or wolf image (or other representation of Odin) to her left. To her right place an image of Thor, or a representation of the Hammer. Before the images are a sword, helmet, and shield.

Have mead or ale available, and a drinking horn or tankard for each person in attendance. Set one additional cup on the left side of the altar in honor of the Great Ones. Include a copy of this rite for the Godi and Godia.

Also, set a candle or torch at each of the far quarters (directions) of the ritual area, while two others will remain on or immediately adjacent to the altar. Light incense.

If a hand-held banner or standard of the Odin Rune is available, the Priest should carry it. Other standards with runes of the High Gods of Valhalla may be carried by the devotees if such are on hand. Play appropriate music if it is available. Wagner's "Entry of the Gods into Valhalla," followed by "Siegfried's Rhine Journey" are ideal, though other music or even nature sounds may be preferred. If possible, the parents should choose the music.

When all is in readiness, the folk assemble. (If there is room, include a Procession of Honor led by the parents carrying the infant, the godparents, the Godi and Godia, and all others following, to end before the altar.) If rune banners are carried, place them in stands to either side of the altar at this time.

As the rite begins, the Godia and Godi face the parents and godparents, as well as the child. The little one may be carried by whomever is best at maintaining a happy and moderately quiet child for the duration of the ceremony.

If desired, a Blot may be held in honor of the young one at this time.

The Calling

At this time the Godia raises her arms in salute and calls:

> *We gather here, in the company of our family,*
> *Our friends, our people, and our Gods*
> *To welcome a small and blessed one*
> *Who is new to the Middle Earth of humankind.*
> *Let us present now the young one*
> *Before the Gods, for their protection,*
> *For all of his/her life.*

At this time the Godi says:

> *O Valfather, Azure-Cloaked Wanderer*
> *From the far, ancient lands of our people,*
> *Lord of the Shining Ones*
> *Who do protect our land, our folk, and our families.*
> *We call to thee to be with us here.*
> *To give thy cloak of protection*
> *About this small and good one.*
> *Grant wisdom, and victory in all things,*
> *Great Odin!*   (End with a salute.)

Then the Godia says:

> *O Lady of magic and beauty,*
> *Leader of the Swan Maidens,*
> *Good and loving mother of the Gods themselves,*
> *Come now, we do ask,*
> *And place thy protection about this*
> *Small and beautiful one.*
> *Grant, if thou wilt, a face and body of beauty,*
> *A mind that many shall honor,*
> *And a charm that none can resist.*

> *Gracious Freya,*
> *Be with us here, in this rite!*   (End with a salute)

Then the Godi says:

> *Strong and laughing One, great hearted and good,*
> *Thou who wander far, thy great Hammer in hand,*
> *Friend and companion to all our people,*
> *Come now, good comrade,*
> *And place thy strong arm of protection*
> *About this small and beloved child.*
> *Grant something of thy vast strength,*
> *Thy joy and thy laughter*
> *That life may be long and rich.*
> *Great Thor, be with us here*
> *In this rite!*   (A salute is given)

Then the one chosen to call to the East says:

> *The skies are blue and open, and*
> *The winds blow free and fair*
> *Over this small and holy one.*
> *Great Ones, keep him/her free as the winds*
> *Which are thy servants.*
> *Hail Odin!*   (salute)

All: *Hail Odin!*   (salute)

Then the one chosen to call to the West says:

> *The waters of our ancient lands*
> *Flow eternally clear and fresh,*
> *And the blue seas wash our far shores.*
> *Grant to this small and holy one,*
> *A soul and spirit ever as pure, and*
> *Ever as new as the streams of life*
> *That flow from far Valhall.*
> *Hail Odin!*   (salute)

All: *Hail Odin!*   (salute)

Then the one chosen to call to the North says:

> *May the forests and the mountains*
> *Give sustenance of the soul and spirit*
> *To this small and holy one,*
> *And the green and golden fields*
> *Provide sustenance to his/her body.*
> *Grant to this small and beautiful one*
> *A healing and a strength*
> *As deep and rich as the Earth herself.*
> *Hail Odin!* (salute)

All: *Hail Odin!* (salute)

The Presentation of the Child

A call is sounded on a horn, and the Godia asks:

> *Who is it that now comes before*
> *The High Gods of Valhalla?*
> *And who speaks for this*
> *Small and sweet one?*

The Mother says:

> *Before those of our family,*
> *Before our good friends,*
> *Before our people,*
> *Before the mighty Gods themselves,*
> *Before those who are seen*
> *And those who are with us in spirit only,*
> *Do I bring forth _____, my child and my treasure.*
> *We have long waited for this small one*
> *And brought him/her forth in love.*

The Father says:

> *Before those of our family,*
> *Before our good friends,*
> *Before our people,*

Before the mighty Gods themselves,
Before those who are seen
And those who are with us in spirit only,
Do I bring forth _____, my child and my treasure.
We have long waited for this small one
And brought him/her forth in love.

Both parents hold the infant, as the Godi comes forth and holds his hands over the child in an attitude of blessing, saying:

May the blessings of the Allfather,
Giver of wisdom and giver of victory
Far-seeing and far-knowing,
Be ever with thee, small friend.

Both parents hold the infant, as the Godia comes forth and holds her hands over the child in an attitude of blessing, saying:

May the blessings of Our Lady,
Giver of love and giver of magic,
Protecting and loving,
Be ever with thee, small friend.

Both parents hold the infant, as the Godi comes forth and holds his hands out over the child in an attitude of blessing, saying:

May the blessings of the hearty and joyous One,
Giver of strength and giver of happiness
Far-wandering and friend of us all,
Be ever with thee, small friend.

The Pledging of the Parents

The Godi holds forth the sword, and the Godia places her hands over his to hold it also. The Godi says to the parents:

In the names of the High Ones,
I ask thee both to place thy hands
On this sword.

Hearken closely to our words,
For bringing into this Mid-Earth of one so small
And linking of one so young with our people
And with our ancient Gods
Is a matter of deepest importance.

Godia: *I call upon thee both to give thy child*
The best of learning to do well in this world.
Yet always keep joy and play
As his/her companions.

Godi: *I call upon thee both to give thy child*
A home of love, warmth and gentleness,
Friends and family that are good
And the best of our people.
Whatever differences thou may have,
Think of thy child, and know that
His/her world must have no disruption.

Godia: *I call upon thee both to know thy child*
As one of our people, unique and individual.
Remember that a small body and a child's ways
Cover a mind of learning and of wisdom
That many may well honor in the years to come.

Godi: *I call upon thee both to listen to thy child,*
And give a fair hearing to all that is said.
Have patience as the young one learns and asks,
And remember how it was
When thou too were a child.

Godia: *I call upon thee both to teach this young one*
The ways of our people, the ways of the world,
And keep always before him/her
The challenge and the vision of far horizons
And of new worlds to explore,
So that thy child may go as far
As his/her own mind and spirit shall lead.
Dost thou hearken to these words?

Parents: *We do.*

Godi: *If thee, as parents of this small and holy one,*
Have resolved to assume this high calling,
Then make thy vows now before
Odin, Thor, Freya
And all the High Ones of Valhalla.

The Godi and Godia hold forth the sword, and the parents place their hands upon it, repeating the words, line by line, spoken by the Godi or Godia:

We, _____ and _____, as parents
of _____, do take this vow
before Odin, Thor, Freya,
and before all the Gods of high Valhalla.

The Godia pours mead into the drinking horn, and each of the parents, the Godi and the Godia drink in honor of the child, saying:

To Odin, Thor, Freya,
And to _____,
The newest of our people.
Welcome, small one!

Pause for 13 heartbeats or more. Additional incense may be put on the brazier or other honorary activities may be added at this time.

Dedication as a Warrior

Bring forth a sword, a shield and a helmet and set before the altar. The Godi goes there and calls:

Bring forth the child,
That, as is the wish of his/her elders,
This young one may receive dedication
As a warrior of Odin, Thor and Freya.

The child is brought before the altar. The Godia holds out the shield so that the infant's hand touches it as she says:

> *This, O young one, is the shield.*
> *Take it and mind that always*
> *Must thou protect those of thy family and folk*
> *Who are less powerful.*
> *Guard always our people, and our faith,*
> *The Way of the Rainbow Bridge,*
> *The Path of Valhalla.*

She puts down the shield and holds out the helmet so that the infant's hand touches it as she says:

> *This, O young one, is the helm.*
> *Take it and mind that always*
> *Must thou protect thyself well,*
> *That thou be always strong, whole,*
> *And ready in the service*
> *Of our people and our Gods.*

She puts down the helmet and holds out the sword so that the infant's hand touches it as she says:

> *This, O young one, is the sword.*
> *Take it and mind that always*
> *Must thou defeatest evil and injustice.*
> *Wield steel, wield silver, wield seid,*
> *That our people may always be free*
> *And always freely give honor*
> *To Odin, Thor and Freya,*
> *And to all our ancient Gods.*

She puts down the sword and takes up the horn of mead, dipping

a finger into it and making with it the Rune of Power ⛭ or ⛭ , with

the words:

> *This small one now wears*
> *The Helmet of Power*

or the Hammer of Thor on the infant's forehead, saying:

> *Before all who gather this dark twilight*
> *Are thou promised truth and arm of might.*
> *Shield to protect and armor strong*
> *In service to thy family and to our people,*
> *To Odin, to Thor and to Freya*
> *Through all of this life.*
> *A bond with thee is sealed by the Gods*
>
> *Until death take thee, beyond the time*
> *That thy parents depart the world of the living,*
> *Though the Ways of Valhalla may vanish*
> *Or the world end.*

Pause for 13 heartbeats. All step back from the altar.

Closing

The child is held up over the altar and the final closing is given:

Godi: *Mark now, Allfather Odin,*
       Giver of wisdom and of victory,
       That _____ has by this rite
       Been dedicated to thee,
       And to our people.
       Hail Odin!
All: *Hail Odin!*

Godia: *Mark now, Mother Freya*
       Weaver of destinies, rider of the winds,
       That _____ has by this rite
       Been dedicated to thee,
       And to our people.
       Hail Freya!
All: *Hail Freya!*

Godi: *Mark now, Thor the Thunderer,*

> *Friend and protector of our folk,*
> *That _____ has by this rite*
> *Been dedicated to thee,*
> *And to our people.*
> *Hail Thor!*

All:　　*Hail Thor!*

Then the Godia says:

> *This rite is ended.*
> *Let us now celebrate in honor*
> *Of _____, the newest and finest*
> *Of our people.*
> *Hail Odin!*

All:　　*Hail Odin!*

Feasting and drinking follow in honor of the child.

Divorce

Not all will desire or be able to stay married. Even with the best of intentions, the differences between a couple may be too great. They should try to their very best to bridge whatever differences they have, and ask friends and kin to help. Each should be willing to yield to the other in the interest of understanding. It is most important to avoid the open anger and hate which so often characterizes a divorce.

Particularly, if there are children there must be a great effort made, for the young need above all to have a home of peace, love and understanding. A couple contemplating divorce should think long and deeply of the harm it may do to their children. If the children are old enough, their wishes should have some impact on the final decisions.

If a divorce seems the only way out, the two must come to a sensible agreement as to the division of property and for continuing support of a partner as long as that one remains unmarried. Kinfolk and friends should help in the writing and witnessing of the document which settles this matter. In particular, any children must be given full consideration, care and support.

It is customary for six witnesses to be present, for both husband and wife. If one is absolutely not available, however, a Godi or Godia may stand in for the missing one at this rite held in the divorcing couple's home.

The Godi holds his right hand aloft and says:

> *In the names of our Gods,*
> *Before Allfather Odin,*
> *Before Freya of love and desire,*
> *Before Goodfriend Thor,*
> *And before Var, who witnesses all oaths,*
> *Do we gather here to sever all bonds*
> *Which remain between husband and wife.*

_____ and _____, *come forward*
And stand before us now.

The two come forward at this time, to stand before the Godi and Godia. The Godia says:

Thou both fully know the importance
Of this final step.
Have thou tried every way to reach an understanding?
     (Both answer)
Has there been a fair settlement of thy properties?
     (Both answer)

And if applicable:

Wilt thy children receive the best possible care?
     (Both answer)

If one or both say nay, then the rite will be halted and an attempt at reconciliation made. If this attempt fails, or if both say "yes," the Godia says:

Then I must ask the woman of the house
To declare the separation,
Three times, in three places,
In the presence of the witnesses
Gathered here.

All proceed to the bedroom, and the woman says:

Before the Gods and before our people
I declare that this marriage is now ended.

All proceed to the place where the man's most treasured belongings have been kept, and the woman says:

Before the Gods and before our people
I declare that this marriage is now ended.

Then all go before the hearth, or into the kitchen and the woman says directly to the witnesses:

> *Before the Gods and before our people*
> *I declare that this marriage is now ended.*

The Godi then says:

> *I ask now for our Gods*
> *And all of friends, family, and folk*
> *To heal the wounds of this parting,*
> *And to give comfort to those*
> *Who do need it badly.*
> *When both have gone their ways*
> *Let understanding and not bitterness remain.*
> *May wisdom be the legacy of this sad time.*

He raises his right hand in a final blessing, and lowers it, saying:

> *In the names of our Gods*
> *And our people,*
> *Thou art free.*

The Godia says:

> *Go now, and go in peace.*
> *This ceremony of divorce*
> *Is ended.*

The Godi, Godia, kinfolk and friends see that all necessary legalities are fulfilled to terminate the marriage.

Funeral Rite

When one of the folk has died, it is proper to give a funeral ceremony before the Old Gods and in honor of the departed. The rite which follows is to be tailored for each individual burial and modified as necessary. If feasible, the headstone or marker is the "man dead" rune (see appendix), either in stone or as a temporary wooden marker for the ceremony. Sprigs of evergreen should be available for the mourners at graveside. Ten or eleven stones about the size of a man's head, plus two others of somewhat larger size, are stacked near the head of the open grave. Prior to the ceremony the Godi or Godia should meet with the respective friends (usually the pallbearers) who will set the stones about the grave during the rite in the approximate outline of a ship.

For a child there should be mention of Odin himself adopting the children who go to him, and of the love of the Great Mother for all of her young. Modify the rest of the rite accordingly.

In the event that this is performed as a private memorial service far from the burying ground, a picture of the one who has died is placed on the altar. After the rite the personal effects and the evergreen sprigs should be buried in some serene and undisturbed place which the deceased enjoyed when in life. Smaller stones may be used for the "soul boat" and candles used instead of torches. The "boat" is similarly re-erected in some remote place. Modify the rest of the rite accordingly.

If there is music, it should be stately and a favorite of the deceased. Otherwise, play "Siegfried's Funeral Music," by Wagner at the memorial service and as a processional to the graveyard. Prior to the closing of the coffin the Godi or Godia calls the mourners to order, and speaks some words uniquely in honor of the departed one. A prayer composed for the occasion is given, to include the following:

In this time of our grief
We call upon our Gods,
In the holiest names of Allfather Odin,
Of Thor the Strong and of the Mother,
To receive the soul of this, _____, one whom
We have loved.
He/She shall be sorely missed.

Yet know full well that the ancient sagas say
That those who are truly worthy
Shall return in time, to family, to friends,
And to his/her own folk.
And we here know full well
That our friend is the worthiest of the worthy.

May his/her spirit help and guide those who remain,
May his/her soul find peace and joy
And the best of company
In the emerald gardens and the golden halls
Of high Valhalla.
This we pray:
So mote it be!

All: *So mote it be!*

The Godi or Godia goes before the open coffin and places a few of the deceased's favorite personal effects therein:

Take this Hammer of Thor, beloved one.
May thy soul be so protected,
Wherever thou travel.

Take this coin of the realm, beloved one.
May it give thee good fortune,
And passage to the Land Beyond.

Take these, the keys to thine own vehicle, beloved one.
May the memory of thine own driving
Make this journey short and easy.

Other items may be added as the situation warrants. Then the Godi or Godia says:

> *Now is the time when the coffin must be closed.*
> *I call upon the pallbearers to come forward*
> *And for the torches to be lit,*
> *That our good friend may begin*
> *This last, long journey.*

Close the coffin and secure it as the pallbearers come forth and take their places. If possible, younger and stronger ones carry the coffin, while elderly or ill friends and relations (selected with their agreement before the ceremony) serve as "honorary pallbearers," walking alongside of those who actually carry the bier of the departed one.

Light the torches, and the torch bearers wait outside the place where the preceding memorial service has been held. They join in with the procession to the graveyard, both preceding the coffin and following it. Have other torches available for those of the mourners who wish to carry them.

All follow the Godi and/or Godia to the burying ground. Once at graveside the coffin is placed in the open grave as the torch carriers, under the guidance of the Godi or Godia, emplace their torches into the ground around the group of mourners. Then the Godi or Godia indicates the stones stacked near to the head of the grave and says:

> *Friends, let us now fashion,*
> *In the ancient way*
> *Of our sea-faring ancestors,*
> *The ship that shall travel*
> *Between the worlds,*
> *With the soul of our loved one,*
> *Our good friend.*

The grave should be set about with a ship-shaped lining of stones; each about the size of a man's head except for the larger stones at the set at the "prow" and "stern" under the direction of the Godi or Godia. When this has been done, the Godi or Godia says:

> *One who is born upon this dim Middle Earth*
> *Has only a few years to live.*

To know the love of family,
The warm embrace of a lover,
And the comradeship of good friends.
To some the years may be long and rich,
To some the years may be all too short.
Yet through it all each does his or her best,
As did this beloved one before us,
So that when finally each does stand before the Gods
It is with pride in self and backed with the loving prayers
Of those known in life.
In time, the others of us are all fated to follow,
There to be reunited with those who have gone before.
To meet again in joy and laughter
In the shining lands of the Gods.

Yet know full well that the ancient sagas say
That those who are truly worthy
Shall be born again.
Returning in time to family, to friends,
And to his/her own folk.

And we here know full well
That our friend is the worthiest of the worthy.
We will meet again, both in the golden lands beyond,
And, in time, here once again.

The legends say that the messengers of the High One
Are about us now, to fetch the true essence
Of a truly good man/woman/boy/girl.
The legends say that on the first night
Shall our beloved one be with Mother Frigga,
The second night with Allfather Odin,
And on the third night in the Shining Lands
Of peace.

So let us now be joyous,
For the soul blossoms as the flower,
It flies as a white bird.
Our good friend has gone to a far better place.
We shall all meet with him/her again,

Both in that shining land
And here, with family and friends, once more.

Let us call now upon our Gods.

After a pause of 13 or more heartbeats, the Godi or Godia says:

O Great Ones, hear our call,
And send forth thy messengers
To be with us here
At this time and in this place.

We commend the soul of _____
To the Gods of High Valhalla,
As we commend his/her body
To the bosom of Mother Earth.

In the holiest names of Allfather Odin,
Of Thor the Strong and of Mother Frigga,
Farewell, good friend.

Some day we will meet again
In the joy of thy friends
And in the love of thy family.
Until then, may all the Gods be with thee.
So mote it be!

All: *So mote it be!*

After a pause of ten heartbeats the Godi or Godia takes up a sprig of evergreen and drops it onto the coffin, saying:

As the tree is green forever,
So may thy soul live to eternity.

The sprigs of evergreen are offered to all. Each mourner takes a sprig and drops it onto the coffin, saying:

> *As the tree is green forever,*
> *May thy soul live to eternity.*

Each torch bearer then moves his or her torch next to the grave, encircling it just outside the stones.

Then all depart for the funeral Blot and feast. If practical, the torches should be left emplaced about the grave and allowed to burn out.

Rite for Healing of the Body

If one has been injured, wounded, or become ill, then the first recourse must be to use modern medical science to the maximum extent possible. When the physicians have done all they can, then the Rite of Healing may be performed. Those closest to the afflicted one should be present, and if possible, members of the family or close friends act as Godi and Godia. As is customary, if a woman of the folk is not available to act as Godia, place flowers before the representation of Freya, and the Godi speaks her words. (This rite may be altered or modified as is appropriate for the special needs of the afflicted one.)

Kindle a ceremonial flame in the ritual area, and place banners or images of the High Ones to the North. Have mead and a ceremonial drinking horn on hand, plus small blocks of wood and writing or scribing implements. (If the rite is held indoors, pieces of clean parchment or paper may be used instead of wood, and burned in a cauldron or brazier.)

After a period of silence for 25 heartbeats the Godi says:

> *Great Odin, we gather here to seek*
> *An end to pain, then peace and healing*
> *For one of our people.*
> *Thine is the wisdom.*
> *Thine is the power to give victory.*
> *Thus we ask for thy help, here and now.*
> *Hail Odin!*

All: *Hail Odin!*

Then the Godia says:

> *Good Freya, we gather here to seek*
> *An end to pain, then peace and healing*
> *For one of our people.*

> *Thine is the magic,*
> *For those who are worthy.*
> *Thus we ask for thy help, here and now.*
> *Hail Freya!*

All: *Hail Freya!*

Then the Godi says:

> *Great Thor, we gather here to seek*
> *An end to pain, then peace and healing*
> *For one of our people.*
> *Thou hast vast strength*
> *And the joy of the Gods.*
> *Thus we ask for thy help, here and now.*
> *Hail Thor!*

All: *Hail Thor!*

Hold a Blot at this time to strengthen the afflicted one and to purify those attending.

Next, after a pause of 25 heartbeats the Godi says:

> *Now let us work the runes of healing,*
> *That strength and healing be done.*

All gather by the fire, as the Godia and Godi explain the nature of the problem. If all in the gathering do not know the one for whom healing is being worked, then he or she is described enough for a mental image to be formed. Pour mead into the gathering's drinking horn, and into the horns or tankards of those in attendance.

One who is closest by blood, or the best friend, takes a block of wood and sketches thereon a symbolic picture of the afflicted person, along with a symbol of the illness, injury or wound. Then he or she sketches a personal symbol of healing, or showing the problem corrected, plus a rune of the God or Goddess who would seem best suited to giving such a healing. Then he or she takes the horn, composes words of request or of spells for the healing, drinks (so also do the others in the group), and puts the wood block into the flames, saying these or similar words:

> *As the flames consume this wood,*
> *May strength and power go forth,*
> *And may healing be done.*
> *Hail Odin!*

The drinking horn is then passed sunwise (clockwise) to the next person, and the Godia or Godi gives another block of wood to the next person for the process to be repeated.

When all have scribed their petitions to the Gods and sent them forth through the flames, other workings may be done, as the members of the Grove so desire. When all has been worked, the Godi says:

> *At this time have we sent runes of power*
> *And of healing, drawing on the High Ones*
> *On the lands, and our people,*
> *That our comrade and friend be made whole again.*
> *I do ask Great Balder, giver of life and of joy*
> *To work with our good friend,*
> *That healing be done, and soon.*
> *Hail Balder!*

All: *Hail Balder!*

Then the Godia says:

> *At this time have we done our best,*
> *And our wills shall ever weave healing, and strength*
> *For our good comrade to be made whole again.*
> *I do ask the Gentle Maiden Iduna, giver of immortality,*
> *To give to our friend some small portion of*
> *The life she gives to the Gods themselves*
> *That healing be done, and soon.*
> *Hail Iduna!*

All: *Hail Iduna!*

The Godi or Godia finally says:

> *This meet of the Gods is done.*
> *May our friend be healed.*
> *Hail Odin!*

All: *Hail Odin!*

Those closest to the afflicted one may be given a torch or candle lit from the need-fire, the flame burned in their own shrines (if it is practical) until healing be done.

Rite for Healing of the Spirit

If one has suffered a battering of the mind, soul and spirit, this rite may be performed as often as needed for the afflicted one to attain a proper balance within. The version of the ceremony given here is only a sample of what is intended, as this ritual, more than most, is to be tailored by the participants, by family and close friends, in order to tailor it more closely to the needs of the afflicted one. Those closest to the afflicted one should be present, and if possible, members of the family or close friends act as Godi and Godia. As is customary, if a woman of the folk is not available to act as Godia, place flowers before the representation of Freya, and the Godi speaks her words.

Kindle a ceremonial flame in the ritual area, and place banners or images of the High Ones to the North. Have mead and a ceremonial drinking horn on hand. Include on the altar before the representations of the Gods a sword, dagger, or other weapon—ideally one with which the afflicted person is familiar. In the days preceding this rite, the afflicted one should have been given further training. If he or she has been hurt or mistreated by others, then strong defense and a ready will to use the weapon with deadly effectiveness is instilled, should the need again arise. Should less definable pressures have caused the pain and inner damage, then the weapons training will be calculated to conquer one's own weaknesses, and to shape events to work in one's favor.

The family, friends and the Godi and Godia counsel the afflicted one and become very close and supportive, ready to help at any and all times in the future. Rearrange life and circumstance so that the harmful situation will not come again, or at least will be greatly limited.

The afflicted one should read or hear several legends, myths or stories of those who have been magically healed, or healed themselves and then went on to do great or heroic deeds. He or she meditates on these stories in dimness or in the dark, hooded and robed.

237

When it is determined that the rite should begin, a muffled drum is slowly beaten. Either the Godi or the Godia (whoever will have the lesser role in this ceremony), hooded, robed, and masked in black, silently goes and brings back the afflicted one, to stand before the one chosen as Godi or Godia for the rite. The slow beating of the drum stops as the Godi or Godia speaks:

I summon thee, _____ of our people,
I am told that thou hast been greviously wounded.
A wound of the soul and spirit.
This is not the first time that thy blood has been shed,
Nor the first time that thy strong spirit has been battered.
But it is one of the very worst,
And the scars may well be with thee for the rest of thy life.

That which can be seen has been healed,
Yet of far greater importance is that which cannot be seen:
Thy spirit, thy pride, thy love of life.
As thou well knowest, these are the most critical by far.

_____, hear me well.
The Dark Chieftain has placed his mark upon thee,
And thou must follow him into the shadows,

If thou canst rejoin those of thine own good people.
As thy chieftain and Godi (Godia) of our family and folk,
I ask thee: art thou healed, and ready to join us again?

An affirmative answer is given.

_____, the Dark Chieftain has placed his mark upon thee,
And thou must follow him into the shadows,
If thou canst not rejoin those of thine own good people.
As thy chieftain and Godi (Godia) of our family and folk,
I ask thee: art thou healed, and ready to strengthen thyself
Both within and without, for thirteen times thirteen moons,
If need be?

An affirmative answer is given.

_____, *the Dark Chieftain has placed his mark upon thee,*
And thou must follow him into the shadows,
If thou canst not rejoin those of thine own good people.
As thy chieftain and Godi (Godia) of our family and folk,
I ask thee: Dost thou now swear upon thy honor,
And before the High Gods of Valhalla,
That thou now relinquishest all within thy body, soul and spirit
Which is injured, all that is weak, all that is sick,
All which is vulnerable and all that is negative?
Dost thou now firmly forswear these?

An affirmative answer is given.

Then remember what thou hast said here,
Before thy leader and Godi (Godia),
Before the High Gods of Valhalla
And before Death himself.
Remember, for they shall never forget thine oath here,
And thou mayst be called to account
If thou dost not always strive to be best!

The subject's weapon is handed to him (or her), and the Godi or Godia says:

_____, *show us how thou hast recovered.*
Show before thine own family, before thy close friends,
Before thine own people, in flesh and in spirit,
That thou art ready and worthy to rejoin us.
That thou art again one of the very best,
Beloved of the High Gods,
And all of us who are thine own people.

Proficiency with the weapon is demonstrated. Then the Godi or Godia says:

What thou hast done is good.
Thou can take thy part to protect thyself
And our people, should the need ever arise.
Before Odin, Thor and Freya,
Thou hast done well.

Now tell to us here, and before the Gods,
Of thine own goals and ideals for the future.

In his or her own words, the subject tells of hopes and plans for times to come. Those in the ceremony may ask further, may make suggestions and generally should be supportive, cheerful and heartily ready to help.

After the discussion, the assembled folk and the Godi or Godia may decide to assign a new quest, or something which must be studied or learned over the next year. When all has been said, the sacramental drinking horn is filled, and the Godi or Godia gives it to the subject, saying:

_____, *we are thy people, and we will always be with thee.*
Thou mayst count on our help, as we may count on thine.
Always remember that we are close to thee,
Though the stars fall or the world end.
I give thee honor in the names of the High Gods,
May youth and joy and love and spirit be ever thine.
May the blessed Iduna give thee a complete renewal.
Drink now, and know that thou wilt never be alone!

After the sacramental drink, the Godi or Godia proclaims:

This rite is ended.
Let us welcome our good comrade
And know good times to seal our bond.
Hail Odin!

All: *Hail Odin!*

A celebration should be held for the duration of the evening. The Godi and Godia and those of family and friends henceforth stay close, in times to come, as long as their support is needed.

The Runner's Seid

Running is an exercise unchanged from the times of our fore-fathers. It is good for the heart, lungs, and indeed tones the entire body. Such exercise takes will power and has a certain amount of dif-ficulty, but the steady, hard exercise of the body can be linked with discipline of the mind and clear visualizations to accomplish goals in ways that may not be obvious.

This rite has the capability of slightly altering the flow of pro-bability so that you will be able to accomplish things that are within the realm of probability. It works, though explaining just how it does so can be difficult.

The best place to run is out in nature, out in the Sun and the fresh air. Warm up as you normally do, and fix in your mind the seid that you plan to work. Just before you begin to run, say quietly or think to yourself these or similar words:

> *Hear me, Beings of Nature!*
> *At this time do I begin to state my need,*
> *Within my mind,*
> *And give thee the power*
> *With every breath that I take*
> *To make it real.*
> *Gnomes of earth and of wood,*
> *Sylphs of air, undines of water,*
> *Creatures of fire that love the Sun,*
> *Use the power I send forth*
> *To work the seid that I image,*
> *That we all may prosper.*
> *As Freya is my friend,*
> *So shall it be!*

Then fix firmly in your mind the goal that you wish to attain, and continue to hold the visualization as clearly as you can for all of the time that you are running.

While you run, imagine clearly that with every breath you take in you draw power from everywhere about you. Hold it within you for just a moment while you impress the image of your goal upon it, and then exhale it.

Inhale pure white energy, feel the pressure within you for a moment while you charge it with your goal, then send it out to be used by the Nature beings. Repeat again and again for as long as you are running. The more exertion, sweat, mileage and will power you put into this spell, the better it will work.

When you finally finish your run for the day, say the following (or similar) words quietly, or think them, while you are phasing down:

> *I've given thee the power, small friends,*
> *Use thy seid and make it happen.*
> *So be it!*

Then as you cool down and shower, put all thoughts of the seid out of your mind for the rest of the day.

Seid: Casting the Ball of Light

The following is an exercise of seid which can help you to attain something which is within the realm of possibility by linking you with Nature and the Gods, and subtly with others of humankind.

The best place to perform this rite is a place out in Nature—in trees and hills and fresh air. It may be done either day or night, as the need dictates, though most will prefer to work the rite by day out in the Sun. If you cannot get to a place of Nature, then use a more or less secluded yard or patio, or a room which is bright and cheerful. When an indoors setting is used for working, it is proper to have banners, statues or other symbols of Odin, Freya and Thor to the north of the ritual area. Some will find the the mood of seid is enhanced when there is incense like the smell of trees, and a candle, to be lit just before beginning the rite.

If conditions are right, you may wish to dress in the garb of an earlier age, something with a feeling of primal strength and simplicity, a costume which tends to "put you apart" from the mundane world. You may wish to refer to some of the sketches elsewhere in this book for some ideas, or be guided by your own instincts and fantasies.

Go to the place which you have chosen and stand at the center of the ritual area, holding the spear in your right hand with its butt upon the floor. Gaze off to the north for the space of 25 heartbeats or longer, placing your mind in a serene, quiet and ready meditative state.

Lift your arms out in salute, saying (or even thinking) these or similar words:

> *With this rite I place myself*
> *In closer touch with all of Nature.*
> *May the threads which weave the world.*
> *And circumstance, and destiny,*
> *Incline to me, that which I need.*
> *So be it!*

Then fix firmly in your mind your goal, and continue to hold the visualization as clearly as you can for the time of the spell.

Draw your hands back and cup them, fingers open, opposite one another before you, not quite touching. As you turn and take three steps to the left (starting with your left foot)—slow, smooth, and easy—roll your hands as though you were rolling within them a round, very soft ball of light.

Just as smoothly, pivot and turn back (stepping off on the right foot) and continue rolling the imaginary ball of light as you step three gliding steps to the right, pivot, and come slowly back again, continuing to roll the ball of light and continuing to bear in mind your goal.

You will feel your palms getting warmer, and feel the pressure of the light ball that you have imaged. The ball of light will become larger and larger, and your hands will tend to move further and further apart as you continue, until eventually your arms are spread wide.

Then come to a halt facing north and slowly, with considerable force, compress the ball of imaginary light tighter and tighter and more intensely until it is finally only about half a foot across. Then impress your thoughts, the seid which you desire to accomplish, strongly into the glowing ball.

And hurl it away with your right hand! You will get the distinct impression that it has flown into countless shards of light. You need only then to say:

So be it!

(It is particularly interesting that, if you are not asking for anything but performing this rite as simply a joyous act out in the open of a park or woodland, the presence of the magical Freya becomes more and more distinctly felt. Sensitive individuals have used this rite as a means of communicating with her.)

Rite of the Flaming Spear

The following is a solitary weapons exercise which has a number of uses and benefits the warrior on several levels. Taken simply as it is given here, the exercise improves coordination and is a mild exercise regimen if practiced often. Also, it will tend to build powers of visualization and memory.

A second result, if practiced frequently over a period of time with similar solitary rites, is a kind of easy and ready confidence and a serene, receptive mind which can quickly and intuitively assess the threat in an emergency situation (whatever it might be) and enable the warrior to take countering action without conscious thought and without the handicap of fear or worry.

A third and equally subtle result is application of a seid in which you can shield yourself with a kind of magic from the bad influences that can converge on you, i.e., pressures of job, debts, disagreements and misguided dislike by others. Practiced until it becomes second nature, and used when a stressful time approaches, this rite has the capability of slightly altering the flow of probability so that you will be guarded and safer, and difficulties, problems and enemies will be turned back on themselves. It works, though explaining just how it does can be difficult.

Setting and Weapon

The best place to perform this rite is a place out in Nature, with trees, hills and fresh air. It may be done either day or night, as the need dictates, though most will prefer to work the rite by night. If you cannot get to a place of Nature, then use more or less secluded yard or patio, or a room which has sufficient space for you to work clearly. When an indoors setting is used for working, it is proper to have banners, statues, or other symbols of Odin, Freya and Thor to the north of the ritual area. Some will find that the mood of seid is enhanced when there are candles placed at North, East, South and West, to be lit just before beginning the rite.

If conditions are right, you may wish to dress in the garb of an earlier age—something with a feeling of primal strength and simplicity, a costume which tends to "put you apart" from the mundane world. You may wish to refer to some of the sketches elsewhere in this book for some ideas, or be guided by your own instincts and fantasies.

The weapon is ideally an iron-tipped spear slightly longer than your own height. The butt of the weapon should be sharpened and perhaps metal tipped also. However, it is acceptable to practice with a quarterstaff or a sturdy pole of this length, since the exercise of mind, spirit, and body is of primary importance here.

The ceremony of the Flaming Spear should be done slowly and deliberately, though as it becomes second nature to you, occasionally it will be worthwhile to do it at maximum speed, to practice precision and force.

The Rite

Go to the place which you have chosen and stand at the center of the ritual area, holding the spear in your right hand with its butt upon the floor. Gaze off to the north for the space of 25 heartbeats or longer, placing your mind in a serene, quiet and ready meditative state.

Lift the spear, take it in both hands, and hold it out in salute at arm's length horizontally before you, saying (or even thinking) in these or similar words:

> *Hear me, O High Ones!*
> *With this rite I do shield myself*
> *And throw back all which is against me.*
> *May this weapon be cast with flames of the spirit,*
> *Sparked from far Valhalla*
> *To burn brightly between the worlds*
> *And which I shall see in the eye of my mind.*
> *Thor, give me strength and a steady hand,*

Freya, give me seid to overcome all obstacles,
Odin, grant me wisdom and victory.
So be it!

Draw the spear back against your body in a "ready" stance, imaging in your mind, as clearly as you can during all of this exercise, that the spear is flickering from point of butt with bright blue flames, a fire which is harmless to you, but which none other can stand.

Step around to face East, still in the "ready" stance. Picture in your imagination that an ominous figure in windy yellow, the image of all which worries and threatens you, is attacking you from the east, with his lance thrusting at your chest. Raise your horizontal spear up full arm's length above you to parry your imaginary opponent's point up and harmlessly overhead. Then bring the spear down hard to your knees to block any low blow. Imagine that your opponent in yellow is staggering back for a moment to regain his balance. Take a step forward and thrust the point of your spear hard into the imaginary yellow figure. Then look the other way (to the West), jerk the spear out, and jam the butt directly into any other figure coming up to attack behind you. Draw back to your ready position facing East, visualizing that the figure in windy yellow is falling and dissolving, and gone.

Step around to face South, still in the "ready" stance. Picture in your imagination that an ominous figure in fiery red, the image of all which worries and threatens you, is attacking you from the south, with his lance thrusting at your throat. Raise your spear vertically and sweep it sharply to one side and then to the other, parrying your imaginary opponent's point harmlessly off to the side. Imagine that your opponent in red is staggering back for a moment to regain his balance. Take a step forward with your spear overhead and thrust the point of your spear hard into the upper part of the imaginary red figure, and work the spear hard from side to side. Then look the other way (to the north), jerk the spear out, and jam the butt into the upper part of any other figure coming up to attack behind you. Again, work it hard from side to side after striking. Draw back to your ready position facing South, visualizing that the figure in fiery red is falling and dissolving, and gone.

Step around to face West, still in the ready stance. Picture in your imagination that an ominous figure in watery blue, the image of all which worries and threatens you, is attacking you from the east, with his lance thrusting at your stomach. Raise your horizontal spear up full arm's length above you to parry your imaginary opponent's point up and harmlessly overhead. Then bring the spear down hard to your knees, to block any possible low blow. Raise your spear up to vertical and sweep it sharply to one side and then to the other, parrying your imaginary opponent's point harmlessly off to the side. Imagine that your opponent in blue is staggering back for a moment to regain his balance. Take a step forward and thrust the point of your spear hard into the middle of the imaginary blue figure. Then look the other way (to the east), jerk the spear out, and jam the butt into the middle of any other figure coming up to attack behind you. Draw back to your ready position facing West, visualizing that the figure in watery blue is falling and dissolving, and gone.

Step around to face North, still in the ready stance. Picture in your imagination that an ominous figure in earth green, the image of all which worries and threatens you, is attacking you from the north, with his lance thrusting at your groin. Raise your spear up to vertical and sweep it sharply to one side and then to the other, parrying your imaginary opponent's point harmlessly off to the side. Imagine that your opponent in red is staggering back for a moment to regain his balance. Take a step forward with your spear overhead and thrust the point of your spear hard into the lower part of the imaginary green figure, and work the spear hard from side to side. Then look the other way (to the South), jerk the spear out, and jam the butt into the lower part of any other figure coming up to attack behind you. Again, work it hard from side to side after striking. Draw back to your ready position facing North, visualizing that the figure in earth green is falling and dissolving, and gone.

Crouch down and stick out the butt of the spear at ankle level and pivot around clockwise one turn completely to trip and crack the ankles or shins of anyone else—perhaps clad in white—who might be attempting one final attack on you. Look around and see that all the figures which have troubled you are now down, dissolved, *and all are gone.*

Lift the spear, take it in both hands, and hold it out in salute at arm's length horizontally before you face toward the North, saying (or even thinking) in these or similar words:

O great Gods, I thank thee,

I return thy flame
With thanks.
Hail Odin!

Imagine that the blue flames of your spear flicker out. Return to the resting position from which you started. Stand for a while holding the spear in your right hand with its butt upon the floor. Gaze off to the North for the space of 25 heartbeats or longer, with your mind in a serene, quiet, and ready meditative state, and savor your victory over all which troubles you.

Advanced Variations

When you have completely mastered this rite and its visualizations with a spear, begin doing it with a lightweight, single-handed sword in lieu of the spear.

As a final phase, ultimately adapt the exercise to using a sword and a lightweight shield (fiberboard or plastic, about 18 inches in diameter, with a leather arm strap and a metal handle).

Lust Seid

This rite is performed under the patronage of the beautiful Freya, before whose beauty and magics neither God nor man could stand. The man and woman who perform this ceremony should best have considerable passion for one another, and one or both should have experience in working seid, second sight, or various forms of divination, if at all possible. If experience is lacking, then more practice may be needed, although this should be no problem for a pair of lovers who truly desire one another!

An entire evening should be allowed for this spell, with the Godi and Godia being alone together and uninterrupted. A copy of this rite should be studied carefully by each in advance, so that the words, meanings and visualizations behind the words are clear. The words that are spoken by each during the rite should be fairly close to the original as written here, but they obviously should not be read.

At the northern wall of the chamber set an altar with a representation of Freya upon it, and a set of horns or antlers about the goddess icon. A symbol of what is desired should be carved, drawn, or assembled from symbols that are meaningful to both the Godi and Godia, and similarly placed upon the altar. Any writing should be done using the ancient runic system. Place several candles upon the altar and about the chamber. Furs should be on the bed and the floor, if they are on hand. Have incense, music, mead or wine, and some food available.

Talismans of the Gods and Norse-style jewelry should be worn, at least at first. Ritual costume, if any is worn, may be a fantasy version of ancient garb—or simply long cloaks worn alone.

The couple may discuss the purpose for their seid, how it ties to their lives, their desires, and to the lives of others. Particularly important points should be emphasized with kisses and caresses.

When all is in readiness, the Godi and Godia should stand or kneel before the altar, touching, as they say, in these or similar words:

Godi
or Godia: *O mistress of beauty and of sensuality,*
We shall work this rite in thy honor,
And with thy warm blessings.
Grant us that which we desire,
For we draw it toward us with the passion
That we have for each other.

Godi
or Godia: *May our ecstasy go forth,*
To worlds beyond worlds,
Carrying our will and our desire
And with thy blessing,
So may it be done!

Each alternately says some version of the following, and tries to feel it within themselves, as they embrace. Each may guide the hands of the other as they speak, so that the feeling of welling power is intense:

I give my love and my passion to thee,
In the name of the lovely Freya,
As we hold each other.
The rainbow light that joins Earth and Sky
Begins to flow through us both.

I feel the rainbow power rise up into my toes,
As mine touch thine
Through my legs, and into my cup (staff),
Pressed with passion against thee.
There to burn with desire
That grows ever more intense.

I feel some of the power rise into
The center of my body, and radiate out like the Sun
As I hold myself against thee,
That thou may feel it also.
It rises into my breast, pressed now against thee.
It rises into my heart, which beats for thee.
Up into my throat and neck, as I kiss thine.

> *The rainbow power glows within my eyes,*
> *As I gaze into thine.*
> *It fills my head and rises through my hair,*
> *To glow and flare above us*
> *As we embrace and kiss again.*
> *By Freya, I desire thee!*

Godi: *Draw this power from me, beloved,*
> *And let me give it back to thee*
> *As we think on our seid, and our desire,*
> *As we make love.*

They embrace and kiss with much feeling.

Godia: *Draw this power from me, beloved,*
> *And let me give it back to thee*
> *As we think on our seid, and our desire,*
> *As we make love.*

They embrace and kiss with much feeling.

At this point the two should endeavor to make the passion within themselves and each other as great and as intense as possible.

Both should make it a point to concentrate on the subject of their seid during lovemaking and especially at the climax. At that time each should feel that power is being pulsed more and more strongly between their bodies, held for as long as possible, then fading away as the vast power goes forth to alter events to accomplish their seid.

When the last flow of passion is spent, each says:

> *The seid which we desire*
> *Is now done.*
> *So be it!*

Relaxation and refreshments follow, with a final review of the goals for this rite.

Lore

Runes

The runic *futhark* (named for the first six letters of the system) is one of the most fascinating legacies of the ancient Norse. It can be used to replace Roman letters when serving as a handy personal code or when inscribing a name or a spell on a talisman for personal use. Each rune can serve as a key center for a spell or talisman.

The runes each have meanings within meanings. The most obvious ones are given here. Anybody interested in pursuing further the metaphysics of the runic systems might want to read some of the specialty books in this field. Some think that valuable clues to runic mysteries can be found in the sections of Robert Graves' masterwork *The White Goddess* which pertain to the Celtic Tree Alphabet (*ogham*). There were certainly contacts between the users of the runes and the users of oghams throughout history in Europe as well as in the British Isles.

A rune is defined as anything mysterious—a poem, secret, spell, song and so on. Historically though, a rune may be a single letter, a long chant, or simply whatever it takes to make a spell.

Although the structure of the runic futhark parallels that of the Roman alphabet, there is a wide variety of additional runes beyond the usual futhark series used for writing. Some of these additional runes, or holy signs, are given here.

Runes come in several different systems, based on their places and eras of origin. A rune can be a symbol of something abstract. There are those simple alphabetical runes of the futhark, and those which have been created to symbolize a situation or a spell. Both are presented here. This section cannot be considered the final authority, but it does reflect an authentic adaptation of the Anglo-Saxon or Old English system in use in the British Isles from about 500 to 1100 C.E. There are other systems, and the reader is encouraged to find one that seems comfortable.

In order to create a runic talisman, take note of the runes corresponding to the letters of the spell you want to write. You may want to make a draft copy of longer spells. Go to some remote or private place where, in your own words, you should call upon the Goddess or God whose good services you wish to borrow. In your own words, invoke your patron deity. Carve the runes onto leather, stone, or whatever material you have chosen. Make a small offering of ale, and begin wearing or using your talisman constantly.

Number	Rune	Description
4		"A" (Ansuz) Signals, receiving messages, gifts, God, source of divine wisdom, explore the depths, experience the divine, also cloak, conceal, protect, shelter.
26		"A" (Asch) Renewing old strength, remembering one's experiences, becoming stronger, good advice, childbirth, naming a child before the Gods.
18		"B" (Beorc) The Sun, beginning or starting something, growth, rebirth, new life; animals, birds, and fish; expansion.
31		"C" (Chalk) Barrenness, poison, noxious vapors, "man dead" rune.
23		"D" (Day) Day, hope, great changes in self, royalty, nobility, king, a doorway or portal, great height and depth in all things.
19		"E" (Eho) A horse, associated with the Sun, transition and change, new home, new attitudes, movement, progress, speed; conquering of death, or old age, loyalty.
1		"F" (Feoh) Material goods, possessions of the family and folk, ambition satisfied, love attained, status gained.

Number	Rune	Description
7		"G" (Gift) A festival, renewal, partnership, a union, sharing, a gift, rewards for loyalty.
9		"H" (Hail) Hail, disruption, natural forces that damage and disrupt, bad luck, abstinence, enforced chastity, damage, bad weather.
11		"I" (Ice) Standstill, the essence of ice, freezing, that which slows or impedes, delay.
12		"J" (Jera) Harvest, a full year, a prosperous year, a good reward for hard work.
6		"K" (Ken) Opening up, a torch or light, enlightenment.
21		"L" (Lagu) Flow, water, sea, waves, primal source of fertility or fruitfulness and/or growth, unpredictable elemental force.
20		"M" (Mann) Self, knowing oneself, one's family or folk, modesty, humankind.

Number	Rune	Description
10		"N" (Need)　Constraint, need, necessity, lessons, cruelty which is a part of the way things must be, sorrow, school of hard knocks, rebirth, changes, delays.
25		"A" (Ac) Golden flowers, initiation into the mysteries of love, inspiration, joy, teaching, finding a teacher, spoken truth.
14		"P" (Peord) Initiation, searching, secrecy.
5		"R" (Ride) A journey, journey of the soul after death, a talisman for luck in traveling, action, message.
16		"S" or "Z" (Sun)　Wholeness, mystic eloquence, female enchantment, recharging, regeneration, creativity.
17		"T" (Tyr or Tac)　Warrior, victory, your guiding star, joyous lust, justice.
2		"U" or "V" (Ur)　Strength, health, male and female principles uniting, passion, the body, that which is sacrificed.

Number	Rune	Description
27		"Y" (Yr) Building, craftsmanship, pride in honest labor.
8		"W" (Wyn) Joy, ending or absence of suffering and sorrow, wonder, well-being.
3		"Th" (Thorn) Irritation, hidden negative forces, hostility, also a portal or transformation, supernatural entity.
29		"Ia" (Iar) The World Tree, magician, godi/godia, concentrated magical wisdom, flexibility, also the danger in gathering wisdom or in exploration.
		"Ea" (Ear) Male lust, angry passion, breaking down the old to make way for the new.
30		"Q" (Quern) The human made perfect, the apple of wisdom.
33		"G" (Gar) Symbol of royalty, scepter, spear.

Number	*Rune*	*Description*
24		"O" (Odal) Retreat, native land, your home, your folk or people, property, inherited possessions.
15		"X" (Elx) Protection through wisdom, defense, control emotions, the bridge, "man alive," the stag or stag-king.
13		"EI" (Eihwaz) Defense, death, rune magic, protective powers.
22		"NG" (Ing) Fertility, a great hero, a God, creative power, new life, a new way.
32		"ST" (Stone) Hardness, steadfastness, resistance to change, permanence.

Rune	*Description*
	WOLF'S HOOK death
	WOLF'S CROSS unchangeable fate
	FIRE EYE far-seeing, second sight, the art of fascination (Freya's magic).
	Healing, rejuvenation, power being radiated out.
	Healing, rejuvenation, power being drawn in.
	Dissipating, radiating.

Rune	*Description*
	Thorshammer—MJOLNIR Thor's Hammer Strength, impact, force, drive, vast force used wisely.
	ODIN'S EYE all-seeing, all-knowing God-presence.
	Odin in his "wanderer" or "mercurial" aspect.
	Rune of Power— Power radiating outwards.
	Death—Disruption, disjointing, termination, destructive piercing, breaking down.

Rune	*Description*
	Gentleness, healing
	MIMIR The mind, meditation, concentration, introspection.
	Odin in the "All-Father" aspect Wisdom, intellect.
	MIDGARD—Middle Earth The Earth, the world, solidity, depth.
	SOL—The Sun Radiant power. The year's cycle.

Rune	*Description*
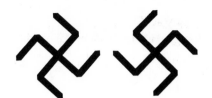	**MUNDILFARI** Raw power, immoderate force, uncontrolled power, creative but violent—a god aspect.
	**MUNDILFARA** Moderated power, gentle force, controlled power, creative and expansive—a goddess aspect.
	**ZIO—the eldest god** God force, power, thrusting, questing, outgoing, conquest, sending out energy.
	**ZISA—the eldest goddess** Goddess force, containing, nurturing, fructifying, inspiring, pulling in energy.
	**VANADIS** Enclosing, fortifying, sealing.

Rune	*Description*
————	**VANAGOTT** Being, existing, suspended, drifting.
	GROTTE—the vast whirlpool of legend. The realms of Hel, drawing in, draining, storing.
	HVERGILMIR—the magic mill of legend The realms of heaven, Valhalla giving forth, creating, giving of bounty.
	**HLUODONIA** Happiness at hearth and home. A Moon rune.
	HLODYN Security and safety. Another Moon rune.

Rune	*Description*

FAGRAHVEL
Success, popularity

MUNDILFARI
Power and magnetism

ODIN'S CROSS
A unity or balance in all things

TRISKELON—Flowing power
Also a place-name symbol in honor
of Odin.
There are many variations of this
rune.

THOR'S HAMMER
Also called MJOLNIR
Strength, power, courage, endurance,
ruggedness, protection.

DRAGON'S EYE
Raw nature, the subconscious, "the
dweller on the threshold" of the
mind.

Rune

Description

THE SIGN OF THE VEHMIC COURTS
Active defense, and active protection.

ACHTWAN: The Great Wheel of Existence
The Wheel of the Year
The Wheel of Life
(A symbol of great antiquity)

Runes symbolizing the Gods and the Festivals

Odin as Wanderer

Odin as Allfather

Freya

Thor

Sif

Loki

Hel

Balder

Nanna

Aeger, Norns

Ran

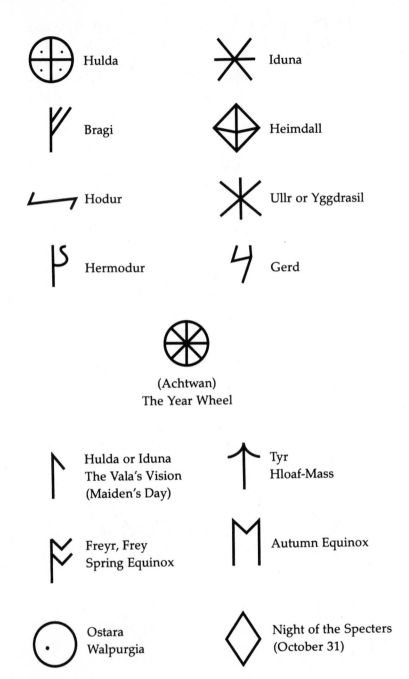

Hulda

Iduna

Bragi

Heimdall

Hodur

Ullr or Yggdrasil

Hermodur

Gerd

(Achtwan)
The Year Wheel

Hulda or Iduna
The Vala's Vision
(Maiden's Day)

Tyr
Hloaf-Mass

Freyr, Frey
Spring Equinox

Autumn Equinox

Ostara
Walpurgia

Night of the Specters
(October 31)

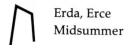 Erda, Erce
Midsummer

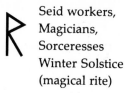 Seid workers,
Magicians,
Sorceresses
Winter Solstice
(magical rite)

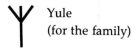 Yule
(for the family)

Rune-Talisman Rite

If you determine that you have need of help or protection or whatever a rune charm can offer, then it is proper to create and to consecrate such a talisman before the Gods. Such a consecration rite is best conducted by oneself in some place of wilderness and solitude such as a forest glade, the top of a mountain, on a river island or some such locale. If such is impractical, then perform it by candlelight in one's own living place.

You may prefer to carve or paint the proper runes on your stone, wooden, or other talisman base before you perform the rite, although if you choose to take the materials with you and create it in the wild, then make an advance sketch to carry along.

Go to the place which you have chosen and spend some time in quiet contemplation of what you want to accomplish. Think over all aspects of your problem. Then find some place which seems right for addressing the Gods, and say these or similar words:

> *Far, clear skies, warm Sun,*
> *Lakes and rivers, far lands and mountains,*
> *Thou art witness to what I do here.*

Then look to the skies and say:

> *Wise Allfather Odin, wanderer and victory giver,*
> *Look favorably on what I do here,*
> *And grant my wishes*
> *That I may ever better be thy friend and comrade.*

> *Strong and hearty Thor, laughing and undefeated,*
> *Look favorably on what I do here,*
> *And grant my wishes*
> *That I may ever better be thy friend and comrade.*

Beautiful and magical Freya, whose powers none can resist,
Look favorably on what I do here,
And grant my wishes
That I may ever better be thy friend and comrade.

Then bring forth your talisman or, if you desire to make it, now is the time to do so. Traditionally the rune or runes symbolic of the seid you wish to accomplish are marked on one side while your name (or the special "Holy Name" by which you want to be known by the Gods) is marked on the other. Most importantly, do what feels right and proper.

When your talisman is ready, sprinkle it with fresh water and hold it up to the skies, saying these or similar words:

Skies, Sun, waters, and lands,
Mark well what I have done here.
Under the rule of the High Gods of Far Valhalla
I call on thee to work for me
To bring to pass that which I have symbolized
With this talisman of strength.

State in your own words what you desire to accomplish. Then say these or similar words:

O High Ones of the Rainbow Bridge,
Thou hast heard that which is my need
And my desire.
Bend thy power that this be done.
And may skies, Sun, waters, and lands
Work as thy servants for so long as is needed
Until all is accomplished.

If you feel it proper to make any special vow before the Gods, any promise that you will make or price you will pay for accomplishment of your need, then now is the time to specify it before Nature and the Gods. Then close by saying these or similar words:

Odin, Freya, Thor, my will is thine.
Grant, I do ask, that which I have requested,
That my powers may be increased

And thine as well,
Upon this Middle Earth.
In the Names of all who are holy and powerful,
So mote it be.

Salute the Gods in your own way, and depart.

For best effect, a rune talisman should be worn or otherwise kept on your person. When you sleep it should be kept next to you or under your pillow.

For so long as you use the talisman, it is well to "recharge" and renew it using this latter invocation and holding it up before the Full Moon. Two weeks later at the time of the dark Moon, use the same invocation while washing it in clear, cold water.

Rune Divination

There are several very effective methods for divination of the future using runestones, and for a thorough study of the matter you should buy one of the excellent books now on the market. Some will even come with a full set of runestones. It is likely that some of the rune meanings may differ from the ones in this book, since these various works have been researched from very different sources and different eras. Familiarize yourself with a couple of systems and see which "feels" better to you, and go with that one.

Divination is a means for foretelling the trends of the future, or things existing but as yet unknown to you, by using the powers of the subconscious mind. (The subconscious is itself the doorway to the paranormal, ESP, magic and such, but that's another story.) Much depends on your own intuition, or "gut feeling," and a lot of practice helps. It's fun, and the practice can be engrossing.

To start, go along a river or a shoreline and make a good-sized collection of flat pebbles, one-half to one inch square, because they appeal to you. Dry them thoroughly and use paint or indelible ink to mark a complete collection of runes upon them, one rune on one side of each stone. Dry them thoroughly while you obtain a soft pouch of cloth or chamois for them.

Keep the stones near you for the first several nights especially. You may wish to consecrate them using the talisman rite as found elsewhere in this book.

To use the runestones, settle down in some quiet place and think for awhile on the matter for which you need divination. Light a candle and concentrate on it, with the matter in the back of your mind. Then reach into the sack without looking and feel the various stones. Sense the one which feels the most "live" to you, and withdraw it, saying: "This is the past." Repeat the process and take out another, saying, "This is the present," and lay it down to the right of the first. Finally, repeat the process for a third and final time, saying "This is the future," placing the third stone to the right of the other two. Then look them over, check out the rune meanings in the book, and form your own conclusions.

Alternately, put a blanket on the floor in some quiet place where you have been considering the matter. Think intensely on your problem as you scoop your stones out of their pouch and cast them all on the blanket without looking. Still without looking, kneel and feel the various stones, picking out the ones that feel "live," as above for past, present, and future.

Practice and you'll be surprised at your good results!

Crafting a Drinking Horn

Perhaps one of the most interesting and pleasing items of an Odinist's personal equipment is a genuine drinking horn. It evokes the atmosphere of times far past, of Pagan celebrations under the Moon or in great halls lit by blazing hearths blessed by the Old Gods, of a dim era of myth and legend, of wilderness and magic.

It's difficult to buy such things unless you frequent science-fiction conventions or Renaissance Fairs. Anyhow, making it yourself is a special way of creating something unique.

Surprisingly enough, it's not difficult. The shopping list is short and simple. Get yourself a horn of cow or bull that is big enough for your purposes—a smaller one for your own personal use or a large one for group ceremonies.

Sketch out any runes or any ancient symbolism you would like to have on your own horn, then pay a visit to a shop that sells jewelry-making supplies for the hobbyist, and purchase what is closest to your needs. This could include some silver foil for the lip, which makes drinking from it easier. Or you can take your time and get thin copper, bronze, silver or gold sheet and carefully work it into the designs that you desire. Also get a pack of epoxy cement and a pound or two of beeswax (if you want to make your horn the ancient way) or use epoxy resin and a can of varethane (if you want modern convenience).

Usually you'll acquire a horn that is good and dry. If not, and if you get one that is very fresh, then make up a pot of water and boil the horn over low heat for several hours, or until it can be thoroughly cleaned.

Clean out the horn thoroughly, scraping and scouring the inside. Make certain your horn is completely dry. If you have doubts, put it up in the attic for a month or two of dry air in the summer. You can use a microwave oven, or place the horn in your oven when you are not baking, as the pilot light will supply warm, dry air for dehydrating it.

277

(Tie a red ribbon or something around the horn and drape the ribbon out the door: you don't want to inadvertently bake it at 450 degrees!) Use care in heating the horn at any time, since horn singes or chars easily.

If the lip is too uneven, you may wish to grind it down somewhat with a file or a grinding wheel, then sand with fine paper to get a comfortably smooth lip on it. Similarly, smooth any rough exterior spots that need it.

Then lay your Odinist symbols on the horn and shape them to the curvature of the horn. Get them all ready and epoxy in place. If necessary, glue a brooch set with a semi-precious stone for the end plug so the wax will form a strong seal. If you can, find or carve a raven or wolf's head to fit the end.

I'm a traditionalist. An untreated drinking horn will have a slight, unique bone-like taste to it, which is the way our ancestors knew it. I personally like the taste, but if the horn has not been very thoroughly dried and cleaned, the taste may be strong. Also, if there is any copper in contact with the contents, that also should be sealed to avoid poisoning yourself. For those of you who wish the interior to be coated, melt the beeswax (or prepare several ounces of epoxy resin).

You may want to wear heavy gloves or handle things carefully, perhaps with kitchen tongs, as you pour the melted wax in the horn and slosh it around. Coat the inside thoroughly, but try not to make the coating too thick. If your horn is long and thin, you may wish to let a wax plug harden down in the tip so that it is easier to keep clean. Wax shrinks when it cools, so after cooling be ready to pour in a bit more wax or the plug may leak.

(I have heard of those who prefer to first put on the runes and decorations, and then instead of using beeswax, mix up several ounces of clear epoxy resin and coat it thoroughly both inside and out, then coat the inside with varethane. Such a coating is very durable and you can wash a coated horn in hot water rather than lukewarm. I prefer things that are ancient, even if they are more trouble.)

Next, mix up some epoxy resin. You have kept the outside surfaces of the horn clean, so apply it carefully to fasten your runic symbols in place. Don't try to do too much, as you might have the temptation to do the whole thing in one sitting and end up with the pieces falling or sliding off and the epoxy dripping or running. Work neatly and slowly. Take three or four sittings if necessary to get everything in place to your satisfaction. Try to make it an aesthetic accomplishment as well as a traditional way to quaff your ale.

If you want a holder, sort of a tripod to stand on with a "V" sticking up to lean the horn against, then carve one from wood, or adapt an appropriate piece of statuary.

A natural stand can also perhaps be found in the shape of a branch of wood. If you spend time in the wilderness and keep your eyes open while hiking or camping, or at outdoor rituals, you will likely come across exactly the right gnome-twisted branch that you want. If you frequent the seashore, look for some driftwood; the nereids can do just as good work as the gnomes in making such things.

It will be used for religious purposes, so consecrate your finished horn in the manner that you and your tradition prefer. You have already given it a good, rough-hewn consecration by all the work and care that you've put into it, and maybe (if you're like most of us) even sacrificed a few drops of blood in those little slips that forever seem to be the lot of home craftspersons.

A formal rite may involve ritual purification by earth, air, fire and water, then libations poured and drink partaken of in honor of Odin, Freya, and Thor—all by the light of the Moon and preferably by firelight out in the wilderness. However you do it, it's yours! Use it well, and enjoy your drinking horn for years to come.

Making a Drinking Horn

Horn with drinking lip, runes & God symbols, and end cap in silver.

Runes are engraved with an awl, then inlaid with epoxied silver foil.

Or design with jewels at end and around middle.

A cut-off horn is plugged with a carved wolf's-head or ravens-head, then the plug is sealed with a quantity of wax or (preferably) epoxy.

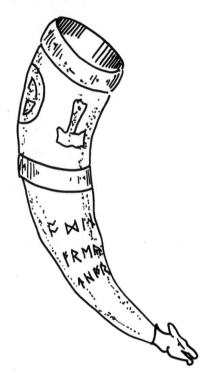

Decorative silver end cap.

Holder of carved wood, driftwood, statuette, or something else appropriate.

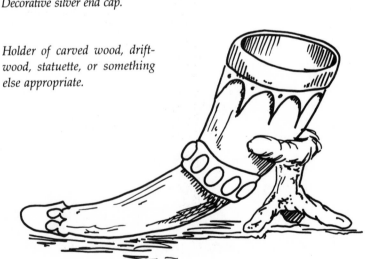

Simple Torches

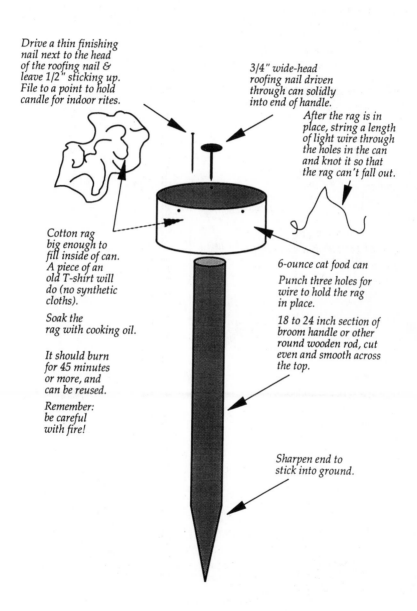

Drive a thin finishing nail next to the head of the roofing nail & leave 1/2" sticking up. File to a point to hold candle for indoor rites.

3/4" wide-head roofing nail driven through can solidly into end of handle.

After the rag is in place, string a length of light wire through the holes in the can and knot it so that the rag can't fall out.

Cotton rag big enough to fill inside of can. A piece of an old T-shirt will do (no synthetic cloths).

Soak the rag with cooking oil.

It should burn for 45 minutes or more, and can be reused.

Remember: be careful with fire!

6-ounce cat food can

Punch three holes for wire to hold the rag in place.

18 to 24 inch section of broom handle or other round wooden rod, cut even and smooth across the top.

Sharpen end to stick into ground.

Typical Banner Construction

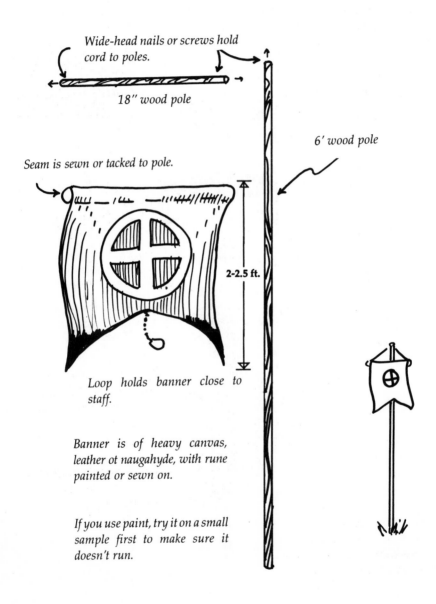

Wide-head nails or screws hold cord to poles.

18" wood pole

6' wood pole

Seam is sewn or tacked to pole.

2-2.5 ft.

Loop holds banner close to staff.

Banner is of heavy canvas, leather ot naugahyde, with rune painted or sewn on.

If you use paint, try it on a small sample first to make sure it doesn't run.

Corner Runes

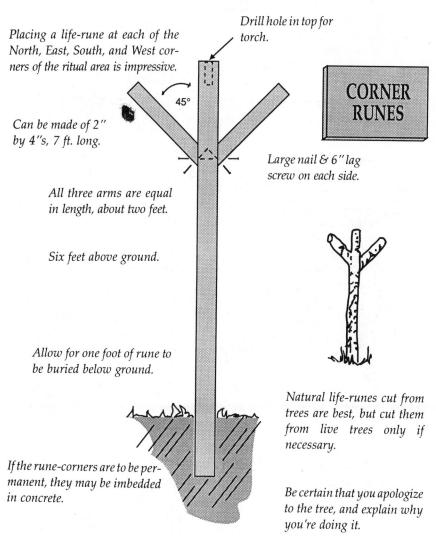

Placing a life-rune at each of the North, East, South, and West corners of the ritual area is impressive.

Drill hole in top for torch.

CORNER RUNES

Can be made of 2" by 4"s, 7 ft. long.

45°

Large nail & 6" lag screw on each side.

All three arms are equal in length, about two feet.

Six feet above ground.

Allow for one foot of rune to be buried below ground.

Natural life-runes cut from trees are best, but cut them from live trees only if necessary.

If the rune-corners are to be permanent, they may be imbedded in concrete.

Be certain that you apologize to the tree, and explain why you're doing it.

More commonly, they can be taken to a ritual site and implanted using a post-hole digger & stored at other times.

Typical Godia Ceremonial Gown

*Long gown worn with necklace
and keys or dagger, with apron
along cape may be worn in cool
or damp weather.*

Godia Ceremonial Dress
Short, or Summer

Short, corded skirt with large
belt plate (preferably with spiral
motif), necklace, and jewelry.

(from Denmark, 800-1000 B.C.)

Typical Ceremonial Garb, Shirt

Peasant-style shirt either belted or tucked. Odin insignia is either a wood or metal pendant, or cloth sewn to shirt. Note trim around all edges.

Godi Ceremonial Garb, Tabard

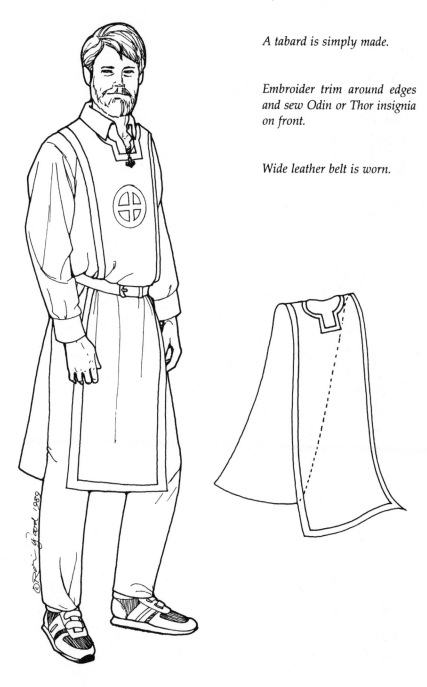

A tabard is simply made.

Embroider trim around edges and sew Odin or Thor insignia on front.

Wide leather belt is worn.

Brewing Your Own Mead

The making of mead, or honey wine, is traditional to those who follow the Norse way. Indeed, this particular kind of brew is probably one of the most ancient known to humankind, yet ever as enjoyable a drink nowadays as it ever has been for thousands of years. Mead is usually the sacramental drink used in Odinist rites. So long as you brew it non-commercially and entirely for the use of yourself and your friends, there is nothing illegal about making your own.

Making good mead is not difficult, so long as you keep all your equipment perfectly clean and so long as you use the best available ingredients.

Whatever kind of honey you use, make certain that it is the best available, preferably bought directly from a beekeeper. Otherwise, a local brand is the next best thing. (Supermarket honey with a national brandname is usually strained, filtered, blended, and boiled entirely too much to be really good!) Generally, the darker and stronger the honey, the more aromatic and full-bodied the mead will be. Amber-colored honeys are pretty much the standard, though I personally have a liking for a strong Eastern variety that I get from a relative in Virginia. The mead made from it is potent, but good!

Use really good and pure water that tastes good. Utilize spring water if you can, and avoid city tap water. Similarly, use the best yeast that you can, buying it from a winemaking supply shop. Although various brands of European yeasts are supposed to be good, it's probably a better idea to buy American brands since they will generally be fresher. Champagne yeast is best for 55 to 70 degree temperatures in your brewing area and emphasizes the flowery bouquet of the mead. Montrachet wine yeast is best for the 65 to 89 degree range and emphasizes the sweetness of the honey, and Tokay wine yeast is for 80 to 100 degree fermenting areas, emphasizing the acidic tang of the brew.

Lemons and tea, or malic acid and grape tannin (or other additives) are used to balance the brew, aid fermentation, and influence flavor, texture and color. I personally like using natural ingredients (the resultant taste and quality is better), but meads made with lemon peel and tea can take up to a year before they are ready to drink, while malic acid, citric acid, or grape tannin will hasten the fermentation so that the mead is ready in only three or four months. Unless you can get lemons straight off the tree, it is wise to soak a store-bought lemon in hot water for a couple minutes before peeling to wash away wax, dirt and insecticide contaminants.

When you add fruit or grapes, the mead that you get will mature more rapidly and be ready in only about three months. Technically, when you add fruits, molasses, herbs, spices, grains, etc., mead becomes something else known by another name, but to us amateurs it's still "mead" as long as the mead contains more honey than these adjuncts. Most will try various fruits to see what comes out best. Add the adjuncts when you are brewing on your stove, then strain out any solid residue after a day or two of fermentation. Grain or hops will give a very bitter taste unless strained off immediately, and herbs should be soaked in the brew while it is cooling. There's a lot more here, but you should consult some texts on the subject to go into the full details of the very wide variety of adjuncts that can be used.

I'd recommend buying a new gallon or five-gallon jug for each batch of mead you make, unless you can throughly scrub down every square centimeter of its inside. Ditto for your hoses. Before using your equipment, wash everything sparkling clean, then sterilize with a teaspoon of household bleach per gallon of water, and rinse thoroughly.

Mead making takes time. After pitching, you should allow at least four months before bottling, depending on how the fermentation goes. Look at your fermentation jug or vat every now and then to keep tab on how it's doing. While the fermentation process is taking place the mead will get very cloudy. Sometimes it will clear up, and then become cloudy once again as secondary fermentation takes place. As a general rule of thumb, the mead should be ready for bottling when you have been able to read newsprint through a gallon jug of it for at least two weeks. (If the mead is a particularly dark variety, you should be able to judge the lack of cloudiness and the clarity by shining a flashlight into the jug or vat.).

Once you bottle it, let the mead age for at least another three months. Have patience, and treat your bottles gently.

Find a good area around your house or garage where you can leave your brewing jugs safe and undisturbed, with a temperature range of 55 to 85 degrees Fahrenheit.

Equipment

The basic hardware you will need for brewing one-gallon batches are easily bought at a wine-making shop:

One-gallon jug
Brewing pot, 4 to 6 quarts (steel or enamel, *not* aluminum)
Clear glass primary fermenter, 6 quart
Fermentation lock and stopper
Wire mesh tea strainer (used for skimming froth from the mead when you boil it)
Long-handled brewing spoon, plastic (if you use a long-handled wooden spoon, you'll have to boil it after each time you use it)
Racking cane
Plastic siphon hose, about 3 feet long and intended for handling foods
Bottle brushes, assorted
Bottles (recycled wine bottles will do)
Funnel, plastic
Corks for bottles
Bottle capper/cork compresser
Sulphite tablets, to terminate fermentation before final bottling (optional)

The brew should be cooled in a primary fermenter before pitching the yeast. With a clear glass primary fermenter, it is possible to siphon the clear mead off from the sediment before you pitch the yeast.

When you transfer the mead from one container to another, whether a jug used for primary fermenting or the bottles in which it will age the final three months or so, always use a siphon to avoid aereating the mead and exposing it to airborne bacteria that could really mess things up!

A racking cane has a cap on the tip and a hole about an inch from the end. When you attach the siphon tube you can draw off the clear mead from the spent yeast and other sediment without stirring up the sediment. Since racking canes are usually long enough for working with a five-gallon carboy or big jug, you should cut it down appropriately for use with a gallon jug.

(As with all other supplies you'll need, locate a brewing supply shop to buy these things. You can improvise or make things up from scratch, but it's harder and much slower.)

Brewing your Mead

There are probably as many recipes for mead making as there are brewers. My own experience has been good with one of the simplest and best from the Brewer's Guild of the Asatru Free Assembly, and I owe them much thanks for the recipe of "Mike's Magic Mead," as created by Mike Murray. To make one gallon:

2 quarts water
2 1/2 lbs honey
about 1/2 cup lemon peels (alternately, 3 teaspoons of malic acid)
1 tablespoon strong tea (alternately, 1 1/2 teaspoons tartaric acid)
1/4 teaspoon grape tannin
1 teaspoon yeast energizer
1 packet mead yeast

Stir the honey and water together, heating slowly. Stir in the lemon peel and tea (or the malic and tartaric acid). When it gets hot, stir in the grape tannin and the yeast energizer. Most brewers will bring the brew to a full boil, though this is not really necessary. Use the tea strainer to skim off the froth that rises to the top. Let it cool for a while, then "rack" or pour into your primary fermenter and let the brew cool overnight. The next day, carefully pour it through the strainer into your gallon fermentation jug. "Pitch" or add the yeast, stirring a packet of yeast into four ounces of 80-degree water (more or less), let it sit for about ten minutes and stir it into your brew.

Carefully move your jug into a dark, moderate-temperature place where it will be completely undisturbed, and put on the fermentation lock. I normally set it in a large bowl of some sort to catch the foam-off that occurs during the first few days of fermentation, and clean it up after a few days. Otherwise the bottle shouldn't be touched except when absolutely necessary.

It's a good idea to keep a log on your mead, noting the amount you've brewed, date pitched, date bottled, your ingredients and your brewing procedure. Also, you may want to give each batch of mead its own name.)

After a few days the mead will start to clear, and there will be a good bit of sediment at the bottom of the jug. Pour the mead into another jug, being careful to leave the sediment behind. Then top off the jug with distilled or purified water, and re-attach the fermentation lock. If after a week or two the mead again has sediment, rack it again into another bottle. It's a good idea to check monthly for sediment, and re-rack if there's more than just a trace.

When your mead has gone for a month without sediment, it's ready to be bottled and corked. At this point many brewers prefer to terminate any residual fermentation by adding a sulphite tablet, crushed and dissolved into two ounces of water, then stirred into the gallon of mead. After allowing the mead to set overnight, it is then funneled into the bottles and corked. I personally like to do things in a more naturalistic way and skip the sulphite tablets, though some other brewers have warned me that one or more of my treasured, corked bottles may explode or blow a cork a few weeks or months later due to pressure buildup by some last bit of fermentation. So far it hasn't happened and I'm continuing to be "organic" in my brewing. If I change my mind (i.e., have to clean up a mess) it will be appended to the next edition of this book!

Let your mead age for three months or more. Then, at some appropriate ceremonial occasion, serve it to yourself and your brethren, and *enjoy*.

I am indebted to the Brewer's Guild of the Asatru Free Assembly for providing me with the instruction to get started with my own brewing, and permission to adapt some of their excellent instructions for publication here.

Readings

The selections which follow are intended to give folklore background on the Way of Valhalla, examining philosophical, social and metaphysical underpinnings of Norse religion. It may surprise the reader that considerable space is spent discussing the goddess-oriented precursors to ancient Odinism, although a bit of reading will show that many of the basic tenets, as well as some rather surprising and obscure beliefs such as Nordic reincarnation, find their explanations here. Also the strong kinship of Gods to men and women is examined.

One of the strongest features of Odinism has always been its strong stress on kinship and families; by reaching into an era before the Aesir we find the reasons for this most strong of all social bonds.

So, read and consider. The sources are not only the Eddas, but folklore from remote areas of north, central, and eastern Europe as well. You may find it interesting and enlightening.

The Philosophy and Theology of the Nordic World Tree

This symbolic tree represents a philosophical scheme which, for this book, is liberally borrowed from the Eddas, from the survivals of pre-Indo European mythology, Slavic mythology, Siberian shamanic cults and many other sources. The Eddas alone are incomplete— portions have been altered and omitted in dealing with the Tree, and there seem to have been several overlays of sometimes conflicting additions to the lore of the World Tree.

According to an ancient Teutonic myth, life was created when the Sun shone upon the ocean. Another variant of this myth states that there was originally a yawning chasm (Ginnunga Gap), and to the north of it was Nifhel, the cold land from which flowed many fountains, and to the south was Muspel, the land of fire. Waters from Nifhel flowed into the gap, where they were met by warm vapors from Muspel. Thus, there was an interaction between the elements of fire and air (masculine), and water and earth (feminine), which produced life in the form of the giant, Ymir.

He was truly bisexual, and from him sprang the first living beings. Ymir was later slain by the Asgardian Gods (reminiscent of how the Olympian Gods slew the Titans, or how the Babylonian Marduk slew Tiamat), and his body was cast into the chasm, filling the gap and thus making the world. (The Eddic descriptions of what became of each part of the body are probably later accretions to the myth and are deleted, having no bearing upon this diagram.)

In the figure which has two sketches to show all the factors involved, the Tree bridges the chasm and is therefore also the body of Ymir, which actually represents man's physical self. (The gender here represented is neutral, of course.) The Tree is the mediator between Heaven and Hel in many shamanic cults, and thus it is here utilized to represent the polarities in Nature and in the human mind. The Tree mediates between Heaven and Hel, Muspel and Nifhel, symbolic south and symbolic north (not the points of the compass), fire and

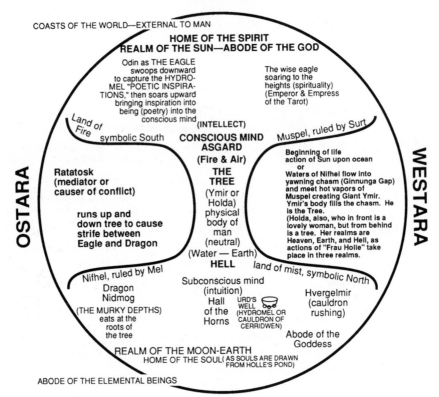

SUDRA

COASTS OF THE WORLD—EXTERNAL TO MAN

HOME OF THE SPIRIT
REALM OF THE SUN—ABODE OF THE GOD

Odin as THE EAGLE
swoops downward
to capture the HYDRO-
MEL "POETIC INSPIRA-
TIONS," then soars upward
bringing inspiration into
being (poetry) into the
conscious mind (INTELLECT)

The wise eagle
soaring to the
heights (spirituality)
(Emperor & Empress
of the Tarot)

Land of
Fire   symbolic South

Muspel, ruled by Surt

CONSCIOUS MIND
ASGARD
(Fire & Air)

THE
TREE

(Ymir or
Holda)
physical
body of
man
(neutral)

(Water — Earth)

HELL

Beginning of life
action of Sun upon ocean
or
Waters of Nifhel flow into
yawning chasm (Ginnunga Gap)
and meet hot vapors of
Muspel creating Giant Ymir.
Ymir's body fills the chasm. He
is the Tree.
(Holda, also, who in front is a
lovely woman, but from behind
is a tree. Her realms are
Heaven, Earth, and Hell, as
actions of "Frau Holle" take
place in three realms.

Ratatosk
(mediator or
causer of conflict)

runs up and
down tree to cause
strife between
Eagle and Dragon

OSTARA

WESTARA

Nifhel, ruled by Mel

Dragon
Nidmog

(THE MURKY DEPTHS)
eats at the
roots of
the tree

land of mist, symbolic North

Subconscious mind
(intuition)

Hall   URD'S
of the   WELL
Horns   (HYDROMEL OR
CAULDRON OF
CERRIDWEN)

Hvergelmir
(cauldron
rushing)

Abode of the
Goddess

REALM OF THE MOON-EARTH
HOME OF THE SOUL (AS SOULS ARE DRAWN
FROM HOLLE'S POND)

ABODE OF THE ELEMENTAL BEINGS

NORDRA

World Tree

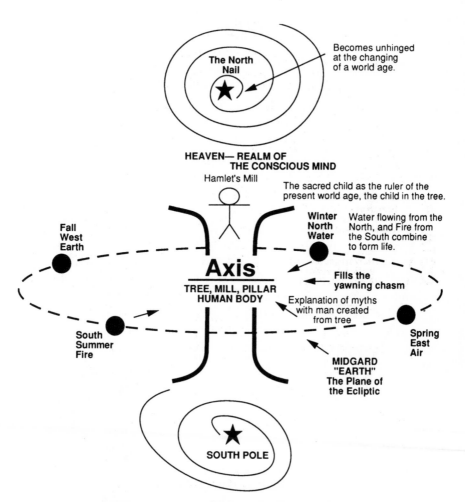

The North
Nail

Becomes unhinged
at the changing
of a world age.

**HEAVEN— REALM OF
THE CONSCIOUS MIND**

Hamlet's Mill

The sacred child as the ruler of the
present world age, the child in the tree.

Fall
West
Earth

Winter
North
Water

Water flowing from the
North, and Fire from
the South combine
to form life.

Axis

TREE, MILL, PILLAR
HUMAN BODY

Fills the
yawning chasm

South
Summer
Fire

Explanation of myths
with man created
from tree

Spring
East
Air

MIDGARD
"EARTH"
The Plane of
the Ecliptic

SOUTH POLE

HELL: realm of the Unconscious Land of the sleeping
King of the Golden Age. Eridu: the place where the waters
converge. Hvergelmir: the rushing cauldron (the
Maelstrom guarded by the Nine Maids of the Island Mill).

water, earth and air, male and female, Sun and Moon-Earth, conscious mind and unconscious mind, intellect and intuition, and so on.

This concept of polarities is particularly relevant where (as often happens in myths of all lands, including Nordic) a God and Goddess are seen as twins, representing masculine and feminine sides of nature, although otherwise unspecialized. This is true of Gode and Goda, Freyr and Freya, Njord and Nerthus, Behrta and Berholt, Zio and Zisa. This is also true of other mythological systems: Janus and Jana, Dianus and Diana, Faunus and Fauna. This brother-sister relationship of God and Goddess is also found in branches of Wicca, where the year is equally divided between the rule of the God and the Goddess.

The pre-Asgardian Goddess Holda could also represent the Tree. Her realm is the three worlds—Heaven, Earth and Hel—as illustrated in the fairy tale "Frau Holle." In the tale, the girl descends into the pond, yet manipulates the elements from the sky; but when she walks out through the gate she is once again on Earth. Also, Holda is pictured as a beautiful woman in front but with the trunk of a tree behind.

This Tree diagram is much different from the tree Yggdrasill as pictured in the Eddas. Snorri's descriptions have been discarded. They elaborated upon earlier conceptions and are not relevant to the conception of polarities represented by this diagram of the World Tree. (The *Prose Edda*'s descriptions of the Goddess Hel, her realm, and her denizens have been discarded from this diagram. Snorri was writing under a very heavy Christian influence in picturing the Goddess and her realm as evil.)

In fact, the name "Yggdrasill" means "the steed of Yggr" (Odin), and represents the shaman-god's horse, the funeral pall. Slepnir was an eight-legged horse. There were four pallbearers at funerals, and a shaman's work often takes him or her beyond the gates of death and back. The World Tree must have been confused with the tree Yggdrasill at an early date.

Hel is represented as the unconscious mind; it is not seen as the Christian place of suffering. The ancients did not see it as a place of torment and punishment; it was simply the place where the dead went. In fact, some folktales picture the "Hollenreich" as a land of beautiful meadows, and when Hermod descended to Hel in search of Balder, he saw a great hall where a feast was being held in honor of Balder. This, however, is not relevant to the diagram, but is meant to emphasize the fact that Hel is not seen as evil.

Below the tree, in Hel, was the hall of the Norns—the Goddesses of Fate. Nearby was the well which they guarded. In the mythology one actually encounters many wells, but here Urd's well, Mimir's well and the others are all the same. Furthermore, the famous cauldrons of Nordic and Celtic mythology are identified with this well. In fact, one name for the well is Hvergelmir, or "Cauldron Rushing." This well is the mystical inspiration which lies deep in the subconscious mind.

However, the dragon Nidhoggr also lurks in the murky depths of this realm, and he gnaws at the roots of the Tree. The subconscious mind holds terror as well as beauty, and will the one who delves into it find the cauldron or the dragon?

Hel is the lunar realm, as envisioned by some occult philosophies. According to these conceptions, the soul went to the Moon after death, whereas the vital spirit returned to the Sun. The idea of unborn souls residing in the Moon is particularly interesting in view of folk beliefs that souls are drawn from Frau Holle's (Hel's) pond. (Although the ancient Germans and Slavs saw the Sun as feminine and the Moon as masculine, at this point we will not strive for mythological accuracy, but utilize instead the conventional occult conceptions.)

At the other end of the Tree is the realm of fire and air, the realm of the Sun (from where the vital spirit comes), the "Asgard" of the Eddas, the conscious mind, the intellect. At the top of the tree sits the wise eagle, sometimes also represented as a falcon or a hawk. When the eagle soars above the tree, he represents the attainment of spiritual heights; no longer in the mind of man, conscious or subconscious, but soaring into the realms of the transcendent. However, not all good is found in the conscious mind. The influences of dissipated thought are represented by four harts who gnaw at the buds and branches of the Tree, just as Nidhoggr gnaws at its roots.

Running up and down the trunk of the tree, trying to cause strife between the dragon and the eagle (i.e., subconscious and conscious minds), is the squirrel Ratatoskr. He represents the brain as a mediator between the conscious and the unconscious mind.

The Tree and the levels of the mind are all internal to man, and are thus contained in a circle. External to man, and therefore outside the circle, "at the coasts of the world," are four quarters and the realms of the elemental beings. This diagram should actually be three dimensional, with the Tree as a vertical pole piercing a horizontal plate, with

Heaven on one side, Hel on the other, and the four quarters dividing the rim. However, although these dimensions are external to man, the realm of the transcendent into which the eagle soars is even beyond them.

Additionally, it should be noted that in this diagram both Asgard and Muspel are represented at one pole of the World Tree. Of course, there certainly is no traditional relationship between Asgard and Surt's realm. Here they are both represented together at one pole because they both, as far as our own purposes are concerned, represent aspects of the masculine principle. Obviously this brings up the point that there is a confusion in sense of direction, as Muspel is the symbolic South, Asgard is represented as being in the heavens, and Hel is both the symbolic North and the nether world. These are some problems in the technicalities that we are trying to work out. However, we've had to rearrange some of the traditions anyway, in order to employ certain symbolic values here.

Surt was considered an enemy of the Gods, but he was a member of the race of giants, and we interpret the giants not as being evil forces but rather as being simply the elder races, much like the Titans in the Olympian mythology or the Fir Bolg in the Celtic mythology. The giants are often represented as very beautiful people with great skills in magic, and they are also tied in with the vala priestesshood. There may be a case for suggesting a God-Goddess relationship between Surt and Hel as the God and Goddess of the Old Race, now long forgotten, employing the concepts of male-female polarities.

Yule Journey

This is a reading for the Yule season, incorporating many features from the folklore of northern and central Europe, and linking them with far more recent traditions in the New World The old crone is Hulda or Holle; the young prince has gone by many names in the vegetation religions which preceded the cult of Valhalla, and existed even alongside it. The Snow Queen was (and still may be) widely honored in central Europe, appearing notably in the folklore of Austria and the Slavic lands. The Giants and Titans of one era may be remembered as lesser godlings and as saints for centuries and even millennia to follow: the genial Old King is one you will know quite well, and was highly honored under many names at the dawn of history and even before. The Mother is of course Erda, or the Earth, and her new child, in folk beliefs and in the Kalevela presaged new beginnings and a new age.

The place in which this story is told should be decorated for the Yule season, with appropriate (more Pagan) songs and carols and the full, rich atmosphere of the season. Before beginning this inner-plane journey, verify that all present are wearing Thor's hammers or other talismans of the Old Ways.

As we listen to this tale, imagine that we are in another time and another place, either far in the past or far in the future; or perhaps simply off in the wilderness, not too far away, on a Midwinter's night. In this story we will both be here and we will be, well, somewhere else at the same time. Let the pictures in your mind drift along with the words, watching and listening as the narration proceeds.

To start with, let us imagine that this room exists in this "other time and other place," perhaps as a part of a stone-and-log house tucked far off in the forest.

At the south of this rustic room we see a heavy, old-looking door set into the wall. It is of heavy wood and hung with a wreath of holly. We go over to the door and push on it: the door opens easily and beyond we see snow, trees, and white-covered hills in the distance under a late-afternoon Sun. Although we know the light wind and the snow about our feet must be must be cold as we step through the door, we still feel warm and comfortable as though the talismans that we wear give all the warmth our bodies, our hands, and our feet need from within. Each of us is dressed as we deem appropriate for this trek through a world of snow and magic. We pull the door shut behind us, noting that it is set into a small stone hut with a straw-thatched roof.

The trees are lightly powdered with snow, and there is the sound of distant wind in the trees. A path leads off to the east, away from the declining Sun, and this we take. The snow crunching under our feet is usually ankle-deep, though sometimes drifting more, sometimes blown away to bare ground beneath. There is a chill and a bite in the air, though the cold does not bother us.

The path leads on down into the snowy forest. Overhead low, heavy clouds are moving in, with the promise of more snow likely. There is the sound of wind in the treetops and somewhere a raven calls in the distance. A few flurries of snow swirl about us as we continue on the trail that slants down farther into the evergreen forest. There are tracks in the snow before us, and we can see that others have been here quite recently.

There is a scent of wood smoke in the sharp, cold air, and ahead we can hear the sound of bells somewhere ahead, and distant voices. The trees open out into a clearing ahead, and we can see a small, ornate village; the picturesque type we would expect to see in the mountains and the snowy forest. They are half-timbered, with slanting roofs of thatch and shingle. Smoke rises from the chimneys, and there are candles in the small windows, behind the thick, tinted glass. Our path becomes the one short street in this little village as we continue along. There are people here, dressed in rough, archaic styles; laughing, drinking and singing, with children yelling and running through the snow and hurling snowballs from time to time. Although this is a village of peasants and foresters, it is a joyous one, particularly at this season. Wreaths of holly and ivy are hung on all the doors and the good smells of cooking waft from within.

A group of men in rough, fur-trimmed coats walk and stagger

past with steaming tankards in their hands, attempting to sing in harmony some song that is festive and almost familiar. Although there are many people about, none seem to notice us as we walk down the packed snow of the street.

Ahead is a cluster of people of all ages, laughing and shouting together, for something seems to particularly spark their merriment. As we approach the children, women and men happen to move apart somewhat and we see that there is an old, bent woman there, leading a goat about whose neck is a garland of straw and ivy. The old woman is laughing with the rest and is obviously the center of attention. She waves her tankard at some of the men and shouts a suggestion that reduces them to laughter. From a large, old bag, once ornately embroidered but now dirty and tattered, she pulls out a small carved toy and gives it to a child, and another to a young girl who takes it and hugs her. She tugs on the rope about the goat's neck and pulls him along toward us. Then the old woman looks up and sees us. She grins a near-toothless grin, pulls her shawl closer about her head and beckons for us to come nearer. She swats at her goat, who has begun to butt against her.

She is cheerful, lively and quite ugly, with warts and even a bit of a beard on her angular chin. Her voice is like a crow, but she is obviously much liked here and definitely the life of the festivities with her raucous and bawdy good humor. She comments that we are very obviously strangers here and that it would surprise the locals if they could see us, as odd as we look. But she welcomes us, then turns toward the forested hills which rise on the other side of the small village; she points with one gnarled, bent finger. The old woman tells us to go on out beyond the town, to the old stone circle on the other side of the hills and wait there. She says goodbye, then cackles with laughter as she turns toward a pair of boys who are pulling on her tattered cloak, threatening to swat them with her broom and turn them into toads. They laugh and run and she talks to her goat, who also has been nibbling on her raggedy clothes. Then she hobbles over to a group of women to begin an animated, loud conversation. We continue on down the street. The people about us seem not to notice us as they celebrate this season, singing and calling greetings to one another.

The tavern, stables and the houses are warm, cozy and ornate, with carved, half-timbered structures and small windows of leaded glass. As we proceed down the street past the last sod-roofed sheds and to the small fields, it once more becomes a path, with snow that crunches beneath our feet.

At the edge of the field the path passes beneath a high portal like an inverted "V," made of two carven logs. We cannot make out any meaning to the angular letters of the strange alphabet carved on the portal, though where the two logs cross near the top the high ends look like stylized hawks or eagles. The last light of the setting Sun breaks through momentarily so that the high gate seems to shine like red gold as we pass through it.

The trail passes through the snow-covered underbrush and then into the blue-grey shadows of the forest, with snow flurries whirling down from the dimming sky overhead through the snow-covered evergreen boughs to either side. The air is sharp and cold, with the slight scent of evergreen and the delicate touch of occasional snow-flakes on our faces.

There is the sound of a bird in the distance, a sort of croaking "caw, caw" that must be from a raven, faint at first, then louder as it approaches. We look up through the snow-flecked dimness to see the dark shadow overhead. The bird obviously sees us and swirls down in our direction in a beating of ebony wings that shakes the snow from the trees all about us so that it falls like a miniature blizzard. The big bird lands on the broken trunk of a dead tree next to us, and the wind stirred by her wings is surprisingly strong. The swirling of the snow fades away and the large black raven is perched on a dead branch near to us, about eye level. The bird cocks its head to the side and looks at us with a quizzical, mischievous expression uncannily like the old crone we had met back in the town. We pause for a couple minutes, looking at the raven as she looks at us. We listen, and perhaps we hear with our minds what the Old One has to say.

(Here the narrator should pause for a while, as all listen to the words of the old one.)

The raven decides that it is time to depart. With a loud, raucous "caw" she spreads her great black wings and beats them powerfully. The snow swirls suddenly about us so that we cannot see the bird, though we can feel the strong wind from her wings, lessening along with the diminishing sound of their beating as she flies away. The snow flakes, soft and cold on our faces, settle about us and the raven is gone, though we can hear her call fading over the dark trees, far away.

We continue walking along the snow-covered road.

The trees overhead are higher and thicker, and the evergreen forest darker and more dense on either side. We can hear the sound of some animal off to the side (perhaps a deer) startled by our passing, as it crashes through the undergrowth and snow falls from the bushes to the ground. There is the sound of wind in the treetops far off, then closer. Here and there sheets of snow fall from the boughs of the trees as the wind stirs them, and we are wrapped in the swirling snow for awhile as we continue. We can see little except for the path as we continue.

The wind fades somewhat, and the swirl of snow from the upper branches lessens. In the deepening dimness we can see that the trail has begun to incline upward and the trees are lower and thinning. We continue further and the darkening sky can be seen more and more. The Full Moon has risen, and floods the sky and the treetops with bright silver light, though the shadows are still deep. The trees thin enough so that we can see we are at the edge of a great, open meadow—perhaps a plain—that stretches far to the north and the east.

A hill rises ahead and to the left of us and, in the still moonlight, we can see a high circle of standing stones atop the hill. We walk toward it through the slightly deeper snow, looking at the symmetry of the standing circle of monoliths and at the sparkling stars beyond, glistening in the bitter night air. All is still, and far overhead we can hear the calling of a flock of birds as they wing south. Their calls fade into the distance as we reach the stone circle, to reach out and touch the icy rock of the first monolith. We walk to the center of the great circle and pause to look around. From where we came we can see the dark forest, and farther to the east seems to be mountains and perhaps more forest. Off to the northeast seems to be some clouds and perhaps a misting of snow.

Somewhere, far off in the distance, we can hear the faint howling of wolves and, somewhat closer, what might sound like the baying of hounds: hunting dogs of some sort. The wind begins again, soft at first from the north across the vast, empty plain. It is bitter cold, though the icy breeze does not bother us as it blows harder, whirling the snow before it so that we feel the cutting sharpness of the blowing snow. The wind is harder yet, with snow whirling about the black stone monoliths, the bright moonlight making it all look like whirls of silvery whiteness with icy spangles dancing between and about the great rocks.

Off to the northeast, from out of the blowing, bitingly cold snow we hear the hounds again, closer now. We hear other sounds from other creatures: yappings, howlings, caterwauling screams, and, as they draw closer, even some gibberings which do not sound like they come from any animals of which we know. Always, there is the deep baying of the hounds in the distance, drawing closer. We ease back across the stone henge through the driving, sparkling snow to one of the great stone monoliths, and stand against it in the shadows to watch what is approaching this place.

From the northeast to the southwest we see something dark and shadowy run swiftly and silently across the center of the stone circle. Then others rush past behind it, both large and small. Some call raucously, others howl and shriek in strange voices. They are hard to make out through the driving snow. Most look like some kind of animals, though many are hulking, misshapen creatures with eyes that glow scarlet in the snowy dimness, and white, long teeth that glisten in the moonlight. The ground rumbles with their passing and the snow swirls all the more densely in and around the circle of dark stones. More of the chaotic, bestial things come, stampeding with the baying of the hunting hounds ever closer behind them. They scream, bellow and even laugh wildly, though there seems to be no intelligence, no mind, no sanity to any of them. We feel the almost physical waves of raw elemental power, chaotic and uncontrolled, that seems to be all about these strange, fearsome things, passing through the dimness of the whirling snow like a wild waterfall of greys and blacks.

The belling of the hounds is close now, and the horde of fleeing, shadowy creatures begins to thin, for most of the herd seems to have gone past, heading off to the southwest into the driving snow. A few last ones come lolliping through, some seeming almost human, some very bestial, others large, huge, and hulking, their jaws slavering and their harsh breath clearly audible through the icy wind. Then for a few moments the stone circle is again empty.

A group of large animals pause at the edge of the circle, and we can sense that they are looking about, sniffing the air, listening for a moment. Then the deep, bellowing bark of the hounds fills the air and they run through the stone circle, eyes glowing yellow in the darkness. One of them passes nearby, sees us and pauses for a moment. It is a very large, powerfully built animal with a massive, thick neck and sharp teeth; its body is dark, but the head is definitely red in color, seeming almost to glow in the dimness. The great hound sniffs the air in our direction, regards us closely with its glowing, yellow eyes and runs off to follow the others of its pack, giving a deep, barking voice as it chases after the chaotic horde.

Again all is still and silent in the stone circle, except for the blowing snow and the silver of the moonlight. Then a glistening figure in silver armor, mounted on a large, white horse, appears between two of the great standing stones nearby. We see the rider's helmeted head, with the broad spread of glistening silver antlers, turn toward us; he snaps the reins and the big horse walks over to halt in front of us in a jingling of harness and with breath steaming in the bitter cold wind. The rider looks down at us.

His full armor glistens brightly in the full moonlight, ornate and finely fashioned armor of a very old style, looking familiar as though we can almost remember having seen it somewhere, long ago. The polished helmet has the visor closed, so that we cannot see his face. The helmet is set with antlers seemingly fashioned of pure, sparkling silver and wreathed in holly and ivy. There is a definite sparkling glow in the air about his head and his antlers. A long sword in an engraved, jeweled sheath hangs by his side, as does a large, ornate hunting horn. He lifts his silver-gauntleted hand and raises his visor with an almost musical chime.

In the full moonlight the face of the horned rider is extremely handsome, almost supernaturally so, as befits the rest of his appearance. From what we can see of his hair it is almost like spun gold, (or of silver, for we cannot really tell in the moonlight). He smiles at us and wishes us a joyous Yule, then adds that not many come here any more, and it is good to see those of the Old Ways once again. He laughs in a voice which is rich and musical and tells us to come again at a time when he is not so busy. He points off to the east and says that if we head off in that direction we will find another who will be happy to see us, just over the next hill and through the veil of snow. He tells us to just remember that space as well as time may vary in these lands, for we are beyond the far boundaries of the world of men.

His great white stallion snorts and stamps the ground restlessly. He reaches forward to pat the neck and scratch the mane of his mount. "Now I must be going. These lands have to be scoured clean by the rising of the Sun." He calls farewell, snaps down the glittering visor of his helmet and slaps the reins, nudging the horse with his boot heels. As the great stallion leaps away he waves to us, the glistening silver of his armor and his antlered helmet almost seems to throw off sparkles in the bright moonlight. While the armored rider disappears between the tall standing stones, he is reaching for the horn that swings by his side. Then he is gone, though we hear the rich, pure tone of his horn, echoing and re-echoing across the snowy plains, and in the far distance the calling of the hounds answers back. Then all is silent and still once more, except for the blowing snow.

We pause for a few moments, listening for faint sounds disappearing in the far distance, then walk in the direction which he pointed. The snow thins as we walk away down the hill from the stone circle, and we see that there is a faint path in the snow; perhaps some sort of a trail which is on the frozen ground beneath. The touch of occasional snowflakes is soft against our faces as we continue, the wind fading and the stars coming out more clearly overhead. It is still and silent by the time that we reach the bottom of the hill and start up the next. Looking up at the sky to the north we notice what seems like pale curtains of light, shifting and shimmering, glowing in rays and sheets of yellow, blue, red, orange, green and violet.

Patterns that are vague, yet bright, seem almost to crackle in the moonlit night sky, ever-changing, far off in the star-spangled night. As we reach the top of the next hill we see that the rippling and changing lights stretch from the horizon to far overhead, spreading to cover the entire northern half and more of the sky constantly moving, changing sheets, flowing beams, and sparkling, iridescent curtains of color crackling above.

The snow crunches beneath our feet and all is bitter cold, though we do not feel the chill. As we start down the hill we see that at the bottom is the edge of a large, hard-frozen lake that extends out to the far northern horizon. The ice is smooth in most places that we can see, and powdered with snow. Far out the ice has broken, by the winds, most likely, and tumbled up into what look like mountains of angular white here and there. These high, tumbled mounds catch the moonlight oddly. Some of them seem to glow from within from pale elf-fires, cold and desolate. We are near the edge of the lake now, and begin to walk alongside it. Examining the lake carefully, we see that between the great ice-mounds the lake surface still has broad and far areas which are smooth and unbroken, glistening in the moonlight with the pale color of the borealis.

We walk farther along the edge of the frozen lake, with the snow crunching beneath our feet. Perhaps it is only a trick of our eyes, but the northern lights seem to grow richer and more vivid in their rippling and flowing colors; although all is silent, it seems as though we should hear a buzzing and a crackling from the brightening colors in the sky.

Looking more carefully out toward the north across the wide expanse of the glittering lake, it seems as though we can make out a sparkling in the north, like stars glimmering just at the horizon. We pause and gaze closely at the sparkling and the glittering, and by degrees we can now make out, far off across the ice, a great, lofty structure which looks to be of crystal, as though fashioned from the ice, the stars and the glowing and shifting lights in the sky.

As our eyes adjust we see it more clearly now, a far distant castle out on the wide lake, or beyond it. Its towers are impossibly high and slender, of pale, icy blue and violet. It is a slender, high sculpture of delicate, crystalline beauty, glistening in the moonlight and the rippling rainbow colors of the northern lights. The great castle is far too delicate, too high and insubstantial a structure to be fashioned by human hands.

There seems a mist of snow out on the lake surface near the castle, and a movement. From out of the mist comes a faint blue-violet glow, brightening as we watch, for out of the glow, something is approaching swiftly across the lake. It comes rapidly, and now we can make out than it is a sled of some sort, drawn by animals. We can now see three of them. It draws nearer, and the sound of sleigh bells becomes clearer, jingling and tinkling across the ice. It is a sled, pulled by three large reindeer hitched side by side under a carven and painted wooden arch, harnessed with many bells which sound constantly in the icy air. We see that the sledge is painted and carven intricately, glistening in the moonlight and the aurora.

There is a nimbus of frosty light about the driver and sole occupant of this now slowing sled, about the sledge itself, and about the three antlered beasts which draw it, their breaths glowing in the cold air like blue fire. The driver of the sled is a woman, we now see, with long, blue-white hair, touched with shadows of gold, blowing over her full fur collar as she rides. She wears a long coat of glistening, iridescent furs and intricately embroidered gloves. The jewels that she wears catch the fire of the aurora borealis, and of the moonlight, glittering like ice at her neck and scattered through her hair. Her features are perfect and finely chiseled, like a sculpture in pale ice; definitely, this being seems to be "not of this Earth."

She comes closer, slowing, and we can hear the thin sound of the sled's metal runners on the ice. The woman pulls back on the reins as she comes near to the edge of the lake alongside us, and her horned beasts slow and stop. They are restless but they wait, their breath misting blue in the moonlight and their eyes the color of the sky-fires above. We walk toward her as she regards us closely, looking at our hammer pendants and magical jewelry. Then in a clear voice like the sound of crystal she tells us that we are welcome in her realms, as are the worthy ones who truly seek the ancient ways.

She looks deeply into our eyes, for we are close now, and her eyes seem like deep pools of luminous blue flame, drawing in a portion of our consciousness. No words are needed as we begin to know of her, for she speaks directly to our minds. She knows of the distant stars, and of the vast distances between them.

Though she is unhumanly beautiful, like the far-flung aurora of the northern skies, we have the feeling that nonetheless she is ancient beyond the ages. All unchanging, she has seen the ebb and flow of vast aeons of time. She has known the times when the titanic mountains of ice stretched to the skies, and marched slowly far to the south. She has known the distant times before that even, when these icy lands were warm, and other strange races walked the emerald-green Earth. Then she speaks more to each of us in the silence. And in the silence, each of us listens.

(Here the narrator should pause for a while, as all listen to the words of the snow queen.)

Then she smiles at us, a cold smile, and points with one elegantly gloved hand to where our path now sparkles in the snow before us, as though frost had marked the way for us to go. She waves farewell and, in a voice like the winter wind, gives us her blessing as she slaps the reins and her great deer begin moving, the sled turning and moving rapidly away across the ice toward the crystalline castle in the distance. We watch her as she disappears rapidly toward the high structure.

Then we notice that the rippling and flowing colors spread across the dark sky have shaped into what seems to be a vortex, a column of intense light and power rising irom the faceted, glowing castle up high toward a bright star directly overhead. A column of light and colour rising from the very core of the Earth perhaps and flowing on out beyond the very stars. Then the icy wind rises, and swirling snow obscures our view again, so that all we can see is the Moon and some of the color flowing in the sky.

We begin walking toward our path marked with the glistening frost. Ahead, just above the horizon, is a single very bright star, and the path points directly toward it as we walk on through the swirling snow blown by the bitter cold wind. We walk up the first hill and down the other side, away from the lake, guided by the glittering trail of frost and the star before us. We go on, and it is as though we are in a trance with what we have seen, knowing only the wind and the blowing snow. If we should happen to stray from the path, the lines of frost will unerringly draw us back again on the path which now inclines more toward the south as the wheel of the sky turns slowly with the Moon. We become conscious that there are low trees now. How much time has passed we are not certain, but we are among hills and low mountains again, and evergreen forests have begun to rise on either side.

We hear the sounds of bells, chiming clear in the cold air and the distant sound of sleigh bells, soft and musical in the distance. We rouse ourselves as we walk and look about to see that the tall pines about us are laced with delicate, misting snow and glittering icicles. The wind has faded and the air is again still. Sparkles of light glisten here and there in the snow and ice ribbons in the trees, reflecting and refracting every color of the rainbow. The bells are clearer, and the glistenings in the trees are more bright; we realize that they are more than simple refractions of the Moon and the northern lights.

We smell wood smoke ahead, and our path breaks out into a good-sized clearing before us. A large, half-timbered manor house stands there, its leaded-glass windows sparkling with candles and many-colored sparkles of jeweled lights glistening even along the flowing curves of the old-style, heavy-shingled roof. The yard before it is bustling with activity as a noisy crowd of short, stocky, gnomish men and women hurry about, preparing for what seems to be some sort of celebration, carrying flickering lamps and gaily wrapped packages, talking and laughing. We can hear cheerful singing in the distance. They do not notice us as we walk toward the big house. There are sleds, and antlered beasts of burden hitched to them.

A figure appears at the door before us, sees us and waves for us to come over to him. He is a big, cheerful man, large and heavy, dressed in brightly-colored, fur-trimmed leathers. His hair and beard are full and white, and when he laughs the windows seem to rattle, so deep and rich is his voice.

He claps us on the shoulders and welcomes us to his place, stepping outside to be with us. He waves toward his many servants, smiling, and says that the place may be rustic, but it's cheerful, warm and quite a change from his more northern abodes. The big man looks around with a smile. "I was a god before there were gods," he says, "Yet still, of them all, I am remembered a little." He pauses for a moment and looks off into the light-sparkling distance, wrapped in his own thoughts. He looks back at us with a deep chuckle and reaches down into a gold-trimmed pouch at his belt, then holds something out for us in his big hand. "Here," he says, "I have something for you." We hold out our hands and he puts something into it that tingles and glows bright, warm, and with every color of the rainbow, its light shining even on the glistening trees about us. We look at it and gaze at the bright, sparkling rainbow light that gives such a feeling of well-being and strength as it rests almost weightlessly in our hand.

He smiles at us through his thick white beard and looks deep within our eyes with his own bright eyes. "Remember," he says. "From the stars you came, and to the stars you shall return. Know full well of your immortality. Keep your sense of wonder, and work your life so that you strive for perfection." He waves his big hand over ours, and the light settles into each of us, pervading us with a feeling of well-being, strength, and wonder as though we could see and know all things. Then it is gone, though we know that his gift is now within each of us.

He says, "Come, I want to show you something." He turns toward the deep, snowy forest where there are lights and sparkles in the trees, and leads us on the path that goes deep within where elf-lights of every color and hue sparkle and glow in and over the trees, within the bushes, and on the snowy ground all around us. The path glistens and glows, sparkling in reds, blues, greens and yellows. There is thick snow on the ground and in the trees the place seems warm and filled with power, growing stronger as we walk onward. The air is filled with sounds of distant bells and music, gentle and soft, like carols we remember hearing years ago.

There is a clearing ahead, and the Ancient King who leads us stops and points at the vast tree, bigger than any redwood, whose base and gnarled roots are before us. Lights and mists are everywhere, as are the sounds of bells, tiny and faint, large and distant. There are scents in the air like incense. The big man points, and we see that the roots of the gigantic tree (lights glisten as high up into it as we can see) enclose a rustic house, stables and sheds as though they had grown from the tree itself. On closer examination, we see that they are indeed part of the gigantic tree.

The glow is bright as the cheerful, big man leads us on into the house within the tree. There are others here, though they are hard to see: people with features so fine and delicate that they could not possibly be human; beings stocky, massive and elementally powerful; animals, and creatures of pure, colored light. The place radiates strength and power from every wall and nook. The others are going where we are going. Music seems to be everywhere.

We have passed on into the structure so that by now we seem to be at the very core of the vast tree, where the branches might go forever above us and the roots forever below. With all the others, seen and unseen, we enter the inner chamber, where the throne is at the heart of it all, rough like that which has grown out of the Earth, with the small bed nearby.

The light is bright, and the air is perfumed. The Mother is there, she who is at the center of all, holding the new Child in her arms. It seems hard to keep our eyes on the Lady, on the Child, for the light is brilliant, and it seems that vast power rises through the very walls and especially the floors of this rustic place to pervade all. It is as though everything is linked with flowing light that passes into and through us all.

We bow and give greetings to the Great Mother. She smiles, and it is as if a forest suddenly burst into blossom. She looks down at her Child, proud of the new life which has come forth to spread everywhere.

Our bearded friend eases back, and we leave with him. We walk back through this place of elemental power and of life, and when we get outside he shakes our hands and clasps us about our shoulders. "It is time for you to go," he says, "but be sure to come back again, to this, the Source." He points the way for us on the path that glistens off indefinitely into the shimmering and sparkling dimness of the forest. We bid him goodbye and walk away, down the path. It goes on, with the lights of all colors fading somewhat, the singing and then the bells fading into the soft and peaceful, glistening night of the enchanted forest.

We walk on, for how far we are not really certain, and then, abruptly, the path ends at a heavy wooden door set into a small stone hut under a small, thatched roof of straw. There is a wreath of holly on the door, and we realize that this is the place from which we started. We push the door open, and see within the room from where we started our journey. Perhaps hours have passed, or perhaps only minutes. We step into the room and push the door shut, then go over to where we can relax for a much-needed rest.

We have returned.

Frau Holle: Folk Tale and Ritual

Frau Holle

(From a recent translation of *Kinder and Hausmarchen,* by Wilhelm and Jacob Grimm)

A widow had two daughters. One was pretty and industrious, the other ugly and lazy. But she liked the ugly, lazy one much more because she was her own daughter, and the other had to do all the hard work and be the ash-girl in the house. Every day the poor girl had to sit down by a well near the road and spin until the blood spurted from her fingers. Now it happened that one time the bobbin got all bloody. She stooped over to rinse it in the well, but it slipped out of her hand and fell in. She ran weeping to her stepmother and told her of her mishap. But the stepmother scolded her harshly and pitilessly, saying, "If you dropped the bobbin in, then get it out again." So the girl went back to the well and didn't know what to do, and in her great distress jumped into the well to get the bobbin. She lost consciousness, and when she awoke and came to her senses, she was in a beautiful meadow on which the Sun was shining, and there were thousands of flowers there.

She walked across the meadow and came to an oven filled with bread, but the bread cried out, "Take me out! Take me out or I'll burn; I've long since been baked!" Then she stepped up and with the baker's shovel took out all the loaves one after another. Then she went on and came to a tree full of apples, and the tree called out to her, "Oh shake me, shake me! We apples are all ripe!" Then she shook the tree, and the apples dropped like rain, and she shook until not one was left on the tree. When she'd gathered them all in a pile, she went on. Finally she came to a cottage, out of which an old woman was looking, but because she had such big teeth, the girl was frightened and was about to run away. The old woman, however, called after her, "Why are you afraid, dear child? Stay with me; if you'll do all the housework properly, you'll be well off. You've just got to see to it that you shake my bed right and shake it up thoroughly so that the feathers fly. Then it snows on Earth. I'm Dame Holda."

At the old woman's kindly word, the girl plucked up her courage, agreed to the proposal, and entered her service. She did everything to the old woman's satisfaction and always shook out her bed so hard that the feathers flew about like snow flakes. In return, she led a comfortable existence there, was never scolded, and always got good food. After she'd spent some time with Dame Holda, she got sad and at first didn't herself know what the matter was. Finally she realized that it was homesickness. Though a thousand times better off here than at home, still she yearned to go back. At last she said to Dame Holda, "I've got homesick, and though I'm so well off down here, still I can't stay here longer, I must go back to my people." "I'm glad you want to go back home," said Dame Holda, "And because you've served me faithfully, I'm going to take you back up myself." Then she took her by the hand and led her to a big gate. The gate opened, and as the girl was standing right under it, down came a tremendous shower of gold, and all of the gold stuck to her, so that she was covered all over with it. "That's for you because you've been so industrious," said Dame Holda, who also gave her back the bobbin that had dropped into the well. Immediately the gate closed and the girl found herself back on Earth, not far from her mother's house. As she stepped into the yard, the cock that was sitting on the well cried out,

"Cock-a-doodle-do!
Our golden maiden's back."

Then she went in to her mother and, because she arrived all covered with gold, she was well received by her and by her sister.

Then the girl told them everything that had happened to her, and when her mother heard how she'd come by such great riches, she wanted to procure the same good fortune for the ugly, lazy daughter. So she had to sit down by the well and spin, and to make her bobbin bloody, she pricked her fingers, thrusting her hand into the thorn hedge. Then she threw the bobbin down the well and jumped in herself. Like her sister she came to the beautiful meadow and continued by the same path. When she got to the oven the bread again cried out, "Oh, take me out, take me out, or I'll burn; I've long since been baked." But the lazy girl replied, "As if I wanted to get myself dirty!" and walked on. Soon she came to the apple tree which called out, "Oh, shake me, shake me! We apples are all ripe!" But she answered, "What an idea! One of them might fall on my head," and walked on.

When she got to Dame Holda's, she wasn't afraid, since she'd already heard about her big teeth, and came to terms with her at once. The first day she restrained herself, was industrious, and followed Dame Holda's instructions whenever she told her to do anything, for she thought of all the gold she was going to give her. But on the second day she began slacking, and on the third even more so; in fact she didn't want to get up at all in the morning. Nor did she make Dame Holda's bed as she should and didn't shake it so that the feathers flew. Dame Holda soon tired of this and gave her notice. The lazy girl was quite content with this and thought that now would come the shower of gold. Dame Holda led her to the gate, but as the girl was standing underneath it, instead of gold, a big kettle of pitch was emptied out all over her. "That's to reward you for your services," said Dame Holda, shutting the gate. Then the lazy girl came home all covered with pitch, and on seeing her, the cock on the well cried out,

> *"Cock-a-doodle-do!*
> *Our dirty maiden's back."*

The pitch stuck to her and didn't come off as long as she lived.

MEANING AND COMMENTARY

Jacob Grimm and his brother Wilhelm are known, or rather mis-known, in this country and indeed throughout most of the world as authors of quite a large number of children's fairy tales. But posterity has done these very learned gentlemen a most considerable injustice, and the true worth of their years of research and compilation has been largely ignored.

The so-called fairy tales ascribed to the brothers Grimm are in reality folk tales researched by them from the country folk in the rural parts of the various German states. They were not meant primarily for children. (Interestingly enough, a great number of these stories were first told to them by an elderly but magnetic woman who lived alone in a cottage in the forest. She was noted for her expert use of herbs for healing, was reputed to be a sorceress of great power, and had an encyclopedic store of folktales. In short, a witch, a godia, or perhaps a vala.)

For one who is interested in researching out signs of the Old Religion in Central and Western Europe there can be no better source than the four thick volumes of Jacob Grimm's *Teutonic Mythology*. These tomes are heavy going, with exhaustive footnotes documenting all sources, and long quotes in a number of languages. But they are thorough and well indexed. The original goddess-worshiping traditions of the Germanic lands—preceding and underlying the faith of Valhalla—show through most clearly. The "Germanic lands," or the areas where this central European culture was (and still is) strong, extend from Roumania to Latvia, and from Poland to Holland and Belgium.

Grimm's researches indicate that the Nordic Gods of Asgard were a relatively late innovation to northern Europe, arriving probably during the great tribal migrations of about two thousand years ago which overlaid but did not materially affect the original goddess-oriented culture there.

One of Grimm's folk tales which is still quite popular in the German lands of Europe is *Frau Holle*. This tale is fully as bizarre and has the same dreamlike quality of much folk literature.

But before one passes it off as just another bit of quaint weirdness, there should be a further examination made of it; for in this case we have a profound spiritual lesson and probably the narrative form of an ancient rite of initiation. Consider further.

Some Background

Holle or Hulda was one of the most common names of the Great Goddess throughout most of central and northern Europe. Folklore names her as the Queen of the Immortals, the Elves, the Dead and the Witches. Throughout the Continent it was originally she who led the dread and awesome Wild Hunt through the thick forest and the midnight snows, leading ghosts, wolves, witches and elves. Frau Holle is equated closely with Artemis and Diana; she seldom was said to have a male consort. (When she did have a male opposite, on those times he was said to be none other than Odin.)

The tool most associated with Frau Holle was the spindle or bobbin, and with such she was reputed to weave the fates of men and nations, and indeed the fabric of the world itself. Her spindle was magically connected, or one and the same, with the axis about which the entire world rotated.

One end of the spindle was set in a well or sacred spring, and the other at the North Star. When it slowly moved, the ages of the world would pass one into the other. (This refers, of course, to the rotation of the sky yearly, and to the gradual precession of the equinoxes, which takes 25,000 years to complete. The concepts are abstract, but never were intended to be taken literally.) Holle controlled all things, then as now.

In the working of magic, it is well known that the drawing of blood gives great (and frequently uncontrollable) power to a ritual, since blood is the essence of life itself. To call spirits forth or to call on the gods, in ancient times it was the practice in high magic to offer a blood sacrifice, usually an animal which could later serve in a pleasurably mundane manner as a barbecued feast for the worshippers.

Blood sacrifices are magically very dangerous and tricky indeed, and students of magic nowadays usually reject such practices as cruel to the victim and hazardous to the practitioners. They feel it is better to work more slowly but to have greater control of all that happens. But in the old days it was not always such.

The Ritual

The folk tale *Frau Holle* makes very much sense as an initiation ritual. Noting first the symbolism of the bobbin as the tool of the Great Goddess, we see a drawing of blood from the initiate to cause a direct manifestation of Frau Holle. The well has a multiple connotation of a sacred pivot-point of the universe, an entryway into the afterworld, and the source of, perhaps, the Water of Life.

The girl who plunges into the well dies symbolically, for any rite of initiation will involve a symbolic death for the initiate. When she awakens, it is in a beautiful meadow in warm sunlight and among thousands of flowers. This was a common image of Holle's realm: a paradisical Garden of the Goddess in which the dead could ease away the memories of a harsh world, but which the living could visit only for a short time.

Then comes the testing, and the proving of character, for none but the finest are to be initiated into the Mysteries. I imagine that the initiate would be asked to remove the bread, and to give its spiritual significance. In the Eleusinian Mysteries, for example, the initiate was given a stalk of grain and asked its significance; the stalk was kept as the symbol of her or his rebirth.

For a head of grain symbolizes the past, as it leads to the present; and even though of the past, reaped of stalks that must die; it is the symbol and source of rebirth and of countless generations to follow, lifetime after lifetime.

Next came the apple tree, and another humanitarian testing, followed most likely by an explanation of the significance. For the apple has always been the age-old symbol of wisdom, and a fruit sacred to the Great Goddess. Cut the sweet fruit crosswise, and you have a five-pointed star of seeds symbolizing a balance of earth, air, fire, water and of the life-force which pervades all things. It is also the symbol of humankind made perfect, of the five fundamental tools of magic and, primarily, the balance that must exist between all things. (In the realm of the Norse Gods, the Goddess Iduna possessed the magical fruit upon which the gods themselves depended for immortality— apples.) There are many other meanings.

Another point is that trees figure very prominently in Germanic mythology. A tree was said to be at the center of all things, both with the Norse Gods and the earlier matrifocal Germanic peoples. Its roots were imbedded in the underworld, and its branches reached up to the sky itself. Groves and individual trees were sacred, and folk tales tell again and again of the wisdom and charm of the wood-sprites who were, to psychically sensitive humans, the intelligent personifications of trees. And a final note: German folk tales tell that Holle created humankind from a tree. So, our kinship to the forest is closer than most of us have known!

And then, of course, the meeting with the Divine itself, and being able to withstand the recognition and realization of something which is almost always beyond human understanding. It takes a strong mind to resist being unhinged.

For the third test of the initiate would be the taking on of the tasks done by the Goddess, or work as a priestess of the Great One: controlling and caring for the weather, for things of the Earth, and so on.

Of course at the end of the ritual must come the change in the individual herself, that pure gold of the spirit which the medieval alchemists sought (not the physical gold which is merely an analogy and which fooled the small-minded, who would have burned the alchemists at the stake for seeking enlightenment outside of the unenlightened Church). The initiation has "taken," and the new priestess or godia has attained a wider and deeper view of the significances behind all things. Her magic and power will thus be strong, and grow ever stronger.

The Failed Rite

The first part of the folk tale tells about the way that such a rite is to be conducted, and what results are to be expected. The second part somewhat humorously, but very pointedly, tells just what can go wrong.

The stepsister is fully as ugly in spirit as the first girl was beautiful in spirit. First, her motivation is merely to get something for nothing—to receive "divine welfare payments," so to speak. She is not interested in the meanings behind things, but only what she can get out of them for as little work as possible.

The kindness shown by the first girl is lacking in the second. The oven's pleadings are ignored, and she never comes to know the symbolism of the grain and the bread. Likewise the tree is passed by, for she could never have understood the balance behind all things, or the concept of humankind made perfect, or of immortality.

Her duties to Frau Holle failed after a short while, as charlatans and easy-buck artists generally seem to fail. Upon her expulsion the grossness of soul which had characterized her only became more pronounced. By failing to rise higher she had fallen only lower: her smallness of mind and thoughtlessness made it permanent. Others could see it as could she herself, and the moral of this tale is most clear.

I feel that the latter section is a sort of "what to look for" listing in evaluating an initiate (as well as its obvious moral value for those who heard it), for any of the stepsister's evils of commission or of omission would be enough to disqualify anyone.

But read the story again for yourself, and for yourself read the meanings behind it!

Principal Sagas

Little of the early literature of Odinism is what could be termed "scriptural," and generally the sagas will give some of the mythology of that era, or illustrate manners and customs.

The Elder Edda	Mythical—no accurate date
The Younger Edda	Mythical—no accurate date

The *Fornaldarsogur* contains:

Volsunga	Partly mythical
Hervara	Partly mythical
Thorstein Vikingsson's	Partly mythical
Ketil Hæng's sons	Partly mythical
Grim Lodinkinnis'	Partly mythical
Fridthjof's	Partly mythical
Hrolf Kraki's	6th century (?)
Half's	6th century (?)
Sogubrot	6th to 7th century (?)
Ragnar Lodbrok's	8th century (?)
Ragnar Lodbrok's Sons'	8th century (?)
Norna Gest's	No date can be assigned
Gautrek's	No date can be assigned
Orvar Odd's	No date can be assigned
Herraud and Bosi's	No date can be assigned
Egil and Asmund's	No date can be assigned
Hjalmter and Olver's	No date can be assigned
Gongu Hrolf's	No date can be assigned
An Bosveigi's	No date can be assigned
Egil's	Middle of 9th—end of 10th C.

Njal's	End of 10th—beginning of 11th
Laxdæla	886 to 1030 A.D.
Eyrbyggja	890 to 1031 A.D.

Islandinga Sogur contains:

I. Hord's Saga	950 to 990 A.D.
II. Hœnsa Thoris' Saga	990 to 1010 A.D.
III. Gunnlaug Ormstunga's	10th to 11th century
IV. Viga Styr's Saga	10th to 11th century
V. Kjalnesinga Saga	9th to 11th century

Droplaugarsona Saga	10th century
Hrafenkl Freysgodi	10th century
Bjorn Hitæla Kappi	First half of 11th century
Kormak's	10th century

Fornsogur contains:

I. Vatnsdæla Saga	Circa 870 to 1000 A.D.
II. Floamanna Saga	Circa 985 to 990 A.D.
III. Hallfred's Saga	End of 10th century
Gretti's Saga	10th to 11th century (Grettir died 1031 A.D.)
Viga Glum	10th century
Hallaljot's	Beginning of 11th century

Vapnfirdinga	9th to 10th century
Thorskfirdinga, or Gullthori's	Circa 900 to 930 A.D.
Heidar Viga (continuation of Viga Styr's)	First half of 9th century
Fœreyinga	Circa 960 to 1040 A.D.
Finnbogi Rami's	10th century
Eric the Red	10th century
Thatt of Styrbjorn	10th century
Landnama (the colonization of Iceland)	9th to 10th century

Islendinga bok	Circa 874 to 1118 A.D.
Ljosvetninga	990 to 1050 A.D.
Vemund's Saga	End of 10th century
Svarfdœla	First half of 10th century

Biskupa Sogur contains:

Kristni Saga	Circa 980 to 1120 A.D.
Sturlunga	Circa 1120 to 1284 A.D.

Fornmanna Sogur contains:

I. Sagas of the Kings of Norway

II. Jomsvikinga Saga	10th century
III. Knytlinga Saga	11th to 12th century
IV. Fagrskinna	
(short history of Norway)	9th to 12th century

Heimskringla Saga contains:

Ynglinga Saga
  (by Snorri Sturluson)   Written during the first half of the 13th century, giving history of the Kings of Norway and Sweden from Odin down to 1177.

Flateyjarbok contains lives of the Kings of Norway, etc.:

Fostbrædra Saga	Circa 1015 to 1030 A.D.
Konung's Sliggsja	13th century
Rimbegla	14th century
Orkneyinga	Circa 870 to 1206 A.D.

Zodiacal Houses

Certain of the Gods and Goddesses were said to have corresponding regions of the sky. In the myths, these were said to have been their residences or great halls in the Land of the Gods. Further research into this area would be interesting, perhaps comparing the stories and personages in the sagas with the respective astrological implications. Some of these entities have replaced earlier ones for various signs, so much study would be required; a relatively late version is shown below.

ENTITY	ZODIACAL HOUSE	EQUIVALENT
Ullur	Ydalir	Sagittarius
Frey	Alfheim (Elvish Home)	Capricorn
Vali	Valaskjali (Valhalla)	Aquarius
Saga	Sokkvaber	Pisces
Odin	Gladsheim (Glad-Home Castle)	Aries
Skadi	Thrym-heim (originally a Giant's castle)	Taurus
Balder	Breidablik	Gemini
Heimdal	Himinbjorg	Cancer
Freya	Folkvangr (the "folk meadow")	Leo
Forseti (earlier, Jord)	Glitnir	Virgo
Njord	Noatun	Libra
Vidar	Landvidi	Scorpio

Recommended Reading

Audrey, Robert. *African Genesis.* New York: Athenium Publishers, 1961.

_____. *Territorial Imperative.* New York: Athenium Publishers, 1966.

_____. *The Social Contract.* New York: Athenium Publishers, 1970.

Landmark works examining humankind's twofold nature of gentleness and ferocity, drawing parallels with the animal kingdom and expanding it toward a greater understanding of today's societal and human problems.

Blum, Ralph. *The Book of Runes (A Handbook for the Use of an Ancient Oracle: The Viking Runes).* New York: St. Martin's Press, 1982.

An easy-to-learn (and effective) system of divination by rune casting. This book can be bought with a bag of runestones so that one can begin using it immediately.

Carey, Diana and Judy Large. *Festivals, Family and Food.* Stroud: Hawthorn Press, 1982.

A very charming and useful contemporary book of seasonal celebrations, customs, games and foods for families with children, as drawn from British traditions. Highly recommended.

Frazier, Sir James, ed. *The Golden Bowl.* New York: Macmillan, 1985.

Either the abridged or the unabridged versions are excellent sources for research or browsing on ancient folk, religious and holiday customs worldwide.

Graves, Robert. *Greek Myths, Volumes I and II.* New York: George Baziller, 1955.

To be read after *The White Goddess*, this book gives most of the important keys for truly understanding mythology. Perhaps someday some other superb scholar will do an equivalent study of northern European myth.

_____. *Watch the North Wind Rise*. New York: Avon Books, 1949.
An enjoyable novel which summarizes and dramatizes several high points in *The White Goddess* while depicting a true pagan society.

_____. *The White Goddess*. New York: Farrar, Straus & Giroux, Inc., 1966.
Long and difficult with some uncertain scholarship here and there, but still the very best book available on understanding ancient myth and its myriad meanings. Importantly, he stresses the importance of including the feminine aspect of the Godhead.

Grimm, Jacob. *Teutonic Mythology, Volumes I–IV*. New York: Dover Publications, 1966.
Very long and very difficult, but some of the very best source books in existence concerning pagan folk customs in central and northern Europe.

Jung, Carl. *The Portable Jung: A Selection of Works translated from the Writings of Dr. C.G. Jung*. New York: Penguin Books, 1971.
His essays and books are difficult reading, but they are major modern works which lay the basis for much of Odinism. Dr. Jung put forth his theory of the human subconscious having a "racial memory" far older than the human race itself, and that the "Gods" are a part of our own subconscious minds. Further, he states that the subconscious is the portal to much which we term "supernatural," and can even allow paranormal phenomenon and face-to-face meetings, at certain times, with our deities and with nature spirits.

Keith, Sir Arthur. *A New Theory of Human Evolution*. Magnolia, MA: Peter Smith Publishing, Inc., 1968.
Excellent anthropological work on the societies of ancient man, and how the multitude of relatively isolated, small human societies existing since the time of the earliest proto-humans (and probably before) aided and hastened the process of evolution. It is an extension of Darwin's basic researches in the 19th century.

Toynbee, Arnold. *A Study of History*. Edited by D.C. Somervell. New York: Oxford University Printers, Inc., 1961.
Either the abridged or unabridged versions are recommended. Toynbee, perhaps the greatest historian of the 20th century, stated and documented

his epochal "challenge and response" theory of history in these books. His bias toward Christianity, obvious here, was recanted and corrected in *Mankind and Mother Earth*, which he published just before his death.

Nietzsche, Friedrich. *The Pocket Nietzsche.* New York: Penguin Books, 1976.
A useful selection of writings by one of the most significant philosophers of the 19th century. Friedrich Wilhelm Nietzsche had his personal flaws and his writings are often misinterpreted, but his concept of reaching beyond the current human condition is still as valid as it always has been.

Wahlgren, Erik. *The Vikings and America.* New York: Thames and Hudson, Inc.
A very good summary of the existing evidence of Norse expeditions to the North American continent, and speculations as to why the Vikings eventually left.

Additional Bibliography

The folklore and legends of Northern Europe include a number of excellent sources for the scholar. These are some source books that have proven valuable in researching the mythology of the northlands:

Armour, M, trans. *The Fall of the Nibelungs*. Everyman 312.

Bray, O., trans. *The Elder Edda*. London, 1908.

Caesar, Julius. *Commentaries*. Everyman 702.

Craigie, Sir W.A. *The Icelandic Sagas*. Cambridge, 1913.

Craigie, Sir W.A. *The Religion of the Ancient Scandinavia*. London, 1914.

Dasent, G.W. The Prose Edda. London, 1842.

Du Chaillu, P.B. *The Viking Age*. London, 1889.

Faraday, W. Divine Mythology of the North. London, 1902.

Phillpotts, Dame B. *Edda and Saga*. London, 1931.

Sykes, E., compiler. *Dictionary of Non-Classical Mythology*. New York: Everyman, E.P. Dutton & Co., Inc., 1952.

Tacitus. *Germania and Agricola*. Everyman 274.

Thorpe, B. *The Saemund Edda*. London, 1866.

Vigfusson and Powell, eds. *Corpus, Poeticum Boreale*. Oxford, 1883.

LLEWELLYN ORDERING INFORMATION

Order Online:
Visit our website at www.llewellyn.com, select your books, and order them on our secure server.

Order by Phone:
- Call toll-free within the U.S. at 1-877-NEW-WRLD (1-877-639-9753). Call toll-free within Canada at 1-866-NEW-WRLD (1-866-639-9753)
- We accept VISA, MasterCard, and American Express

Order by Mail:
Send the full price of your order (MN residents add 6.5% sales tax) in U.S. funds, plus postage & handling to:

> **Llewellyn Worldwide**
> **2143 Wooddale Drive, Dept. 978-0-87542-224-4**
> **Woodbury, MN 55125-2989**

Postage & Handling:

Standard (U.S., Mexico, & Canada). If your order is:
$24.99 and under, add $3.00
$25.00 and over, FREE STANDARD SHIPPING

AK, HI, PR: $15.00 for one book plus $1.00 for each additional book.

International Orders (airmail only):
$16.00 for one book plus $3.00 for each additional book

Orders are processed within 2 business days.
Please allow for normal shipping time. Postage and handling rates subject to change.

NORSE MAGIC
D. J. Conway

The Norse: adventurous Viking wanderers, daring warriors, worshippers of the
Aesir and the Vanir. Like the Celtic tribes,
the Northmen had strong ties with the
Earth and elements, the gods and the
"little people."

Norse Magic is an active magic, only for
participants, not bystanders. It is a magic
of pride in oneself and the courage to face
whatever comes. It interests those who believe in shaping their
own future, those who believe that practicing spellwork is preferable to sitting around passively waiting for changes to come.

The book leads the beginner step by step through the spells. The
in-depth discussion of Norse deities and the Norse way of life and
worship set the intermediate student on the path to developing his
or her own active rituals. *Norse Magic* is a compelling and easy-to-
read introduction to the Norse religion and Teutonic mythology.
The magical techniques are refreshingly direct and simple, with a
strong feminine and goddess orientation.

0-87542-137-7, 240 pp., illus.   **$5.99**

NORTHERN MYSTERIES & MAGICK
Runes & Feminine Powers
Freya Aswyn

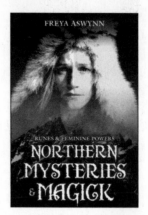

A classic contribution to rune lore . . .

The runes are more than an ancient alphabet. They comprise a powerful system of
divination and a path to the subconscious
forces operating in your life. *Northern
Mysteries & Magick* is the only book of
Nordic magick written by a woman, and it is the first to offer an
extensive presentation of rune concepts, mythology, and mag-
ickal applications inspired by Dutch/Friesian traditional lore.

Discover how the feminine Mysteries of the North are represented
in the runes, and how each of the major deities of Northern
Europe still live in the collective consciousness of people of Northern European descent. Chapters on runic divination and magick
introduce the use of runes in counseling and healing.

1-56718-047-7, 288 pp., 6 x 9, appendix, bibliog.   **$14.95**